Blessed Is He Who Watches

The book of Revelation —
A historicist interpretation

"Blessed is he who watches, and keeps his garments,
lest he walk naked and they see his shame." (Rev 16:15)

Carol White

Blessed is He Who Watches

Print Edition 2019

Copyright: Carol White 2006

ISBN: 9781075151019

For other material by the same author, please see end of book
and our website:
http://www.blessedishewhowatches.org.uk

To contact us:
contact@blessedishewhowatches.org.uk

Contents

Preface

Today, there is no shortage of teaching commenting on the events of our day and outlining what is to happen in the future. Very often, this is associated with the claim that Christ is coming soon. Clearly, all such teaching should be approached with caution, especially when predictions are made or a detailed scenario is given of what is to take place before Christ returns.

At the same time, however, such teaching serves as a reminder that there is a place for keeping aware of world events, and for considering the possible end-time significance of these. Such an awareness is important, not least because it can help us to remain faithful to Christ in our time.

It is here that the book of Revelation has a vital role to play. Revelation is a prophetic book revealing things to take place in this gospel age. Therefore, it has a special part to play in helping us to understand rightly the time in which we live. Of course, prophecy of things to come is also found in the gospels and the letters. However, Revelation is unique among the New Testament books in being a prophetic book. Therefore, it is this book especially that will assist us in correctly perceiving the events of our day.

This study of the book of Revelation has been written in the hope that it will help the people of God to understand this present time, and to be better equipped to serve God and to stand in the midst of the testing days in which we live.

The approach taken in this commentary

Firstly, as stated above, this study of Revelation has been written with a view to understanding the time in which we live. However, attention has not been limited to those parts of the book that especially throw light on the events of our day. Instead, what is presented here is a commentary on the whole book. A complete commentary has been undertaken because all of the book can assist us in walking in faithfulness to Christ in the midst of all that is happening in our time. However, it has also been undertaken because it is only by progressively following through the things prophesied that we can understand the prophecy of the book and discern with confidence those parts that specifically throw light on the events of our day.

Secondly, foundational to the way in which Revelation has been interpreted here are two basic convictions. The first is that the book of Revelation contains a revelation and prediction of the most important events affecting the church during the course of the gospel age. The second is that featuring prominently in the book is the Antichrist, who can now be identified as the pope of Rome. Neither this view of the overall scope of Revelation, nor the belief that the pope of Rome is the Antichrist of Scripture, is at all novel. However, many readers will be unfamiliar with these views. Therefore, for a discussion of these matters, the reader is referred to: 'The historicist approach' (which follows the General Introduction), and 'Antichrist Revealed', 2017, by the same author.

Finally, it is recognised that interpreting the symbolism of Revelation is challenging, and it would be naïve for anyone to think that his or her interpretation is correct in every detail. In view of this, it is hoped that anything disputable in the detail will not prevent the reader from giving fair consideration to the overall focus and interpretation offered here. It is this, above all, that leads to an understanding of our time and that is especially commended to the reader.

General Introduction

1. The author

The book of Revelation itself makes clear that the author is John (1:1,4), and the earliest tradition has it that this is the apostle John. Some people argue that the language, style and thought of Revelation are not like the other writings of John, and conclude it is by a different author. However, there is no real reason not to follow the traditional view that this is the apostle John. The difference in style can be explained by the different nature of the book. Also, it is unlikely that such an important prophecy would be given to someone other than one of the twelve apostles, on whose teaching the church is founded (see Jn 16:13 — Jesus' promise to the apostles that the Holy Spirit would tell them things to come).

2. The date

The date of the writing of Revelation is not given in the book, but there are clues to this. Particularly, there are indications in the book that it was written when the church was entering a time of persecution; and based on this, and its authorship by the apostle John, two dates are most often suggested — the end of Nero's reign (54–68AD), or the latter part of Domitian's reign (81–96AD). Comments by some early writers concerning the banishment of John to Patmos (John was on Patmos when he received the revelation — 1:9) indicate that the later dating is to be preferred.

3. The purpose of the book

From the book's own testimony it is clear that, first of all, the book of Revelation is a prophecy making known to the church things which (from the perspective of John's day) were shortly to take place (1:1–3,19; 22:6–7,10). What is not made clear, however, is the exact scope of what is prophesied; and here views differ, resulting in there being various approaches to interpreting the book (see below). Here a historicist approach is advocated, and in accordance with this, the book is understood to be a revelation and prediction of the most important events affecting the church during the course of the gospel age.

However, the book is not simply a revelation of things to come, but it also gives spiritual understanding of these things. Furthermore, it contains much in the way of comfort for the church: for example, it makes clear that God is on the throne and that all that is to happen is according to his purpose; it shows God keeping and delivering his people and judging his enemies; and it portrays the church's heavenly hope. So, it portrays fundamental spiritual truths for the comfort and strengthening of the church.

Moreover, all of this together serves the vital purpose of helping the church to stand. Of course, all of Scripture contains guidance and encouragement for the church to help it to stand in the midst of this world. However, the knowledge and understanding that Revelation provides concerning the major events of this age, has a unique and essential part to play in the church standing firm and remaining faithful to God in the midst of all that happens.

4. Interpreting the book of Revelation

The revelation given to John was conveyed to him through a series of visions, by means of symbolic pictures and language; and when interpreting the book of Revelation, it is vital that this is kept in view. It means that we must beware of interpreting things literally, and we must seek to discern what the symbols are intended to represent and convey. Moreover, to do this, we need to apply certain principles.

Firstly, in some cases the book itself gives the meaning of a symbol (eg, 1:20; 17:15). In such cases we must simply use the explanation given, and resist any temptation to add our own ideas to this.

Secondly, in some cases the same symbolism appears in other parts of Scripture, notably the prophetic books of the Old Testament. In such cases, it is important to look at the other instances where the symbolism is used, and to be guided in our interpretation by its use and meaning elsewhere (eg, the symbolism of beasts and horns).

Thirdly, in all cases it is vital to give the symbolism its most natural meaning in the context, taking into account that this is symbolism concerning the things of God and his people, and the things of the devil (eg, Sodom used symbolically is a figure for great wickedness and immorality).

Also, before interpreting the book in detail, it is important to consider the overall purpose and scope of the book, and to determine the correct general approach to interpretation. There are four main approaches to interpreting the book of Revelation, and it is necessary to decide between these.

(i) The idealist approach. This does not regard Revelation as predicting specific events in history; rather, the book is viewed purely as portraying timeless spiritual truths, and depicting types of happenings characteristic of the whole gospel age.

(ii) The preterist approach. This regards the main part of Revelation as depicting things that have to do with the church and the pagan Roman Empire in the first century; thus, from our perspective, it puts the fulfilment of most of the book in the past.

(iii) The futurist approach. This places the fulfilment of the main part of the book in the time just before Christ's return.

(iv) The historicist approach. As noted above, this regards Revelation as a revelation and prediction of the most important events affecting the church during the course of the gospel age; it sees the prophecy of this book being fulfilled in the unfolding history of this present age, from the time of John receiving this revelation to the return of Christ.

As already indicated, it is the historicist approach that is being followed here. A discussion of why this approach is preferred is included next, for the benefit, especially, of those who are unfamiliar with this way of interpreting Revelation.

The Historicist Approach

The historicist approach to interpreting the book of Revelation is not new. It was popular at the time of the Protestant Reformation and for some time afterwards (into the 19th-century); moreover, it is still followed by some who stand in the Protestant or Reformed tradition. Essentially, however, it is not a common or familiar approach in today's church. Here, the grounds for following this approach are discussed. The weaknesses of the other approaches are also touched on.

1. Why the historicist approach?

As already noted, this approach takes Revelation to be a revelation and prediction of the most important events affecting the church during the gospel age; it sees the prophecy of the book being fulfilled in the unfolding history of the Christian age. There are a number of reasons for advocating this approach, which together provide strong grounds for following a historicist interpretation of Revelation.

(i) Any interpretation of Revelation must do justice to the clear claim of the book that it is a prophecy (see 1:3; 22:7,10, 18–19), and that it is an unveiling of things to come — things which (from the perspective of John's day) must shortly take place (see 1:1; 22:6; also 1:19; 4:1; 22:10). The historicist approach definitely does this.

(ii) The historicist approach also does justice to the whole matter of prophecy being fundamental to God's relationship with his people. From the beginning, the people of God have been blessed with prophecy, and a basic aspect of God's dealings with his people has been that he has told them beforehand what he will do (see Amos 3:7). We see this in both the Old Testament and the New Testament. Of course, spanning the whole of the Old

Testament are all the predictions concerning the coming of the Messiah/Christ and his kingdom. However, the Old Testament also contains many other prophecies concerning God's dealings with Israel and the nations around. During their history the Jews were shown beforehand such major events as their bondage in Egypt and their release from Egypt, their exile into Babylon, and God's judgement of Babylon and their return to the land; there were also prophecies of God's judgements on the nations surrounding Israel; and Daniel prophesied about the great kingdoms that would follow Babylon and dominate the world of God's people until the coming of God's kingdom. Moreover, in the New Testament we see a continuation of this: Jesus himself spoke about the Jews' rejection of himself and the gospel, about the fall of Jerusalem, and about the gathering in of the Gentiles; and the apostles predicted the falling away of the church and the coming of the Antichrist.

Against this background, it can be seen that to interpret Revelation historically is totally compatible with God's way of revealing the future to his people. In fact, knowing God's way of working, we might expect that before the death of the last apostle and the time when God's revelation to man was complete, God would have given to his church, for its guidance and strengthening, a prediction of the major events that would affect the church in the gospel age. We find a precedent for this in the visions given to Daniel concerning events in the inter-testamental period. Many years before the events happened, Daniel was given prophecies about the replacement of the Medo-Persian Empire by the Greek power, and its replacement by the Roman power; he was also given prophecies about the oppression of the Jews under Antiochus IV (see Daniel chapters 7 and 8). Moreover, he was given these at a time of revelation for a coming period of prophetic silence, for the guidance, encouragement and strengthening of the Jews who would live through those times. It is in harmony with this to hold that similarly, at a time of revelation, for the time when revelation was complete (ie, the post-apostolic age), John was given a prophecy concerning the major events affecting the church in the time to come, for the church's guidance and strengthening.

Essentially, therefore, a historicist approach to interpreting the prophecy of Revelation is in keeping with the whole nature of biblical prophecy; also, it is in harmony with the expectation that arises from this, that, before revelation finally ceased, God would have given to the church a prediction of the major events of the church age.

(iii) The historicist approach to interpretation sits most compatibly with the understanding that the pope of Rome is the Antichrist of Scripture. In Revelation, the Antichrist and his dominion are portrayed under the imagery of 'the beast'. This beast is first mentioned in chapter 11; it is then described in all its evil and power in chapter 13; and it then features throughout chapters 14–19, where its judgement/downfall is depicted. This is very harmonious with church history and the progress of the papacy. With the benefit of two thousand years of church history to survey, we can now see clearly the rise of the papacy and the Roman Church, and the papacy's domination of the Christian world in the Middle Ages; its exposure as the Antichrist at the time of the Reformation; and the subsequent decline in papal power in the centuries after this. The parallel between these known events that cover numerous centuries, and Revelation's depiction of the beast over successive chapters in the second half of the book, is very confirming of the stance that the historicist approach to interpreting Revelation is correct.

(iv) Weight should also be given to the fact that the historicist interpretation was common at the time of the Reformation among the Reformers, and for some time afterwards among those who stood in the Protestant or Reformed tradition. This, of course, does not prove that the historicist approach is correct. However, in a day when this approach is an uncommon and unfamiliar one (and, with the modern theological mindset, seems implausible), it is important to recognise that in the past it was not an uncommon or unfamiliar approach; rather, it was followed by many church leaders and denominations, especially those that correctly identified the papacy as the Antichrist of Scripture.

Finally, we should address some of the major objections to the historicist approach to interpreting Revelation.

(i) Firstly, some argue that the historicist approach has discredited itself because it has resulted in many different interpretations, often with each commentator making his own day the very end. The answer to this objection must be that, while there have been differences in interpretation, there has also been a notable amount of agreement; also, a lack of complete agreement between interpreters is not a valid reason to abandon the historicist (or any other) approach. Moreover, this objection implies that within each of the other approaches to interpretation there has been a consistency of interpretation, which is far from the case.

(ii) Secondly, some question the validity of a historicist interpretation on the ground that it focuses mostly on events in western Europe (ie, on the progress of the Roman Empire and the papacy, and the church's relationship with these); they object that its narrow scope means it ignores God's activity in the rest of the world. This objection, however, fails to take into account that God only shows us the history we need to know about. Particularly, it fails to take into account the vision of the four beasts given to Daniel (see Daniel chapter 7) — where the fourth, Roman beast (which has existed first as imperial Rome and then as papal Rome) is shown to be, from its rise until the return of Christ, the final power of significance as far as the people of God are concerned (see 'Antichrist Revealed', 2017, by the same author, for a discussion of Daniel's four beasts).

(iii) Thirdly, some argue that the historicist approach cannot be correct because it means that the people of John's day would not have understood Revelation, and all Scripture must have meaning and relevance to the people of the time. This argument has a number of weaknesses.

First, it takes no account of the fact that predictive prophecy is found throughout the Bible and is a distinct feature of God's dealings with his people; throughout Scripture we see God showing his people things that related to future events, and that would not have been fully understood by the people to whom the prophecy was delivered.

A further weakness of this argument is that it assumes that predictive prophecy is of no benefit to those who live before the time of its fulfilment. This is to fail to appreciate that warnings of things future are meant to affect the way we live in the present (so, predictions of opposition to the church in the future can be the basis of a present earnestness to stand firm in the faith). Also, this argument assumes that the early believers had no comprehension at all of future events, and that Revelation would have been altogether obscure to them. This is far from the truth. From the teaching of the Old Testament and the apostles, many of them had an expectation of the fall of the Roman Empire, the replacement of this by Antichrist and his kingdom, and the replacement of this by the kingdom of Christ (again, see 'Antichrist Revealed'). They would, therefore, have been able to view Revelation at least in these broad terms.

Essentially, it is entirely compatible with God's way of working to find the early church being given a prophecy of things yet to happen.

2. Why not the other approaches?

a. The idealist approach

This does not regard Revelation as predicting any specific historical events. Instead, it views the book as simply portraying happenings characteristic of the whole gospel age, and picturing timeless spiritual truths (such as the reign of God, the opposition of the devil, and the triumph of Christ and the church over evil) — all shown in order to help believers to stand in the midst of the trials and suffering of this present age. Today, this approach is followed by a good number of evangelicals, including some Reformed teachers. In the right hands, it can provide some very good teaching for the strengthening of the church. Moreover, it provides a reminder of the importance of drawing general lessons and encouragements from Revelation. However, there are some serious objections to the idealist approach.

First of all, while idealist interpreters will draw examples from history, the fundamental weakness of this approach is that it denies the book any specific historical fulfilment (there is an absence of any anchorage to specific historical events). This means that the idealist approach fails to do full justice to the explicit statements in the book that it is a prophecy, and that it is an unveiling of things to come — things which (from the perspective of John's day) were shortly to take place.

Furthermore, this lack of anchorage to specific events results in an understanding of Revelation that does not give due place to the Antichrist/the papacy (the great enemy of the church), to the progress of his dominion, and to his false church. Moreover, associated with this is a failure to do full justice to such things as: the symbolism of beasts and horns which, in Daniel, refer to definite kings and kingdoms existing in time and dominating the world of God's people; the development of events in the book (the beast is absent at the beginning, appears in the middle, and then features until the end); and the fact that the church age has had a very distinct, progressive history involving highly significant developments and events affecting the church (especially those related to the papacy and the Roman Catholic Church).

Thus, while some helpful teaching has come out of the idealist approach, this approach is flawed in some significant ways.

b. The preterist approach

This approach takes the view that Revelation is to be understood exclusively in terms of its contemporary setting: it regards the main part of the book as depicting things that have to do with the church and the pagan Roman Empire in the first century. Thus, for anyone living after that time, it places the fulfilment of most of the book in the past. This means that Revelation serves principally as a book of general teaching, with nothing specific to say concerning the unfolding history of the church age. This view was reputedly spread by Jesuits after the Reformation, and in recent times has been quite common in the church. It is compatible with the liberal outlook of many today (an outlook which dismisses predictive prophecy), and with an approach to biblical interpretation that says that Scripture must have a meaning and relevance to the people of the time.

The great weakness of this approach is that it does not do justice to the book's claim to be a prophecy. Also, it makes the book say nothing about the papacy — the Antichrist of Scripture and the greatest enemy of the church. We must also be suspicious of any approach to interpretation that reputedly was spread by the Jesuits, who were intent on countering the Protestants' identification of the pope as the Antichrist. For all of these reasons, this approach to interpretation is not considered correct.

c. The futurist approach

This approach places the fulfilment of the main part of the book in the very last days, and it sees most of the events portrayed as taking place in the time immediately before Christ's return. Especially, it sees the book warning of a future political Antichrist who is to come just prior to Christ's return. This approach to interpreting Revelation was also reputedly propagated by Jesuits following the Reformation. It then became popular among those who followed the dispensational, premillennial interpretation of Scripture, and has been passed down to the present time. Today it is a popular view among evangelicals, especially in America.

Although this approach treats Revelation as a book of prophecy, it makes the book jump from John's time to the very last days; thus, it does not do justice to the indications in the book that the things prophesied were shortly to take place (see 1:1; 22:6,10). Also, it is associated with a faulty understanding of the Antichrist, and one that deflects us from identifying the Antichrist as the pope of Rome. Moreover, again we must be suspicious of any teaching that reputedly was propagated by the Jesuits. For all of these reasons, this approach to interpretation is not considered correct.

In view of all this, the approach to interpretation advocated and followed here is the historicist approach.

Chapter 1
Christ among his churches

John's introduction (1:1–3)

v1,2. By way of introduction, John begins by giving a general description of the book. He says it is "the Revelation of Jesus Christ". This could mean that it is an unveiling of things 'about' Jesus Christ (as we will see, it concerns his government of all things); however, in this context, more probably it means that it is an unveiling or disclosing of things 'by' Jesus Christ — things that otherwise would be hidden from or unknown to us. Moreover, John tells us this revelation was given to Christ by God to show his servants "things which must shortly take place". As mediator between God and man, Christ was given this revelation by the Father for the purpose of making known to his people things to occur in the future, things which shortly and surely would come to pass. Thus, this is a book of prophecy (see v3) speaking to the church of things to come.

John then goes on to relate how Christ conveyed the revelation to his church. He tells us Christ sent the revelation and made it known through the agency of an angel (a messenger of God), and he sent it to his servant John. John then bore witness to all he saw (which he equates with him bearing witness "to the word of God, and to the testimony of Jesus Christ"). Thus, John fulfilled the role of a prophet, receiving revelation from God and then faithfully passing it on to God's people. And this John did by writing down the revelation and sending it to the churches (see v4,11). Moreover, John's record of the revelation has been preserved in the canon of Scripture for us to receive, and it should be received by us as God's word to us and the testimony of Jesus Christ.

v3. John then speaks of the blessing associated with this book. When John mentions here "he who reads and those who hear the words of this prophecy", he probably has in mind his written record of what he saw being read to the churches (most probably by one of their elders or overseers). And he tells us that those who read and hear, and keep the things which are written (that is, retain them in their hearts and live by them) will be blessed. Of course, knowledge of and obedience to God's word always results in blessing. However, this promise of blessing is notable because no other book of Scripture has a specific promise of blessing attached to it. Therefore, we should inquire into the purpose or significance of this promise.

First of all, it is an encouragement to look into this book and study it, and not be put off by the difficulties associated with its interpretation. It is a promise of rich reward if we will have faith that we can understand it, and we persevere in our study and application of it.

Particularly of note, however, is the association John makes between this promise of blessing for those who hear and keep the words of this prophecy, and the fact that the time is near. The things revealed would soon begin to come to pass, and this revelation was given by Christ to his church to prepare it for all that was to happen, and to help it to stand in the midst of all that was to come. Thus, those who knew and kept this word would be blessed because they would be prepared for and strong in the midst of all that lay ahead. A neglect of this revelation, however, would mean that they would be inadequately prepared and therefore vulnerable. This must spur us on to study this book of Revelation. For us the time is not simply near, but we are in the midst of the things prophesied, and we will be greatly helped to stand in our time if we will give ourselves to understand and live by the words of this prophecy. A neglect of this book, however, will leave us inadequately equipped for the battles and trials of our day.

John's greeting to the seven churches (1:4–8)

v4–6. Following his introduction, John then begins to address directly the churches to whom this message is to be sent; and he begins his communication in the customary way. First he gives his name, "John"; then he names those to whom he is writing, "the seven churches which are in Asia". This is the first occurrence of the number seven, which features much in the book of Revelation. It is a number which stands for completeness and perfection, and is of significance here. Undoubtedly this communication from John was intended for the seven specific churches named (see v11). However, the choice by Christ of seven churches (there were more than this in Asia) indicates that this was not just a revelation for them, but it is for all the church — it is for every church of every day, including ours.

Then, as part of his greeting, John proclaims grace and peace to them from God. This is not a priestly blessing, but is more of a prayer and an affirmation of truth to encourage and confirm the believers in it. God's desire is that we know his saving grace — his undeserved and unmerited saving favour and kindness; also, that we know his peace — an assurance of forgiveness and reconciliation with him.

Moreover, in speaking of this grace and peace from God, John sets forth a glorious description of the triune God which is unusual but, as will be seen, is drawn from the things shown to him in this revelation.

First, this grace and peace is said to be "from Him who is and who was and who is to come". This is a description of God the Father, and it expresses the eternal existence and unchangeableness of God. Grace and peace come to us from the eternal, unchanging God, who purposed our salvation even before the world was made and most surely will complete it.

This grace and peace is also "from the seven Spirits who are before His throne". This is a description of the Holy Spirit, and it portrays the Holy Spirit in the fullness of his grace and power, and as the one who performs the will of God. We have grace and peace from the Father through the working of the Holy Spirit, by whom we experience the saving grace of God in all its various aspects.

This grace and peace is also "from Jesus Christ". Here, the Lord Jesus Christ is described as: "the faithful witness" — he is the perfect revealer of God in his person, his teaching and his works; "the firstborn from the dead" — having died for our sins, Christ is risen and in heaven as the forerunner of his people; and "the ruler over the kings of the earth" — Christ is now seated on his throne, over all earthly powers and governing all things. Here is Christ, our Prophet, Priest and King. He is the one by whom and in whom we are saved and have all grace and peace.

This glorious description of the triune God, and affirmation of his grace and peace, is set forth by John for our encouragement. It should lead us to a contemplation of our God in all his wonderful attributes and works, and serve to confirm us in God's grace and peace. It is also something to be kept in view as the potentially disturbing prophecy of the book unfolds. For John, contemplation of these things leads him to burst forth in praise of Christ. In this praise John speaks of what Christ has done for us: he "loved us and washed us from our sins in His own blood" — by his sacrificial death, Christ freed us from our sins; and he "has made us kings [or a kingdom] and priests to His God and Father" — he has formed us into his kingdom, and has enabled us to approach God and offer to him acceptable sacrifices of worship and service. To the one who has done all of this, John says, "be glory and dominion forever and ever. Amen".

v7. From contemplating what Christ has done for us, and what we have been made in him, John's thoughts turn to Christ's return — the time when he will come as Judge, and when our salvation will be completed. First, with the call "behold", John calls our attention to Christ's coming; then he describes Christ's coming in a glorious but sobering way. John speaks of him "coming with clouds", and says "every eye will see Him, even those who pierced Him" — unlike Christ's first coming, this coming will be in majesty and glory (see Mk 13:26), and it will be an event known to all, even to his enemies. John then adds, "all the tribes of the earth will mourn because of Him" — this is a scene of great grief, anguish and despair, and it portrays Christ's coming being a devastating time for those who then see him, but who rejected him.

So John points to our great hope, but also to a day that will be terrible for the unbelieving world. Nevertheless, John adds, "Even so, Amen." Although this will be a terrible event for unbelievers, John gives it a double affirmation. This was not because John gloried in the anguish and destruction of the wicked, but because this will be the day when God and his church will be vindicated, and there will be the final triumph of truth and righteousness. So this day is humbly and soberly to be welcomed.

v8. With all of this in view, Christ then declares, "I am the Alpha and the Omega, the Beginning and the End...is and who was and who is to come, the Almighty" (alpha and omega are the first and last letters of the Greek alphabet). So, Christ ascribes to himself the same honour and power as the Father — he is God, from everlasting to everlasting, the origin of and Lord of all (see Is 41:4; 44:6; also 43:10), the eternal, unchanging, all-powerful God. This is the one who has saved us; and this is the one who is coming again at the end of the age and to whom all men will have to give account.

Vision of Christ in the midst of his churches (1:9–20)

v9. Following this inspiring greeting, John then begins to relate how he received this prophecy for the church. First, he describes himself as their "brother and companion in the tribulation and kingdom and patience of Jesus Christ". Here, John identifies himself with those to whom he is writing. He and they are one family in Christ, and he with them is having to suffer and endure much for the kingdom of the Lord Jesus Christ.

Then, he says he was "on the island that is called Patmos [which is in the Aegean Sea] for the word of God and for the testimony of Jesus Christ". This statement, combined with John's prior reference to tribulation, is widely understood to indicate that this was a time of persecution (most probably the persecution of Domitian's reign — 81–96AD) and that John had been banished to Patmos because of his faithful witness to the Lord Jesus Christ. This is probably the case. However, there might also be a suggestion in John's repetition of the phrases "word of God" and "testimony of Jesus Christ" found in verse 2, that he had also been brought apart to Patmos by God to receive this revelation.

v10,11. John then says that he was "in the Spirit on the Lord's Day". On the day that the church called 'the Lord's Day' (the first day of the week — the day associated with Christ's resurrection, on which it was customary to gather for worship — see Acts 20:7), John was engaged in his devotions and enjoying communion with God by the Holy Spirit, when these extraordinary visions broke in upon him.

First, John heard behind him a loud voice like a trumpet — a voice of power and authority summoning him to listen. And he heard the speaker announcing himself as "the Alpha and the Omega, the First and the Last", and then telling him that what he saw he was to write in a book and send to the seven churches which are in Asia. This was the Lord Jesus Christ revealing himself to John as the eternal God and Lord of all, and instructing him concerning his prophetic task.

v12–16. For John, this voice was so loud and startling that it seemed as if someone was literally standing behind him; so he turned to see who was speaking to him. It was then that he saw the first vision. He saw seven golden lampstands, which represent the seven churches (see v20), and in the midst a glorious majestic figure. This was a vision of the Lord Jesus Christ portrayed in a manner that displayed his glorious attributes.

John describes the one he saw as "One like the Son of Man". Christ had announced himself to John as the eternal God; however, when John turned to see the one speaking to him, he saw a vision of Christ displaying him as the Son of God incarnate — the one who became flesh to redeem us. This was the same one who John had walked with on this earth, and heard and looked upon and touched (see 1 Jn 1:1). This was the same one who John saw laying down his life for men's sins. And this was the same one John had seen risen from the dead, and who he saw ascending bodily into heaven. At that time Christ's glory was veiled; but now John saw a vision of this same Christ, who is now in heaven, portraying his glory and majesty.

John says he was clothed with a garment down to his feet and had around his chest a golden band. This is a garment of rank and honour — a priestly or kingly robe, and one appropriate for Christ, our High Priest and King.

His head and hair were a dazzling white (see Dan 7:9). This signifies his antiquity and his perfect wisdom.

His eyes were like a flame of fire. This signifies his penetrating insight. Christ knows all and sees all; nothing is hidden from him and he sees even into the hearts of men.

His feet were like pure fine brass, depicting him as strong and steadfast, and one who subdues (treads down) his enemies.

His voice was as the sound of many waters (it sounded like loud roaring water), signifying the authority and power of his word.

He had in his right hand seven stars — which later we are told represent the angels (or messengers) of the seven churches (see v20). These angels/messengers are variously understood, but the best interpretation would seem to be that they signify the elders or overseers in the churches who would read this prophecy to the churches.

Coming out of his mouth was a sharp two-edged sword (see Is 49:2; Heb 4:12). This signifies the living and powerful word of God with which he searches and judges the hearts of men. God's word must be proclaimed in the churches, but it is effective only by God's power.

His countenance, his whole appearance, was like the sun in full strength, too bright to gaze upon. This signifies Christ's dazzling glory — his purity and splendour which is too glorious for man to behold.

v17,18. John then tells us that when he saw this vision of Christ, he fell at his feet as dead (like a dead man). Quickly, however, Christ comforts and strengthens John. First, Christ lays his hand on him and tells him not to be afraid; then, declaring again that he is the eternal God and Lord of all ("the First and the Last"), Christ calls John's attention to his resurrection life and his power over death. He announces he was dead, but now he lives and is alive for evermore. And he has "the keys of Hades and Death" — he has authority over Hades (the abode of the dead) and death, and power to release people from death. At the sight of Christ's splendour, purity and power, John had been overwhelmed with awe and fear; but Christ, in tenderness, calmed his fear and strengthened him with words reminding him that he is our God and Saviour. It is right that a person who belongs to Christ should contemplate and gaze upon him with reverence and awe. However, there should be no gripping fear, because the one beheld is not only the glorious and majestic Lord of all, but also the one who died and rose again, and has saved his people from sin and death.

Thus, John's commission to bring the revelation of Christ to the church (see v11) came directly from Christ and was accompanied by this glorious vision of the Lord Jesus Christ. This would have greatly encouraged and confirmed John in his prophetic task. Moreover, this was important to authenticate this revelation as truly the word of Christ to the church. It had been the role of the apostles to receive from Christ an understanding of his saving work and to teach this in the church, and this they had done. However, here was now a sudden breaking in of further revelation; and John's commission from Christ, accompanied by this vision of Christ, authenticated this as truly Christ's word to the church.

v19. Having comforted John, Christ then repeats his instruction to John to write down the revelation, now indicating to John all that he is to record. First, he tells John to write "the things which you have seen". By this, Christ means the glorious vision of himself which John has already seen. So, Christ makes clear that this vision was given to John not just for his own blessing, but also for him to share with the churches for their encouragement and edification. The churches at that time were in a time of trial, and great trials were ahead. This vision of Christ displaying his power and glory would have brought great reassurance and comfort to them. Moreover, it is recorded for us to contemplate, for the strengthening of our faith.

Christ also tells John to write "the things which are". Most probably, here Christ is referring to his individual messages to the seven churches (recorded in chapters 2 and 3) which concern the state and circumstances of the churches at that time.

Christ also tells John to write "the things which will take place after this". By this, Christ is referring to the whole series of visions he will give to John concerning events affecting the church in the time to come (see 4:1). Thus, this book is truly a word of a prophecy, speaking into the current situation and foretelling things to come.

v20. Christ then makes known to John the meaning of the seven stars in his right hand and the seven golden lampstands. The seven stars represent the angels/messengers of the seven churches (ie, the elders or overseers in the churches who would read this prophecy to the churches), and the seven golden lampstands represent the seven churches. This explanation is helpful not only because it gives the meaning of the lampstands and the stars, but also because it draws attention to them. John had been overwhelmed with the vision of Christ; and when we read John's description of what he saw, we too can tend to focus on the description of Christ alone. However, the vision John was given was not simply a vision of Christ, but a vision of Christ in relationship with his churches, and the explanation of the lampstands and stars reminds us of this.

In short, what was signified to John was the seven churches with Christ in the midst — the churches being represented as golden lampstands, symbolising their role, by the power of the Holy Spirit, to hold forth the light of the gospel in this dark world. So this vision is a reassurance of Christ's presence with his churches; and it is a reassurance that, just as the priests in the temple tended the lamps and kept them burning, so Christ is constantly tending his churches and sustaining their life and witness. Also, John was shown the churches' leaders, signified as stars, in Christ's right hand — showing that they are in his keeping and under his government, and all their light and influence is from him. Thus we are meant to contemplate the whole vision, and be encouraged not simply by the revelation of Christ's majesty and power, but also by the reaffirmation that this Christ is with his people, and that he watches over us and tends us, and sustains our life and witness. Moreover, all that is subsequently to be revealed (the things which are and the things to come) must be received against the background of this vision of Christ and his presence with, oversight of and care for his churches.

Chapter 2
Letters to the churches

General comment on the letters

Before unveiling the things that are to take place in the church age (4:1), Christ first gives to John a series of messages to the seven churches. Before considering these in detail, it will be helpful to consider the destination, format and purpose of these messages.

The destination of the messages — Undoubtedly, these messages are messages from Christ to the seven individual named churches. However, they are also messages from Christ to every church of every day. As already noted, this is indicated by Christ's choice of seven churches (the number seven signifying completeness). It is further indicated by Christ's statement at the end of each individual message that this is what the Spirit "says to the churches" (eg, 2:7). Thus we must read these messages not purely as messages to the various named churches, but also as messages from Christ to be applied to ourselves and to the wider church today.

The format of the messages — Each of these messages of Christ to the churches follows a similar format.

First, instructing John to write, Christ specifies the church to which the particular message is directed. It is notable that each message is initially said to be to the angel/messenger of the church, rather than to the church itself. So, each is addressed to whoever would read the message to the church; however, clearly, each message was for the whole church to hear and heed.

Then, beginning with the statement "these things says", Christ introduces himself as the one from whom the message comes, in each case by means of a different title or description of himself. In most cases, the particular title or description chosen by Christ is taken from the glorious vision of himself already described and is of relevance to the exhortations or admonitions contained in the message.

Following this, there is then a comment by Christ on the state and circumstances of the church, beginning "I know your works". In each case, this involves a statement of things for which Christ commends the church, and/or a statement of things that Christ has against the church. Then, where relevant, there is a call to repent and a warning of what will happen if this is not done. Christ's comments on the state of the churches remind us that Christ knows and takes note of all the deeds of his people, both the good things and the bad things. They also remind us that, no matter how good a church is, if there is something wrong in it this is a serious matter in Christ's sight, and if it is not dealt with it will eventually bring the church's downfall (any sin is dangerous and can destroy even good churches). We must not imagine that Christ weighs everything up together, and if there is more good than bad he is pleased with us and overlooks the bad things. Rather, he sees the good things for what they are and is pleased with them, and the bad things for what they are and is displeased with them (one does not negate the other). Moreover, he will chasten us for the bad things.

Finally, following Christ's comments on the state of the church, there is then an exhortation to hear (in some cases this comes at the very end). There is also a promise of reward to the one who overcomes (who repents of the sin or stands firm in the trial). Generally, the promised reward bears some relation to the rest of the message; also, all of the rewards are blessings that we have in Christ, that will be ours in fullness in eternity but that we have also entered into now.

The purpose of the messages — Taking into account the content and context of these messages to the churches, two main purposes can be suggested.

Firstly, these messages served to prepare the churches for receiving Christ's revelation of things to come; also, they served to strengthen them to stand firm and maintain their witness in the testing days that lay ahead. As already noted, at that time the churches were suffering considerable opposition and persecution, and further trials lay ahead. Moreover, as we will see, some of the churches had fallen into serious sin and error. All of this, and especially the sin and error, would have made the churches vulnerable to rejecting God's word and to falling away (sin and error is always a hindrance to a believer receiving and obeying God's word; also, it makes a church more vulnerable to temptation and deception, and it harms the witness of a church). In view of this, it would seem that these messages of Christ were given to correct and strengthen the churches so that they would receive and keep all that Christ was about to show them, and so that they would stand firm and be his witnesses in the testing time to come. Moreover, it follows that these messages serve a similar purpose for us; therefore we should read them as messages of correction and encouragement, examining ourselves in the light of them, and seeking to be corrected and strengthened by them. Then they will prepare us to receive and obey Christ's revelation; equally, they will help us to stand and to be Christ's witnesses in our present situation and in all that lies ahead.

Secondly, these messages are also a help to understanding the state of the church today. As already noted, the seven churches are representative of all churches, and Christ's messages are for the churches in every place and every time. In view of this, it would seem that these messages also serve to give us insight into the major errors, dangers and trials confronting and affecting the churches during the gospel age. This means we must guard against reading these messages simply as interesting insights into the state of the churches at that time. Rather, we must also approach them as messages that show us the main dangers confronting the church today, and that give us insight into what is happening in the church.

(NB: It would be generally accepted that the messages to the seven churches are both messages to the actual named churches, and messages to every church of every day. However, some commentators find in them a third level of meaning. These hold the view that these messages also run in a series, and they progressively outline and unfold the course of church history down the centuries, from the apostles' day until the return of Christ. This understanding of the messages is not addressed in what follows.)

Finally, it should be stressed that all of these messages were delivered to the churches to renew, strengthen and help them, not to condemn them. Moreover, there is reason to think that, by the grace of God, those who truly belonged to Christ did hear and overcome (it is the believer who, by God's grace, has ears to hear and is an overcomer — see 1 Jn 5:4–5). Therefore, we must approach a study of these messages with faith, knowing that by God's grace they can be to us a means of renewal and strengthening, and can serve to fit us to meet all that confronts us in our day.

Christ's message to the church of Ephesus (2:1–7)

v1. Ephesus was a very wealthy and large city. It was also a city given over to idolatry and magic arts. We know from Scripture that a number of prominent Christian leaders had been there, notably Paul and Timothy (Acts 19:1ff; 1 Tim 1:3).

To this church, Christ describes himself as "He who holds the seven stars in His right hand, who walks in the midst of the seven golden lampstands". Thus this church's attention was called to their relationship with Christ: to the fact that the churches' leaders are in Christ's keeping, and all their power and influence is from him; also that Christ is present with and watches over his churches, and all their light and witness is from him.

v2,3. Christ then says that he knows their works, and he has much to commend them for. All of the things he mentions here are an example to us, and a reminder of what our life in Christ should be.

He commends them for their labour; also, that they had laboured for his name's sake and had not become weary. So, this was a church that was putting a great deal of effort into serving Christ and his cause; it was a church that was serving with diligence, and with sustained enthusiasm and vigour. All of this is an example of self-denying devotion to the service of Christ, and it is a real challenge to us. Many will do some work for Christ, but few will labour for Christ in this manner.

Christ also commends them for their patience and perseverance. As a church, they had suffered hardship and difficulties for Christ's sake. However, they had endured these trials and had remained steadfast under the weight of suffering and hardship. They had gone on in their walk with Christ and witness to him, and had not given up.

He also commends them that they cannot bear (or endure) those who are evil. This cannot mean that they hated unbelievers and would have nothing to do with them. Rather, it means that the Ephesian believers had a real aversion to everything that was not of God and was opposed to God (they appreciated its evil nature and harmfulness); so, they resisted and would have no part in such things. Here it is notable that Christ later commends them for hating the deeds of the Nicolaitans, which he also hates (see v6). The Nicolaitans are mentioned again in Christ's message to the church in Pergamos, and the things that they stood for will be discussed there. The important point here is that the Ephesian believers detested and resisted the things this group did because those things were not of God. They hated the things God hated. This is a challenge to us. We need to ask ourselves if we sufficiently hate and resist all that is not of God and is opposed to God.

Lastly, Christ also commends them for testing those who claimed to be apostles but were not, and finding them to be liars (to be false apostles and deceivers). This was all part of their detestation of evil. Because of their awareness of the evil nature and harmfulness of false teaching, they tested all who claimed to preach the word of Christ and resisted all who were found to be false. This is a great challenge to us in a day when there is a great reluctance to test teachers and to oppose those who teach falsehood.

So we see that this was a faithful church. It was a church that Christ could commend for its hard work, its perseverance, and its concern for righteousness and truth. In short, this was a church zealous for the things of God; and clearly, all of this stands as an example and challenge to us.

v4. However, this church had one major fault which Christ highlights to them. They had left their first love — they had departed from the fervent love for Christ that they had at first. This does not mean that they had no love for Christ, or that their works were done hypocritically or were empty. It is clear from what has already been said that the Ephesian believers had a genuine devotion to Christ (they wanted above all to honour and serve him, and they were concerned for his righteousness and truth). Moreover, the works they did sprang from this devotion, and Christ commends them for all they have done for him. Nevertheless, there was something radically and seriously wrong, and this was that they had departed from the fervent love for Christ that they had when first they knew him. Essentially, what they no longer had was that fundamental desire for Christ himself, the desire to know him and to commune with him; what they now lacked was that fundamental appreciation of Christ and delight in him for who he is and all he has done.

This departure from their first love was a very serious matter because it involved a departure from Christ's fundamental purpose for the church, which is that we should love him. Christ laid down his life for the church not that we might serve him, but that we might be his and live with him in a relationship of love and devotion through all eternity (although, loving him we will obey him and serve him). This is expressed especially in the whole biblical imagery of the church as Christ's bride for whom he laid down his life that he might purify her and bring her to himself (it is notable that Paul wrote in these terms in his letter to the Ephesians — see Eph 5:25–27). Therefore, if we lose our personal love for and devotion to Christ himself, we have fallen away from the very essence of our relationship with him.

Sadly, it is not uncommon for Christians to fall away from their first love. When a person is first converted there is usually a great desire to commune with Christ, and a great enthusiasm for and appreciation of Christ and his saving love, out of which flows a great devotion to serving him. Too often, however, the same person is to be found some time later still working hard for Christ (and perhaps even doing more than before), but having lost the personal appreciation of and desire for Christ himself which he had at first. This is what had happened in the Ephesian church, and this has been a constant danger since.

v5. Having exposed their condition, Christ then sets before them the remedy. First, he tells them to "remember therefore from where you have fallen" — he calls them to remember how they used to be, comparing their present state with this. In doing this, they should see their backsliding, feel grieved and ashamed by it, and truly desire to be restored. Then he calls them to "repent and do the first works" (the things they did at first). They needed to confess how far they had fallen and sincerely seek God for a renewing of that first love. Also they needed to devote themselves to such things as meditating on Christ revealed in his word, and to worship and prayer. These were the things that would help their hearts be warmed again to a fervent love for Christ. This is not to imply that the Ephesian believers had stopped reading God's word and praying and so on — undoubtedly they still did these things. What is likely is that this had become very lacking in real contemplation and worship of Christ himself, and it was this that needed renewing.

Christ then warns them of serious judgement if they do not repent and stir themselves to a renewed love for himself: he says, "I will come to you quickly and remove your lampstand from its place". The consequence for this church, if they are impenitent, will be that Christ will suddenly and surprisingly judge them by withholding his influences so that they will no longer be an effective witness. Christ may also mean that the church will cease to exist. Certainly, this would be the eventual consequence of their witness no longer being effective; with no new converts being added to it, the church would eventually die out.

This seems a very severe judgement, especially in view of the fact that this church had so much to be commended for. However, it is a just judgement. Moreover, its severity highlights the seriousness of this sin. As noted, this was a failing which struck at the very heart of their whole relationship with Christ. It also undermined both their witness and their fitness to be a church to which Christ added new believers (a church that is lacking in heartfelt love for Christ will not be a fit place for new believers to be nurtured, no matter how commendable its works may be). Moreover, this failing was also serious because a lack of love for Christ will lead to other sin. (In fact, it may well be that this is the first of the seven messages because a loss of love for Christ is a factor in all other backsliding; conversely, a renewed love for Christ is the key to throwing off other sinful ways, and to knowing a new devotion to righteousness and truth and to serving Christ.)

v6. Christ then returns to a matter for commendation — they hate the deeds of the Nicolaitans, which he also hates. Here we see the loving way Christ reproves this church, which had many good ways. He reproves them in the midst of showing that he also takes note of the good things they do. Christ combines reproof with commendation, and this is an example to us.

v7. There is then the call to hear. It is notable that it is addressed to "he" who has an ear. The message is to the church, but it is each individual believer's responsibility to respond to Christ's message.

Christ's message is also termed "what the Spirit says to the churches", reminding us that this is for all churches to heed.

Thus our response should be to examine ourselves in the light of this message. Especially, we need to examine ourselves concerning our love for Christ; then, as necessary, we need to heed the call of this message to repent and to do what is needful to be stirred again to a fervent love for Christ.

Finally, there is the promise of reward for the overcomer — to him Christ "will give to eat from the tree of life, which is in the midst of the Paradise of God". Using the garden of Eden as imagery, this is first of all a promise of eternal life in heaven, which is ours through Christ (the real tree of life). However, since we have a foretaste of that life now, it also contains a promise of a present closer communion with Christ and strengthening of spiritual life. The overcomer will be restored, and more than restored, to the relationship with Christ he once knew; and with this will come a renewed longing and hope for his eternal destiny.

Christ's message to the church in Smyrna (2:8–11)

v8. Smyrna was a church that was suffering considerable trouble and persecution. Of note, however, is that this is one of the two churches (the other being Philadelphia) to which Christ speaks no words of rebuke. Very often a church keeps its purity best in the heat of persecution.

To this church, Christ describes himself as "the First and the Last, who was dead, and came to life". So, this church's attention was called to the fact that Christ is the eternal God and Lord over all, and that he overcame death and rose up to life (he is the firstborn from the dead and has power over death — 1:5,18). This description of Christ contains great encouragement for a persecuted church.

v9. Christ then begins by making clear to this church that he knows all they are enduring. He says he knows their tribulation — the trouble and affliction they were having to endure. Here we should take this to be referring not to the trials common to all men, but troubles they were having to endure for

Christ's sake (because they were Christians). These, it seems, were great; but Christ says he knows, which would have been a great comfort to them.

Christ also says he knows their poverty (their material poverty) — again, something they were suffering for Christ's sake. The cause of this poverty is not indicated. One possibility is that they had suffered the spoiling or confiscation of their goods at the hands of those who were enemies of the gospel (see Heb 10:34 for an example of this). Another possibility is that they had little work because they would not attend the idolatrous and immoral trade guild banquets, which were key to gaining work and earning a living (the guild banquets are discussed later, in the message to Pergamos — see 2:14). Whatever the cause, this was a people suffering significant material loss and lack because of their Christian faith. However, Christ comforts them by showing them that he knows. Moreover, he adds that really they are rich — they have spiritual riches that no one can keep from them or take away.

Christ further makes clear that he knows the falsehood, opposition and wickedness of their enemies — "the blasphemy of those who say they are Jews and are not, but are a synagogue of Satan". Here Christ is referring to the Jews who rejected him and the gospel — those who were Jews racially, but who, by rejecting Christ and not believing in him, showed they were not true Jews (not true children of Abraham or the true people of God). Such Jews were amongst the fiercest opponents of the churches; and it seems that in Smyrna these Jews were vehemently opposing the church — speaking against and slandering the believers (probably Christ was being blasphemed and the believers were being accused of being heretics who had departed from God). However, Christ shows them that he knows the wickedness and opposition of these unbelieving Jews. Moreover, he makes clear how he views them: they are a synagogue of Satan — they were not a congregation belonging to God and serving God, but a congregation belonging to Satan, serving his purposes and furthering his interests.

In all of this there is warning, challenge and comfort for us. This message serves as a reminder of some of the things that we are called to suffer for Christ's sake — and that we will suffer if we fulfil our calling to live godly and righteous lives in the world and to serve the cause of the gospel. If we do this we will suffer much tribulation for Christ's sake; we may suffer material loss; and we will suffer persecution of one kind or another. Moreover, this message also sets before us something important for us to recognise and accept, which is that the persecution we suffer may include persecution by the merely religious — that is, by individuals and churches that call themselves Christian but are unbelieving and are engaged in a mere form of religion. However, there is also encouragement here — the assurance that whatever trials and difficulties we have to endure for Christ's sake, Christ knows and cares about all we are going through.

v10. Having shown them that he knows their present troubles, Christ then forewarns them of a great future trial, encouraging them to stand. Here is further comfort — to know that Christ not only knows our present trials and sufferings, but he also knows our future trials and will prepare us for them.

Christ tells them not to fear any of the things they are about to suffer. This, of course, was not something they could do in their own strength but only through the truth and power of God. However, it is notable that Christ had already set before this church truths that, by his grace, would serve to calm their fear (the fact that he is Lord over all, that he has overcome death, and that he knows all of their trials). This is an encouragement to us to know that when we have to face great trials, Christ by his word and his Spirit will enable us not to fear but to be strong.

Christ then tells them that the devil is about to throw some of them into prison, that they may be tested. This reminds us that although we suffer persecution at the hands of men, it is the devil who is behind this. It is he who stirs people up against the church, although they are culpable participants as they give vent to their own sinful hatred of God. However, Christ also makes clear that although the devil's intent was evil, this trial was not for their harm. Rather, it was to befall them that they might be tested — that their faith and endurance might be proved and increased, and they might grow in character, to the glory of God. So we see that God uses even the deeds of the devil and of evil men to serve his purposes and our good.

Christ also tells them that they will have tribulation ten days. This time is probably not meant to be taken literally but as an indication that God, not the devil, is in control. This short, precise time period indicates that this trial is by God's will, that the time is limited, and that when God's wise and perfect purpose has been served, God will bring it to an end. Here is further encouragement to strengthen us — the reminder that all we have to endure, including severe persecution, is under Christ's lordship.

Christ then calls and encourages them to be faithful until death. This is the ultimate victory in persecution. When the devil persecutes the church, one of his great goals is to cause believers to deny their faith and to forsake Christ. For the believer, to overcome persecution and have the victory is not to escape persecution, but to maintain their confession of faith and walk with Christ in the midst of it, even unto death. So, Christ calls these persecuted believers in Smyrna to be faithful until death. Moreover, he encourages them to be faithful with a promise of great reward — the crown of life. A person forfeiting his life for Christ's sake does not suffer loss, but gains the blessing of eternal life.

v11. Finally, there is the call to hear and the reward for the overcomer. "He who overcomes [who endures and remains faithful to the end] shall not be hurt by the second death." The second death is a term Revelation uses for the final fate of the wicked — a fate of everlasting punishment (see 21:8). The overcomer (which, by God's grace, the true believer will be) will not have to suffer this fate; rather, his destiny is life in God's presence forever. So, here is further comfort for believers enduring great trials for Christ's sake: the assurance that whatever suffering or loss they have in this life (even the forfeit of life itself), ahead is no loss but only blessing and gain — life with God forevermore.

Christ's message to the church in Pergamos (2:12–17)

v12. To this church, Christ describes himself as "He who has the sharp two-edged sword" (see 1:16). So, this church's attention was drawn to the living and powerful word of God by which God judges the hearts of men. Christ drew attention to this because in his message to this church there was going to be an exposing and judging of their deeds.

v13. However, in many ways this was a faithful church, and Christ begins with words of commendation. He makes clear to them that he knows their difficult situation, and he has seen and taken note of their faithfulness in the midst of it.

He says they dwell "where Satan's throne is", and "where Satan dwells". It is not certain precisely what this refers to. Possible explanations are that in Pergamos was a temple to the principal Greek god; or this was a centre of Emperor worship; or the Roman governor of the city was a violent enemy of the church (and the seat of persecution is Satan's seat). Whatever the specific meaning of this might be, the important point here is that this was a city where Satan's hold and influence was particularly great; it was a city of particular godlessness and wickedness and opposition to God. Therefore, this was a place where it was especially difficult to be a Christian, and where it was particularly hard for Christians to maintain their godly life and faithful witness. Yet, in the face of this, this church was remaining faithful to Christ. The believers were holding fast to his name — against all difficulties they were continuing to confess Christ and were not shrinking back from being identified with him. Moreover, they did not deny their faith in him even in the days when Antipas was martyred — even when one of their

notable people was martyred for his faith, they did not shrink
back from confessing and following Christ, but remained
faithful. For all of this Christ commends them.

So, here we have an example of faithfulness in a situation of
great godlessness and wickedness, where temptation and
opposition are great. Also, we have a reminder that churches and
Christians differ in their circumstances, and some have to
maintain their life and witness in much more difficult situations
than others. However, Christ knows if a church's situation is
especially difficult. Not only that, he takes special note when his
people remain faithful in the midst of such circumstances. This
is a great comfort and encouragement to a church that is having
to remain faithful in a situation of great godlessness and
opposition to Christ.

v14. However, while sustaining this faithful witness to
Christ, the church in Pergamos had allowed itself to become
infiltrated with error and was tolerating this; and for this Christ
admonishes them.

First, Christ says they have there "those who hold the
doctrine of Balaam, who taught Balak to put a stumbling block
before the children of Israel, to eat things sacrificed to idols, and
to commit sexual immorality". This is a reference to an incident
recorded in the book of Numbers. Balak, the king of Moab,
commissioned Balaam to curse the Israelites, but God did not
allow this. Following this, it seems that Balaam advised Balak
that he could cause the Israelites to come under God's judgement
if he could induce them to worship idols; and it seems that this
counsel was acted upon, with some success. Moabite women
went to the Israelites and invited them to the sacrifices of their
gods. By this means the Israelites, who most probably had no
intention of committing idolatry, were enticed into eating food
sacrificed to idols (and so into idolatry) and into sexual
immorality (which was part of these feasts), for which God
judged them (see Num 25:1–5; also 31:16). In this way Balak put

a stumbling block before the people and they were caused to stumble.

From this we see that, in essence, the fault in Pergamos was that they had in their midst people who were advocating and encouraging involvement in worldly ways and pursuits, and so were encouraging compromise with the world (all worldliness is both harlotry, ie, unfaithfulness to God, and idolatry, ie, serving something other than God). This, of course, is contrary to the way we should walk as Christians. Our calling is to be in the world but not of the world; so we are to cast off worldly ways, to keep ourselves unpolluted by the world, and, as far as possible, to keep apart from things which can draw us into compromise and sin.

More specifically, however, these people were probably advocating attendance at the trade guild banquets. At that time, nearly every trade had its own guild with its own patron god and guild temple, and belonging to a guild played an important part in earning a living. However, membership of a guild involved attending the guild banquets at which food offered to idols was eaten and sexual immorality indulged in. Clearly, for Christians, attendance at these banquets was unacceptable. However, refusal to attend made it hard for Christians to earn a living (we have already noted that this could have been the cause of the poverty at Smyrna). Consequently, a temptation the early Christians faced was to compromise in this matter. And it is probable that this is what those who held the doctrine of Balaam were doing — they were maintaining that attendance at the trade guild banquets was acceptable (perhaps they argued that an idol was nothing). Moreover, by this they were putting a stumbling block before others — they were encouraging others to participate in something that could lead them into idolatry and immorality (and very probably they were causing some believers to stumble).

Here we see one of the great ploys of the devil to lead God's people away from God — which is to infiltrate the church with teachings and ideas that, rather than encouraging separation from false religion and worldly ways, encourage involvement in or association with these things. Those advocating such things place a stumbling block before others which can lead people into sin and compromise with the world.

Clearly, this state of affairs was displeasing to Christ. Of note, however, is that Christ's words of disapproval are directed not just at those holding this harmful doctrine, but at the whole church. This suggests that Christ's displeasure was not just with those spreading error, but it was also with the church in general for tolerating them. The church should have responded by addressing the error and warning those in error, but they had not done this. Why this was, is not clear. It could be that they did not recognise the error; or, unlike the Ephesian believers, they lacked a right detestation of error; or they were avoiding the unpleasant task of exercising discipline. It is also possible that they did not deal with the error because it enabled them to attend the guild banquets and so avoid material loss. What is clear, however, is that they were at fault in tolerating in their midst and not disciplining those who held and spread this error.

This, therefore, is a fault that we must guard against by keeping alert to teaching and ideas that encourage compromise with the world, and by dealing with those who are spreading error and placing a stumbling block before others. Today, this is something few churches seem willing to do. However, it is something that must be done, remembering that both worldliness and toleration of error displease Christ.

v15. Having addressed this error, Christ then goes on to say that thus (in this fashion) they "also have those who hold the doctrine of the Nicolaitans, which thing I hate". Most take the connection between this verse and the previous verse to indicate that the doctrine of the Nicolaitans was akin to (although not identical to) what is termed here 'the doctrine of Balaam'. However, it is held by some that this was a different teaching, which set forth a special priestly order in the church and led to leaders having a wrong authority over the people (this is deduced from a possible translation of the word 'Nicolaitans' which is, 'subjecting the people or laity'). Certainly, this is something that quite early on did develop in the church, deviating it from the true form of leadership. Whatever this doctrine was, however, Christ here is admonishing the church for also tolerating in their midst those who hold this doctrine, which he says he hates. Christ hates all that is opposed to his truth and that leads his people into sin and bondage.

v16. Christ then calls the church to repent. They must stop tolerating this error in their midst, and they must discipline those who hold these harmful doctrines. This was vital to maintain the purity and witness of the church, and also for the sake of those in error. Christ also warns them of serious and sudden judgement if they do not do this. He says "I will come to you quickly and will fight against them [those who hold these doctrines] with the sword of My mouth." This, in part, must mean that if the church will not deal with those who are holding false doctrine and putting a stumbling block before others, then he will deal with them himself — he will expose their sin and judge them. However, since the call to repent was directed at the whole church, we need also to see this as a judgement that will in some way affect the wider church. Most probably, Christ's intervention to deal with those in error will bring for the whole church a time of great turmoil, disharmony and disarray. It must stand as a sobering warning to us that a church tolerating serious error will come under Christ's chastening.

v17. Finally, there is the call to hear, and the promise of two things for the overcomer. Christ says that to him who overcomes he "will give some of the hidden manna to eat". This contrasts with the food associated with idol worship, and speaks of Christ, the bread of life. Those who overcome will know spiritual nourishment and strengthening of their souls now, and Christ's sustenance eternally. Also, the overcomer will be given "a white stone, and on the stone a new name written which no one knows except him who receives it". The significance here of the giving of a white stone is uncertain, and numerous different explanations have been offered. The fact that the stone is said to have a new name written on it known only by the recipient, indicates that essentially this in some way is signifying the believer's adoption into the family of God. So, this reward for those who took a stand against the erroneous doctrines that encouraged compromise with the world was a greater assurance of belonging to God and a sure inheritance in heaven.

Christ's message to the church in Thyatira (2:18–29)

v18. Thyatira was a trading town, and is mentioned in Scripture as the town from which Lydia came (see Acts 16:14). To this church, Christ describes himself as "the Son of God, who has eyes like a flame of fire, and His feet like fine brass" (see 1:14–15). By this description, Christ drew attention to his divinity and majesty, to his penetrating insight, and to his steadfastness and judgement. He is God who sees and judges with perfect wisdom and strength. This description of Christ indicated that judgement was at hand.

v19. First, however, Christ has things for which to commend the church, things which therefore stand as an example to us. The qualities for which he commends them are their love, service, faith and patience. These perhaps should be understood together. They had a disposition to do good to others, even at personal cost; they gave of themselves in the service of others; they did this out of faith in and devotion to Christ; and they did this with steadfastness and perseverance. Christ also commends them that their works have increased ("the last are more than the first"). They were growing in fruitfulness.

v20. However, there were things for which Christ had to admonish this church. He says they were allowing "that woman Jezebel, who calls herself a prophetess, to teach and seduce My servants to commit sexual immorality and eat things sacrificed to idols". This is a reference to Jezebel, the pagan wife of Ahab (see 1 Kgs 16:31). She was a worshipper of Baal, and she practised and promoted the worship of Baal in Israel. So, heathen religious practices were encouraged in the midst of the people of God.

Using Jezebel as a figure, Christ is admonishing this church for allowing a certain person (or persons) who claimed to have God's teaching for the church, to teach things that brought sinful practices into the church and that enticed the people into sin. Here, we could take literally the reference to sexual immorality and eating things sacrificed to idols. However, what is said here can also be taken figuratively to indicate that this teacher was promoting pagan or worldly ways and practices in the church, thus creating a mixture of Christianity and the world (as already noted, all worldliness is both harlotry and idolatry). Certainly, this is a trap that the church of all ages has fallen into.

The most significant example of this is to be seen in the development of the Roman Catholic religion during the earlier centuries of the church. At the beginning, the church had a simple form of worship, and a simple faith and life. Some centuries later, however, we find a church with worship full of ritual and symbolism, priests in ornate robes, the cult of Mary, Saints' days, prayers for the dead, belief in purgatory, and much more. Essentially, there had been great change in the church's worship, faith and life — change which at first sight is difficult to comprehend. However, when we look at the world in which the church was living, we can see that much of this change came through the church absorbing and Christianizing pagan beliefs and practices — the product of which was the Roman Catholic religion which is essentially a mixture of Christianity and the pagan world.

Thus the problem in Thyatira, like that in Pergamos, was that the church had in its midst a person or persons who were encouraging worldly ways. Moreover, the fact that this was a second church that Christ had to address concerning this, highlights the great danger that worldliness is to the church. However, while there is some similarity between what was happening in the two churches, there is also a significant difference. Comparing the illustrations used (Balaam and Jezebel), it seems that in Pergamos they had in the midst people who were spreading ideas that encouraged the believers to participate in things in the world around them that could lead them into sin. In Thyatira, however, there was an actual teacher who was teaching error that was bringing pagan or worldly beliefs and practices into the church itself (into its worship and life); so, they were leading the church away from the true faith and true way into a mixture of Christianity and the world.

In this we see another of the great ploys of the devil to lead God's people into sin and error: it is to infiltrate the church with false teachers who introduce false religion or worldly beliefs and practices into the life of the church. Of note, however, is that what is foremost in Christ's rebuke is not his displeasure with the one introducing error, but his displeasure at the church for tolerating this teacher and allowing error to be taught. Basically, the church should have stopped this person teaching error, but for some reason they did not. It is possible that they allowed this teaching because it justified them engaging in worldly ways, or it brought them acceptability in the world. Alternatively, there may be a clue to the reason for their failure to discipline this false teacher in the description of this person as 'Jezebel'. Jezebel was a very formidable, powerful woman, who not only promoted Baal worship in Israel but also persecuted the prophets of God (1 Kgs 18:4). Therefore, it could be that this teacher was a forceful, overpowering person who was difficult to stand against. Certainly such people can be found in all walks of life, and in the church can be powerful instruments for harm. However, even if this teacher was like this, the church should have dealt with this person.

From this we see the importance of testing the doctrine of teachers, and of dealing with any teachers who are teaching error. Particularly, it reminds us of the importance of both watching for, and protecting the church from, teaching that would bring false religion or worldly beliefs and practices into the worship and life of the church.

v21. Christ then warns of the judgement that will befall this church if this situation goes on. First, Christ says he has given this seducer of the people time to repent, but there has been no repentance. Here we see the great mercy and patience of God in being slow to judge and giving a time of opportunity for repentance. This was also a time, of course, when the church had opportunity to deal with this false teacher, but they had not done this.

v22. Christ then describes how, unless there is repentance, he will deal with this false teacher, and with those who have been seduced and have embraced this false teaching ("those who commit adultery with her"). Christ says he will cast Jezebel "into a sick bed". This could literally mean that this false teacher will be given over to physical sickness; or it may mean that this person will be completely turned over to their sin, which will bring only harm and pain. He also says he will cast those who have embraced Jezebel's teaching "into great tribulation". Again, this could literally mean that God will cast them into actual trials; or it may mean that they also will be turned over to the ways they have chosen, which will cause them only great trouble. However, still, right up to the last moment, Christ is holding out the opportunity for repentance. All of this may be avoided if they repent.

v23. Christ also says he will "kill her children with death". This seems to refer to a different category of people from those who commit adultery with Jezebel. Most likely it refers to the really devoted disciples of this false teacher (they are being created in Jezebel's likeness). These, Christ says, he will kill with death. This could mean that, given over to their sin, their lives will become a complete ruin; it could also mean that they will suffer the second death — that is, they are not saved ones and are destined for everlasting punishment (see 21:8). Certainly, a person who follows false teaching in the way that these did, gives evidence of not truly being saved.

Christ further says that this judgement will serve to show all the churches that he is "He who searches the minds and hearts" — he knows and examines the thoughts and intents of men. This should cause all to rightly fear God and cleanse themselves from sin. However, with this Christ also makes clear his impartial justice — he says he will "give to each one of you according to your works". As Christ looked upon this church he saw each person individually, and he knew the one who taught this error and seduced the people; he knew who were zealous disciples of this false teacher; he knew who in weakness had been seduced into this error; and he knew which ones had kept themselves apart from it. He saw and would deal with each one accordingly. So, we should be comforted in the knowledge of the equity of Christ's justice. However, this should also stand as a warning to us of serious judgement if we embrace ungodly, worldly teaching.

v24,25. Christ then addresses those who have not embraced this false teaching. These he describes as those "who have not known the depths of Satan, as they say". This description makes clear that Satan, their adversary, was behind this false doctrine (and is behind all mixture in the church). It also indicates that this teaching was presented as bringing them deep mysteries and insights. To those who had not embraced this error Christ says he will put on them no other burden, but they must hold fast what they have until he comes. Christ was not going to burden them with new teachings or commands. They had the faith, and all they needed to do was to give attention to this, to live by it, and to hold fast to it until the end. This is the responsibility of us all. There will be no new doctrines to receive or practices to obey. Our faith is set down in Scripture and we must endeavour to know this and keep it to the end.

v26,27. There then follows the reward for the overcomer — for the one who remains free of or rejects these false doctrines and worldly ways, and who keeps on to the very end in the way that Christ has set down. To him Christ says "I will give power over the nations...as I also have received from My Father". This is a promise that the overcomer will share in the victory of Christ over this world and over those opposed to God.

v28. Christ also says he will give to the overcomer "the morning star". Christ is the bright and morning star (22:16). He brings to us the day — he brings the light of truth and holiness to our souls now, and he will bring us to dwell in perfect truth and holiness in the life to come. So, the reward for the overcomer who rejects these worldly teachings will be more grace to his soul now, and the eternal destiny of heaven where there is eternal day, and truth and righteousness dwell in full measure.

v29. Finally, is the call to hear. In the previous three messages this came before the reward for the overcomer. In this message, and the remaining three, it comes at the very end. This highlights that it is important to pay attention to the promised rewards as well as to the instructions and warnings Christ gives. Of course, we should cast off sin and obey Christ because this is right to do. However, we are also moved to do this by the present spiritual benefits that obedience brings and the eternal blessings to come. Therefore we need to pay attention not only to Christ's admonitions and warnings, but also to his promised rewards. Together they will spur us on to a godly and pure life.

Chapter 3
Letters to the churches (cont.)

Christ's message to the church in Sardis (3:1–6)

v1. To this church, the Lord Jesus Christ describes himself as "He who has the seven Spirits of God and the seven stars". So, Christ depicts himself as having the Holy Spirit with his various operations and graces, thus drawing attention to the fact that the gift of the Holy Spirit is bestowed by him. Also, he draws this church's notice to the fact that the churches' leaders are in his keeping and under his government, and all their light and influence is from him. This was very appropriate for this church. This was a church and ministry that was languishing; and this would remind them of the source of the church's life and power, and the source of a reviving work of God among them. All of our life and power is from Christ by the power of the Holy Spirit.

Then, as with all the other churches, Christ says he knows their works — he has seen and taken note of all the circumstances and deeds of this church. However, whereas in the previous messages Christ begins with a word of commendation, here there is no word of commendation; rather, he begins with a sharp reproof. No doubt there were some good things in this church; nevertheless, the overall, general condition of the church was poor and deteriorating, and Christ addresses this urgently and directly.

He says to them "you have a name [or a reputation] that you are alive, but you are dead". From this we can conclude that outwardly this church appeared to be a good church with a lively religion, so that people seeing it could conclude that it was alive. So, no doubt, there were gatherings for worship and for prayer, the word of God was preached, the Lord's Supper was observed, there were bonds of friendship between the people, concern was shown for the lost — and everything was done with a kind of enthusiasm for the things of God. Consequently there was an appearance of life. However, the verdict of Jesus, who sees all things truly and who sees into the hearts of men, was that they were dead. This does not mean that the people were spiritually dead, but the church was dead, in the sense that the things they did were lifeless.

Essentially, the problem with this church was that it had decayed into a mere outward form of religion. So, worship services and prayer meetings were held but they were lifeless — not in the sense of dull (they may have been lively), but in the sense that the worship was not heartfelt and true, the preaching was not with power, and the prayer was lacking in fervour and faith. Similarly, there was a kind of godly living and devotion to serving God, but not true holiness of life and dedicated discipleship. Also, there was a bond between the believers and they enjoyed meeting together, but there was a lack of true fellowship (of sharing in the things of Christ, and having common desires, goals, hopes and concerns). And, there was some concern for the lost, but a lack of real zeal for evangelism and fruitfulness in evangelism. So, Christ says they are dead. He saw the true condition of the church. They may have been able to give a false impression to others, and even fool themselves into thinking that they were in a commendable condition, but nothing is hidden from Christ.

The condition of this church must stand as a warning to us that it is very possible for a Christian or a church to have an appearance of life, when really there is very little spiritual life and fruit. Therefore, we must always guard against the life of the church becoming or being only an outward form — a condition which is especially dangerous because it can fool us and others into thinking all is well when it is not. However, Christ is not fooled — he sees, and mercifully he acts to make known his assessment of things and to revive his people.

v2. Christ then makes clear to this church what it needed to do for its condition to be remedied (for it to be revived). First he tells them to "be watchful" — they needed to wake up and examine their life, and become aware of their condition. For them this was a vital first step to seeing and repenting of their backsliding. However, being watchful is important for the church at all times because of our constant tendency to backslide. Church history gives numerous examples of new movements or churches that at first were full of life, but some years later were to be found having only an outward form remaining. One of the things that contributes to such a decline is a failure to be watchful. And one of the reasons for the poor condition of the church in Sardis was that it had stopped being watchful.

Christ also tells them to "strengthen the things which remain, that are ready to die". There was still some true spiritual life and fruitfulness in Sardis, although this was about to expire, and Christ tells them to strengthen this. They must recognise what constitutes true life and fruitfulness and endeavour to increase in this. Christ adds, "for I have not found your works perfect before God". In the eyes of others this was an admirable church; but in Christ's assessment this church might have done more for him, and what they had done might have been done with greater uprightness and sincerity. Essentially, their works did not measure up to the standard of life, fruitfulness and holiness God wants from his people.

v3. Christ then calls them to "remember therefore how you have received and heard". This is a call to remember both the message that brought them salvation, and also the effect the message of salvation had on them. So, part of the remedy to their condition was contemplation of the truth concerning Christ and his saving work. It is by means of this truth that God first saves his people; and it is this same truth that is the means by which a church that has fallen into great deadness and decay will be brought to repentance, and enter into a renewing of spiritual life. A further part of the remedy to their condition was to recall the impression the gospel of Christ had had on their souls when first they believed, and to remember the affections and devotion it had stirred in their hearts and the fruit it had borne in their lives. A remembrance of this would help them to see their present condition and long to be revived. It is notable that Christ's call to remember how they have received and heard shows that this church had once known powerful gospel preaching, and the people knew what it was to have their hearts moved by God and their lives changed. However, this had been lost.

Christ then tells them to "hold fast and repent". They must keep a firm hold on what they have so that they do not lose everything, and they must repent. All that Christ had already said was aimed at leading this church to repentance, and now they must repent: they must truly confess before Christ their backsliding, and deadness, and fruitlessness; and they must seek Christ for a renewing of spiritual life and a new fruitfulness.

Christ then warns them of what will befall them if they will not watch (if they will not examine themselves and see their condition) — he will come upon them as a thief, and they will not know what hour he will come upon them. If they refuse to recognise and acknowledge their deadness and fruitlessness, Christ will judge them — most probably he will remove from them their remaining enjoyments of him and their remaining fruitfulness. Moreover, this will happen suddenly and unexpectedly because they have not heeded Christ's word and are still unaware of their condition.

v4. Yet even in this church there were a few who had maintained their life and fruitfulness. Describing this, Christ says that the church has "a few names...have not defiled their garments". This description of these as "a few names" shows that they were personally known to Christ. He not only views the church as a whole but he sees each member individually. Moreover, even when a church is in a generally dead state, Christ sees and takes note of those who are maintaining their Christian life. And there were some even in Sardis.

Moreover, these faithful ones are said to have not defiled their garments. These garments cannot be garments of justification because the righteousness imputed to us in Christ, by which we are justified, cannot be tainted. Rather, the garments here must signify their practical holiness. It was this that was not defiled. Of course, this does not mean that they had not sinned, for even the most devoted believer sins. Rather, this means that these ones had been watchful of their lives, and they had sought to walk in Christ's ways and to keep themselves free from the pollution of the world; moreover, when they had sinned they had been aware of this, and had confessed and turned from their sin and known God's forgiveness and cleansing.

Christ's recognition of these faithful ones would have been a great encouragement to them. However, it also gives us some insight into the cause of the deadness in Sardis. It suggests that the root cause of the church's spiritual deadness and fruitlessness was that the believers were living lives tainted by ungodly and sinful ways. A slipping back into such ways will always lead to a decline in spiritual life and fruitfulness (it is notable that this message comes after those to Pergamos and Thyatira, which concerned the introduction of worldliness into the life of the church). However, some in Sardis had lived lives of real practical holiness and kept themselves unspotted from the world. And these, Christ says, "shall walk with Me in white, for they are worthy". They would know the blessing of a close walk with Christ, a clear conscience, and Christ's power in their lives to walk in holiness and to overcome sin and the world (Christ's statement that they are worthy, does not mean that they had merited this walk with Christ; rather, they had lived lives that made them fit to walk with Christ in this way).

v5. There then follows the promised reward for the overcomer (for the one who will take an honest look at himself, and confess his spiritual deadness and fruitlessness, and devote himself afresh to walking in God's ways). Christ says the overcomer "shall be clothed in white garments". Such a person would know the blessing of their sin forgiven, and Christ's power in their life to walk in holiness. They could also be assured of the blessing of purity, dignity and honour in the life to come.

Christ also says he "will not blot out his name from the Book of Life", but he "will confess his name before My Father and before His angels". This cannot possibly mean that the believers were at risk of losing their salvation, but if they overcame this would not happen. No one whose name is written in the Lamb's book of life can ever have his name erased. Rather, this should be understood in a similar way to Christ's promise to the church in Smyrna, that he who overcame would not be hurt by the second death (see 2:11); it should be seen as an encouragement that the true believer will overcome. True believers will respond to Christ's call to repent, and they will walk with Christ in white garments of real practical holiness. They will prove they are saved ones by the purity of their walk, and on that day when all men are judged, Christ will confess before his Father that he knows them and they are his, and they will enter into their eternal reward.

v6. Lastly is the call to hear what the Spirit says to the churches. Again, the call is not just to this church, but it is a call to "the churches" to pay careful attention to this message. Thus it sets before us the challenge to examine ourselves (both as individuals and churches), and to consider to what degree it is true of us that we have an appearance of being alive but really we are dead — that we have an outward form of religion but are lacking in true spiritual life and fruitfulness. Facing such a challenge will not be easy; however, we need to remember that Christ gave these messages to the churches not to condemn them, but that they might be purified and strengthened. Thus, he wants this message to be to us a means of purifying and strengthening; and, by his grace, it can and will be.

Christ's message to the church in Philadelphia (3:7–13)

v7. To this church, Christ describes himself as "He who is holy, He who is true, He who has the key of David, He who opens and no one shuts, and shuts and no one opens". This portrayal of Christ as having the key of David expresses the fact that Christ has authority over the church, and the government of the church belongs to him (see Is 9:6–7 and 22:22). Similarly, the description of him opening and shutting expresses Christ's absolute and irresistible power. Christ has absolute sovereignty over his kingdom and no one can thwart his purpose. He opens the door of the kingdom of heaven to those he is saving, and he shuts the door to impenitent sinners. He opens doors of opportunity for individuals and churches (see 1 Cor 16:9; 2 Cor 2:12), and, if he pleases, he shuts doors of opportunity. Moreover, what he has purposed to do or to come to pass, no one can prevent; equally, what he does not purpose or brings to an end, no one can make happen. However, all of this is in accordance with his holiness and truth — he is holy and true in his nature, and in all his words and deeds, and thus he governs with justice in everything. So, Christ draws this church's attention to his sovereign and just government of the church, and the infallibility of all he wills and does.

v8. Then, again making clear that he knows all about this church, Christ calls them to see that he has set before them an open door that no one can shut. By this, we should probably understand that Christ had set before this church an opportunity for fruitful evangelism, which he assures them no one can deny them or thwart.

Christ also indicates the reason he has given them this opportunity: he says they have a little strength, have kept his word, and have not denied his name. In what respect they had a little strength is not clear; possibly they had little in the way of resources and advantages. Whatever this means, however, the commendable thing would seem to be that, while having little strength, in the midst of opposition and difficulties they had held to the truth and had remained faithful in their walk with and witness to Christ. And for this faithfulness, Christ has given them this opportunity for effective witness. Of course, this is not to imply that they had merited this. Essentially, the opportunities any church has are purely according to Christ's sovereign will and purpose. However, Christ is pleased to bless faithfulness, and to this church that was faithful to Christ and his word, Christ had been pleased to give a great opportunity for effective witness.

v9. Christ also tells them that he will make their enemies (those of the synagogue of Satan) "come and worship before your feet, and to know that I have loved you" — he will cause their enemies to recognise and acknowledge they are truly God's people. We cannot expect always to be vindicated in this life; however, it would seem that to this faithful church, God's validation is promised. Here we see another reference to the unbelieving Jews who claimed to be the true people of God, but who had rejected Christ and who opposed the church (see 2:9). To the church in Philadelphia Christ promises that these enemies of God and his church will, when they see what Christ does through them, have to humbly acknowledge that Christ has loved them and his blessing is upon them. Moreover, Christ's words could also indicate that some will actually receive the church's testimony, and repent and believe in Christ.

v10. Christ further says that because they have kept his command to persevere (because they have been loyal and steadfast in their Christian life and witness, and have not been drawn aside by the tests and trials that have come upon them) he will keep them "from the hour of trial which shall come upon the whole world, to test those who dwell on the earth". We do not know the exact nature of this great and testing trial. However, the important point here is that they had already been tested, and had been proved to be faithful. Therefore, now they would be given persevering grace in the trial to come, and they would not stumble. In the trials God brings, sometimes he allows his people to stumble to teach them; but the Philadelphian believers had been proved and would be given grace to stand. So we see an example of the principle that to him who has, more will be given (see Mt 13:12; Mk 4:25).

v11. Christ then calls their attention to his return. And he tells them to "hold fast what you have, that no one may take your crown" — he urges them to be steadfast, and to continue being faithful. This exhortation was important because, no matter how faithful a believer or church may have been, there is always the possibility of falling away from this. And so Christ urges them to continue. Moreover, he does this in association with calling their attention to his return. A great motivation for a believer to persevere and be faithful is the certain hope of Christ's return and the life to come, when we will be relieved of all suffering and trials, and our faithfulness will receive its final reward. Therefore, we must keep Christ's return set before us at all times. It will help us to persevere to the end. And, of course, by God's grace, the true believer will persevere, and will win the reward of life in heaven.

v12. On top of all the blessings already promised to this church, Christ still has a promise of reward for the overcomer. Here, the overcomer would seem to be the one who remains faithful to the very end. Christ says he will "make him a pillar in the temple of My God, and he shall go out no more". The overcomer will have a firm and permanent place in God's presence; also, he will be a monument to the grace and power of God. Christ also says he will "write on him the name of My God, and the name of the city of My God [the New Jerusalem], and My new name". The name of God indicates that the overcomer belongs to God; the name of the city of God signifies that he is a citizen of the new heavenly Jerusalem; and, "My new name" would seem to indicate that the overcomer belongs to Christ, and has a share in his redeeming work and victory. So, the overcomer will know a present real assurance of and experience of belonging to God and his kingdom, and have the certain destiny of a place in heaven.

v13. Finally is the call to hear what the Spirit says to the churches. Here, as in all the messages, we are to hear what the Spirit "says" (not what he "said") to the churches. God is always speaking this word.

This message, therefore, holds out wonderful promises to all who presently are being faithful to Christ and to his word — who are holding to and defending the truth, and who are being faithful in their Christian living and witness in the midst of the trials and temptations and doctrinal error of our day. To such as these, the promises of God set forth here apply. They will be given by God opportunities for effective evangelism. Also, they will know some vindication before their enemies (every church that proclaims, defends and lives by the truth will experience opposition, including from churches that have merely an outward form of religion or that have departed from the truth; however, God's blessing upon his faithful people in the midst of this will show that they are his people, and may cause even some opponents of the church to come to true faith in Christ). Added to this, those churches that have been remaining faithful to Christ and his word, God will keep in the midst of the tests and trials that are to come. Such churches, however, must take care to heed Christ's word to hold fast; they must continue in these good ways, looking to Christ's return.

Thus, this message to the church at Philadelphia is especially a message to those churches who, in this testing time, have been standing firm, holding to the truth, defending the faith, and maintaining their Christian life and witness. To such churches come the great promises here of fruitfulness in evangelism, of God's validation and of persevering grace, as they continue in faithfulness to Christ and his word.

Christ's message to the church of Laodicea (3:14–22)

v14. Laodicea was a wealthy, well-to-do city, famed for its resources and wealth. It was noted for its banking, for its manufacture of clothing, and it had a famous medical school. The church in this city is mentioned in Paul's letter to the Colossians, from which we see that this was a church that had received good teaching (see Col 4:16). By this time, however, it was in a very poor state.

To this church, Christ describes himself as "the Amen, the Faithful and True Witness, the Beginning of the creation of God". As a description of Christ, "the Amen" speaks of him as true and faithful, and speaks of the sure accomplishment of all God's purposes and promises in him. "The faithful and true witness" sets him forth as the one who has perfectly revealed God in his person, words and deeds, and whose testimony of God to men should be fully believed. "The beginning of the creation of God" could be a description of Christ as the creator and governor of all creation, but it also points to him as the source and head of the new creation, the church. So this church's attention was drawn to Christ's faithfulness, to his fulfilling of God's purposes, to his perfect revelation of God to men, and to God's new creation in him. All of this was an important reminder for this lukewarm church.

v15,16. Christ then, as in the other messages, describes their works. And for this church there is no word of commendation. Neither is there any mention by Christ of any individuals who have remained faithful, as was the case with the church in Sardis (v4). Rather, there is only a word of sharp rebuke for the whole church. This is because, as Christ looked upon this church and saw its works, he saw one overall and overriding thing — and that was lukewarmness. So this is what he highlights — he says that they are "neither cold nor hot", but they are "lukewarm". Essentially, these were Christians who were very half-hearted in their walk and witness as God's people. They were neither truly zealous for God, nor completely unconcerned. They professed a devotion to Christ, and lived in a certain fashion as Christians; but in their hearts there was a lack of real fervour for God and the things of God, and in their Christian living there was a lack of real devotion to following and serving Christ. This was a terrible condition to be in.

Moreover, commenting on this condition, Christ adds that he could wish they "were cold or hot" — either firmly and clearly against him, or firmly and clearly for him. This seems a strange thing to say, but it makes sense when we remember that matters to do with God, belief and religion are the most important matters, and they should elicit a strong reaction, for or against. They warrant being met with either earnest devotion if a religion is true, or earnest resistance if it is false. Anything less than this does not ascribe to these matters the importance they should have. Essentially, lukewarmness and religion are two things that do not belong together. Moreover, lukewarmness in Christianity is the worst possible thing because it dishonours Christ. It devalues Christ and his salvation by making this something of small importance and consequence, and less than worthy of full devotion. It is better to be openly antagonistic than lukewarm, because at least this ascribes significance to Christ.

Christ also says that because they are lukewarm, and neither cold nor hot, he will vomit them out of his mouth. By this graphic picture, Christ is making clear that in this condition they were distasteful and unacceptable and repulsive to him, and he could not bear them. Christ wanted them to know how grievous and intolerable their lukewarmness was to him, that they might repent.

v17. Having exposed their lukewarmness, and shown them how grievous it is to him, Christ then begins to counsel the Laodiceans concerning what they needed to do. He begins by contrasting their assessment of themselves with his assessment of them. And we see from this that this lukewarm church was also very self-deluded about its condition, and very self-confident, self-satisfied and complacent. The church says of itself, "I am rich, have become wealthy, and have need of nothing". The church considered itself to be a mature church, spiritually rich and with no need of anything more. However, Christ's assessment of the church, which is the true assessment, is quite different. He says that they do not know that really they are "wretched, miserable, poor, blind and naked". They are wretched — they are afflicted and pinned down by temptation; they are miserable — they are to be pitied; they are poor — they are spiritually poor and experiencing little of God's grace; they are blind — they are lacking a clear perception of Christ and his salvation, and are deluded about themselves; they are naked — they have no works or accomplishments and are in a sinful, shameful condition. This was a devastating assessment of the true state of the church; but Christ made this known not to condemn them, but to shake them out of their complacency and make them see their true condition, that they might repent.

v18. Having clearly set before them their self-delusion (they considered themselves to be rich and in need of nothing, but really they were poor, blind and naked), Christ then counsels them to buy from him the things that would remedy their condition and make them truly rich. Here he uses the riches of the city to speak of the spiritual riches they were to obtain from him, thus highlighting that it is his riches that are the true riches. Moreover, he calls them to "buy" from him what they lack. Of course, there was nothing they could give to procure the spiritual riches there are in Christ. Rather, as in Isaiah 55:1, this was an invitation to the spiritually needy to bring their need to Christ, and to receive freely from him all they lacked.

So, Christ calls them to buy from him gold refined in the fire, that they may be rich — they are to come to Christ and receive from him true riches, the spiritual riches that are in him. Also, they are to buy from him white garments to cover their shameful nakedness — they are to come to Christ to receive his cleansing, and to receive from him power to live holy lives of true devotion to God. He also counsels them to anoint their eyes with eye salve, that they may see — they are to come to Christ and receive from him revelation of the truth and a new comprehension of Christ and his salvation. So we see what it is that comprises true riches, and what we should all be desiring and seeking from Christ.

All of this begs the question: 'Why was this church lukewarm, and how could it be so self-deluded and think it was rich and lacking nothing?' A clue to this comes in the counsel Christ has just given them. Christ's use of the material riches of the city, as figures for the spiritual riches they lacked and should receive from him, points to the fact that their fundamental problem was that they still loved and lived for the riches of this world. This is a potential snare for all Christians; however, it is a particular snare for a church such as this that had been gathered out of and was living in an affluent, self-reliant society. Christians who have plenty of money and possessions, and who have accomplished much in this world (with all this brings in terms of comfort, security and status), will have to battle with a love of the things of this world in a way that Christians who are not in this position will not. And, if a Christian or church fails in this, the result will be lukewarmness. Scripture is clear that a person cannot love both God and the world, and that where a person's treasure is, there his heart will be also (see Mt 6:19–21,24; 1 Jn 2:15). Therefore, if a man's heart is set on the things of this world, it follows he will be cool towards God. And it would seem that this was the fundamental cause of this church's lukewarmness and accompanying spiritual poverty — it was that the believers' hearts were still set on the things of this world. Moreover, it seems their material wealth and human accomplishment distorted their assessment of themselves as a church, causing them to have an over-inflated opinion of themselves.

From this, we see that absolutely key to avoiding lukewarmness is that we guard against having our hearts set on and living for the riches this world gives (money, possessions, status, worldly pursuits and pleasures). Also crucial is that we keep watch over ourselves, and we make sure we are valuing and desiring above all things the spiritual riches there are in Christ. We must set our hearts on these things, and then not only will we have real enduring riches, but the things of this world will lose their value in our sight and their hold over us. A question every Christian needs to keep asking himself is: 'What is my treasure — is it Christ and the things of Christ, or the world and its riches?' Notably, there is a great contrast between this church in Laodicea which was materially rich and spiritually poor, and the church in Smyrna which was materially poor but spiritually rich. Too often material wealth and spiritual poverty go together, and a church in an affluent society needs to be aware of this special danger.

v19. Having counselled them concerning their true condition and their need, Christ then gives them a wonderful reminder that God disciplines those he loves. Christ had had to speak stern words to this church, but he wanted them to understand the loving purpose behind it — that this stern word was given not for their condemnation, but for their spiritual good. This stands as a reminder to us that one of the great outworkings of God's love for his children is his chastening; therefore, we should always be thankful for God's chastening, knowing it is designed only to benefit us.

Christ then calls them to "be zealous and repent". He calls them to a life of fervent and enthusiastic devotion to him; and he calls them, as the first step towards this, to an act of sincere repentance. They needed earnestly to confess before God their lukewarmness, their love of the world, and their proud complacency; and they needed eagerly to seek Christ for his spiritual riches, and to devote themselves afresh to following and serving him.

v20. Christ then portrays himself to them as standing outside the door, knocking to come in. This is a picture of Christ coming to his people (which he does by his word and his Spirit) calling them to respond to him. And he promises that if anyone hears his voice and opens to him, he will come in and dine with him, and he with Christ. Up to this point Christ had addressed the church as a whole. Now he calls the members to an individual, personal response, promising them that all or any who respond to his word to the church, will know the blessing of a close communion with him and spiritual grace in union with him.

v21. There is then the reward for the overcomer (for the one who will see his lukewarmness, and be zealous and repent). Christ says he will grant the overcomer "to sit with Me on My throne, as I also overcame and sat down with My Father on His throne". Here, the overcoming of Christ refers to his overcoming the world. When he walked in this world he overcame every temptation to have worldly power, riches, fame or pleasure and, obediently, he walked the path to the cross, where he laid down his life to save his people. So God exalted him to the highest place, seated at his right hand. And the reward for those in Laodicea who repented of their lukewarmness, and set themselves on a path of eagerly following and serving Christ, would be a share in Christ's victory over the world. They would share in his dignity and honour in all eternity, and would know power in Christ now to overcome the temptations of this world.

v22. Christ then ends with his final call to "hear what the Spirit says to the churches". This message has set before us a stark warning about the problem of lukewarmness in the church. And, clearly, the challenge that comes to us through it, both as individuals and churches, is to take stock and to consider if it is true of us that we are lukewarm in our devotion to Christ (alternatively, we might ask to what degree we are zealous for Christ and the things of Christ). Moreover, in doing this it is good to remember that lukewarmness is very displeasing in the sight of God, not least because it dishonours Christ, who gave himself for us and to whom nothing less than full devotion is fitting.

-o-

So, Christ completes his messages to the seven churches — messages that were not just for them, but are also for us to heed.

In these messages are challenges about such things as lack of love for Christ, toleration of evil, toleration of false teachers and teaching, compromise with the world, spiritual deadness, lukewarmness, and a love of the things of this world. They also contain encouragements to stand firm in trials and persecution. And they set before us, as an example, such things as dedicated service, faithfulness, perseverance, and a zeal for righteousness and truth. Thus these messages can serve to expose our sin that we might repent; and they can serve to encourage us to continue and increase in those things in our lives which are commendable. Especially, they are given to remove any hindrances to us receiving Christ's revelation of things to come (and thus to us receiving an understanding of the time in which we live), and also to help us to stand and to be Christ's witnesses in our day. Therefore, it is vital that we give time to considering these messages, ready and willing to be challenged and encouraged and changed by them.

Chapter 4
A vision of heaven

Vision of God enthroned in heaven (4:1–11)

v1. After receiving Christ's messages for the seven churches in Asia, a new set of visions then began to open up to John. And as we will see, John was now to be shown the things to come: he was to be shown the most important events affecting the church during the gospel age (this begins in chapter 6).

First, however, by way of preparation for this, John was given a vision of heaven. Having recorded the last of Christ's messages to the churches, John says he looked (as if to see what God had to show him next), and he saw "a door standing open in heaven". Then he heard a voice like a trumpet (the voice of the Lord Jesus — see 1:10–11) saying to him, "Come up here, and I will show you things which must take place after this" (see 1:19). This door standing open in heaven, and the summons to come up to receive the revelation, shows us that the revelation of future events that John was to receive was from heaven. Moreover, it serves as a reminder that we know nothing of future events unless they are disclosed to us by God. It also reminds us that what happens on earth is first settled in heaven; hence, the things John was to be shown about future events were things that "must" take place — they had been preordained by God to serve his wise and perfect purpose, and they would certainly come to pass.

v2,3. John then tells us that immediately he "was in the Spirit". In some way, John was taken up by the Spirit into heavenly realms to receive the revelation Christ had for him. And the first thing he then saw was a scene of the throne-room of heaven — the seat of government of all things (in fact, to John it must have seemed as if he was actually entering the throne-room).

Describing this, John says he saw "a throne set in heaven, and One sat on the throne". This portrays God's power and dominion. Then, describing the one who sat there, John tells us he was in appearance "like a jasper" (a stone clear as crystal, that reflects many colours) "and a sardius stone" (or carnelian — a transparent red stone, that shines a brilliant red). This is a depiction of God the Father (the Holy Spirit and Christ are mentioned later), symbolised to John by means of the appearance of dazzling, precious stones, and portraying God's transcendent glory, splendour, purity and beauty. Moreover, the use of the appearance of precious stones to portray God also reminds us that God is Spirit and has no form, and he dwells in unapproachable light: so he was not symbolised by any living image, but simply as the brilliance and beauty of precious stones, to show his dazzling glory and majesty.

Then, continuing his description, John also tells us that around (encircling) the throne there was a rainbow, "in appearance like an emerald". A rainbow is the sign of the enduring covenant God made with Noah and his posterity (Gen 9:8ff) and, in this context, it is a fitting sign of the everlasting covenant God has made with the elect in and through the Lord Jesus Christ. It reminds us that it is only on the basis of this gracious, merciful covenant that we have access to the presence of God. Moreover, the rainbow's appearance as an emerald (another transparent precious stone) would seem to further display God's glory. God's glorious attributes are supremely manifested in his work of salvation in Christ.

No doubt, for John, this glorious throne that he saw before him must have been a gripping sight. However, there was more for him to see and describe, and he goes on to describe the scene around and in front of this glorious throne.

v4. First, John tells us that around the throne were twenty-four thrones, on which were sat twenty-four elders, clothed in white robes, and with crowns of gold on their heads. These twenty-four elders depict the twelve patriarchs and twelve apostles, and together they represent the entire church made up of the saints of both Old Testament and New Testament times. So, God's people are depicted as crowned and sitting on thrones around the throne of God. This denotes: the honour and high estate accorded to the church; the church's relationship to God and nearness to him; and the sight and enjoyment God's people have of him. Moreover, the white robes depict the righteousness that the saints have in Christ, which is the only basis upon which the church can dwell in God's presence.

This depiction of the church should be regarded as portraying the whole church of God. Essentially, it portrays the church triumphant in heaven. However, the church on earth is also described as seated in heavenly places in Christ (Eph 2:4–6); therefore, we can see ourselves as part of this church in heaven gathered around the throne of God, clothed in Christ's righteousness, and accorded dignity and honour.

v5. Next we are told that from the throne "proceeded lightnings, thunderings, and voices". This reminds us of the giving of the law at Sinai (Ex 19:16; 20:18), and it symbolises the awesome authority and power of God, and the declaring by God of his sovereign will and purpose. It sets before us the power and authority of God's word, and the certain accomplishment of his sovereign purposes; also, it sets before us our need to hear and obey God's word with reverent fear.

Also, we are told that before the throne there burned seven lamps of fire, "which are the seven Spirits of God". As previously, this depicts the Holy Spirit (see 1:4), now represented pictorially as seven lamps of fire before the throne. This is a reference to the golden lampstand in the tabernacle, which had seven lamps (Ex 25:31–40). So, of all the manifold graces distributed by the Holy Spirit in accomplishing God's saving work, special attention is drawn here to the illumination given by the Spirit — the light he brings to believers and, via them, to the earth. God's word has great power and authority, but we receive and understand it only by the illumination of God's Spirit.

v6–8. Following this, we are told that before the throne "there was a sea of glass, like crystal". This is understood by many to be a reference to the bronze sea sited before the temple (which took the place of the laver of the tabernacle), in which the priests carried out their ablutions before they went to minister before the Lord (see Ex 30:17–21; 1 Kgs 7:23–26). If so, this represents the cleansing, by the blood of Christ, that is necessary for admittance into God's presence. And, as with the rainbow that appeared like an emerald, the sea having an appearance like crystal would seem again to highlight the glory of God manifest in his saving work.

Then, last of all, John tells us that in the midst of the throne, and around the throne, were four living creatures, the first like a lion, the second like a calf, the third with a face like a man, and the fourth like a flying eagle. He also says they each had six wings, and were full of eyes; and they were offering unceasing praise to God — extolling the holy, sovereign, all-powerful and eternal God. These living creatures bear some similarity to the seraphim that Isaiah saw (Is 6:1–3). Particularly, however, they are similar to the living creatures Ezekiel saw beneath the throne of God, which he terms "cherubim" (see Ezekiel chapters 1 and 10), and it seems right to identify them with these. In view of this, some understand that these represent a high order of angelic being. However, another view is that they do not represent any type of real being, but they were merely an emblem employed by God to visibly represent to fallen man the prospect of being restored to life and wholeness in God's presence. This explanation is preferred here, as explained below.

First of all, the likeness of the living creatures to certain animals and man connects them with the earth and creation. Moreover, the specific creatures that they resemble would, at that time, have been counted as the highest kinds of creaturely existence on earth. The lion was considered the highest among the wild beasts, and representative of kingly majesty and peerless strength. The eagle was counted as pre-eminent among the birds, and was especially distinguished for its acute vision and powerful flight (its flight being emphasised here). Man is the highest of all God's creatures, unique in intelligence and feeling. The calf would seem to correspond to the ox in Ezekiel's vision, which was considered the highest of the domesticated animals and epitomised patient and productive labour. So, these living creatures display the highest creaturely capacities.

Furthermore, these living creatures are also portrayed possessing both life and knowledge. They are called "living" creatures, stressing that possession of life is their characteristic feature. Also, one of their prominent features (notably, mentioned twice) is that they are "full of eyes" ("in front and in back", and "around and within" — v6,8), depicting them possessing a fullness of knowledge and understanding. So, life and knowledge characterise these living creatures.

Lastly, also notable is the position of these living creatures. John describes them as in the midst of the throne and around the throne; so they are portrayed in close proximity to the throne and to the presence of God.

In summary, therefore, these four living creatures are pictured near to the throne of God; they are characterised by the possession of life and the possession of a fulness of knowledge; and they portray the highest capacities of creaturely existence. And all of this is strongly supportive of the understanding that these living creatures portray the fullness of life, knowledge and capacities that will be known by those dwelling in God's presence, and that they are an emblem employed by God to visibly set before fallen man the prospect of being restored to life and wholeness in God's presence.

Moreover, if we identify these living creatures with the cherubim, this understanding fits well with other places in Scripture where we see cherubim. Here, of particular note is that cherubim are said to have been placed by God at the east of the garden of Eden, after man had been expelled, to guard (to keep or preserve) the way to the tree of life (Gen 3:24). Also, by God's design, two golden cherubim were placed over the mercy seat in the Most Holy Place of the tabernacle, with their faces towards the mercy seat; and God said that it was from there (above the mercy seat and between the cherubim) that he would meet with and speak to the people (Ex 25:17–22; Ps 80:1). And, in both of these cases, the cherubim can very fittingly be understood as an emblem of mercy, giving promise of a return to God's presence, and setting forth the prospect of man being restored to life and wholeness in the presence of God.

So, understood in this way, the living creatures (cherubim) held the promise of redemption. What John saw, however, was much more than this — because when he saw the church and the four living creatures around the throne in heaven, he did not merely see the emblem that promised life and wholeness in God's presence; rather, he also saw the fulfilment of this — God's people (represented by the twenty-four elders) restored and exalted, dwelling in the presence of God. Moreover, the unceasing praise of these living creatures depicts man's restoration to life and wholeness in God's presence being perpetually to God's praise and glory.

v9–11. Following this, John then tells us that whenever the living creatures give glory and honour and thanks to God, the twenty-four elders (depicting the church) also fall down and worship God (they join in the perpetual worship of the living creatures). An association of the worship of the four living creatures (the emblem promising redemption) and the worship of the church (the possessors of redemption) is also found elsewhere (see 5:8,14). This reminds us that it is only by the redeeming work of God that we can come before God's presence and worship him.

Furthermore, also instructive is how the church's worship is depicted. The twenty-four elders are said to "fall down before Him who sits on the throne" — which is an act of profound adoration, and an act of humbly reverencing God, and exalting and magnifying him. They also "cast their crowns before the throne" — which is a symbol of giving God all the honour and glory, and an act of acknowledgement that all that has been bestowed upon them in the way of honour and blessing is from him. Moreover, they do this extolling him as the creator of all things, and thus the one worthy to be worshipped, and to receive glory and honour and power.

So, here is a picture of the church engaged in constant worship and praise at the throne of God. And it sets before us the fact that we should worship God constantly — which is to say that all of our living (all we are, and think, and say and do) should be to the praise and honour of God, because he made us, and has redeemed us, and we belong to him. So we should live constantly as before God's throne, honouring him and giving him glory in everything.

Chapter 5
The Lamb and the scroll

The Lamb takes the scroll (5:1–14)

v1. After gazing upon this glorious vision of God on the throne, and the church in his presence, redeemed and worshipping him, John then tells us he saw "in the right hand of Him who sat on the throne a scroll written inside and on the back, sealed with seven seals". This scroll signifies the preordained purposes of God for the gospel age. The fact that it is completely covered in writing shows that everything is determined. And its place in God's right hand shows that God will execute his purposes. So, the scroll in God's right hand symbolises the preordained purposes of God for this gospel age, which God will bring about.

However, this scroll was sealed with seven seals. This symbolises God's purposes being unrevealed and unexecuted (conversely, the opening of the seals will symbolise the revealing and execution of God's purposes).

v2,3. After seeing the scroll, John saw a strong angel proclaiming with a loud voice (so all hear), "Who is worthy to open the scroll and to loose its seals?" This is a general challenge concerning who is worthy to reveal and execute God's purposes for this age.

However, no one was found, not in heaven or on the earth or under the earth, who was able to open the scroll, or to look at it. There were none of God's creatures — no angels, or men living, or spirits of men departed — who were worthy to reveal and execute God's purposes, or even to look into what God had purposed.

v4,5. John was very distressed by this (he "wept much"). This distress most probably was because John longed to know the purposes of God, and he longed for these purposes to come to pass, but it seemed they were to remain sealed up. However, quickly John's distress was calmed.

One of the elders tells John not to weep, and he calls his attention to the Lord Jesus Christ as the one who is worthy to open the scroll and to loose its seven seals. Here Christ is described as "the Lion of the tribe of Judah" (see Gen 49:9–10), "the Root of David" (see Is 11:10 — Jesse was David's father). These are Messianic titles for Christ that point especially to his kingly office and his divinity (they speak respectively of Christ as the king in David's line, and Christ as David's origin/creator).

Moreover, John is told that Christ is worthy to open the scroll because he has prevailed — because of his victory. Christ prevailed or conquered through death. His death upon the cross seemed like a defeat, but by it he triumphed over Satan and redeemed his people; therefore God exalted him to the highest place, seated at his right hand, and placed all things under him. So, it is by virtue of his saving work that Christ is worthy to reveal and execute God's purposes for this gospel age.

v6. Having had his attention drawn to the Lord Jesus, John then looked, and in the midst of the throne and of the four living creatures, and in the midst of the elders, he saw Christ. However, he did not see Christ depicted as a king in regal majesty, but he saw him depicted as "a Lamb as though it had been slain". This portrays the Lord Jesus as the one who laid down his life as a sacrifice for sin, but is now alive and reigning with God the Father. This reinforces the fact that Christ's victory and reign came through his sacrificial death. Moreover, the Lamb that John saw had "seven horns [a horn is a symbol of power] and seven eyes, which are the seven Spirits of God sent out into all the earth". This depicts Christ's perfect kingly power and perfect wisdom to execute all the will of God, which he carries out by the Holy Spirit.

v7. Then, as John looked, he saw the Lamb come and take the scroll out of the right hand of him who sat on the throne. This depicts Christ receiving and accepting from the Father the government of all things, and the task of revealing and executing God's preordained purposes for this gospel age. Of course, when John saw this, Christ was already governing all things — he received the government of all things when he ascended into heaven and sat down at the right hand of the Father. However, it was very appropriate for John to have this portrayed to him as he was about to receive Christ's revelation of the things that were to happen in the future — it makes clear Christ's government over all that was to come.

v8–10. Upon Christ receiving the scroll, John then saw great praise being offered up to Christ. Here it is impossible for us to imagine the sound John heard. But, as we will see, this praise began with the church, was then added to by the angels, and then reached a crescendo with all creation adding its voice — and so this must have been an overwhelming experience for John.

Describing this, first John tells us, "the four living creatures and the twenty-four elders fell down before the Lamb, each having a harp, and golden bowls full of incense, which are the prayers of the saints". Previously, the church was shown falling down and worshipping the Father on the throne (4:9–11). Now, following Christ taking the scroll, the church is shown falling down before Christ, and offering up before him praises and prayers. Moreover, we are told "they sang a new song". Christ was made known in Old Testament times in prophecies and types, but it was not until he accomplished his saving work that he was really known; and then the church had a new song to sing — a song extolling the Lord Jesus Christ and giving praise for his salvation. So, in this song, Christ is worshipped as the one worthy to have the government of all things and to execute God's purposes for this age because of his victory through death; and he is worshipped for redeeming us out of all the peoples of the earth, and making us one people in the kingdom of God who share in his victory and worship him. Again, we must see ourselves as having a part in this praise before the throne, and give of ourselves, by God's grace, to honour and worship Christ our Lord and Saviour.

v11,12. After this, John looked again, and he heard the voice of innumerable angels around the throne, with one voice joining in the worship of the Lamb. These are depicted further away from the throne than the church, showing that redeemed man has a higher place than the angels. Moreover, having never fallen and been the subjects of salvation, the angels are not singing the same song as the church — only the church can sing a song of salvation. However, they also worship Christ, ascribing to him all the honour that is his due.

v13. Following this, John then heard every creature worshipping God and the Lamb, ascribing to them the honour that is their due. Of course, the animal creation cannot literally proclaim worship to God; nevertheless, this reminds us that all that God has created manifests his glory and glorifies him. It also reminds us that God's rule extends to all things, and that creation itself is awaiting the redemption of God's people, when it will be set free from its present bondage to decay (see Rom 8:19–21).

So, the Lord Jesus Christ, together with the Father, was shown as a focus of all the praises of both heaven and earth; all is created to praise and glorify God and the Lord Jesus — all men, and especially the redeemed, all angels, and all his creatures. For us, Christ's saving work and his sovereign government of the world should be a constant cause for great praise, and a constant motivation to live our lives for Christ, and to honour and glorify him in all things.

v14. Finally, John heard the four living creatures say, "Amen!" And he saw the twenty-four elders fall down and worship God. Here again, we see the four living creatures (the symbol of redemption) and the church (the possessors of redemption) associated in worship. So, the final act of worship shown to John was the worship of the church, the redeemed people of God. All creation glorifies God, but it is the church that supremely does this, and will continue to do so through all eternity.

So, before receiving Christ's revelation of things to come, John was shown (in chapters 4 and 5): a marvellous vision displaying the majesty, glory and sovereign rule of God; the church in God's presence through the redemption of Christ; Christ's government of all things by virtue of his saving death; and all of creation, and especially the church, glorifying and honouring God and Christ. All of this is to be contemplated by us, and forms an important background to all that is to come.

Chapter 6
The opening of the seals

Introduction to the unfolding of events

Having had set before him Christ's government of all things
in this gospel age, John was then shown the things that were to
come. Now begins a gradual and progressive unfolding of things
to happen from John's time to the end of history.

Before looking at this, however, it will be helpful to say a
number of things by way of introduction.

The place of hindsight — Important to remember when
interpreting Revelation, is that the precise fulfilment of the
events symbolised and prophesied can only be known once the
events have happened. This means that the believers of John's
day would have had limited understanding of the fulfilment of
these things (although the visions that follow would still have
held much to encourage and warn them). In contrast, we have
the benefit of looking back on two thousand years of history.
Consequently, from our perspective, it is possible to see the
fulfilment of a large proportion of these prophesied events. At
the same time, however, there are portions of the prophecy that
are yet to be fulfilled. Therefore, when we come to these, we will
need to guard against undue speculation and be content to have
only a limited understanding (although, in these portions, there
will still be much to encourage and help us).

The history covered — As will be seen, here the revelation
given to John concerning the future is interpreted with a focus
first on events to do with the Roman Empire, and then on the
progress of the papacy and its dominion. This focus is by no
means novel. However, for those unfamiliar with such an
interpretation, it can seem too narrow (ignoring, as it does, other

important events in church history), and also somewhat arbitrary. However, there are good reasons for this focus and, before going on, it will be helpful to set these down.

Firstly, from an overview of church history it can be seen that the greater portion of church history has been shaped first, in the early centuries, by the church's relationship with the Roman Empire (which was the world of the early church), and then, following this, by the progress of the papacy and its dominion. Therefore, any historicist interpretation of Revelation will be majorly concerned with the Roman Empire and the papacy, and the church's relationship with these.

Secondly, from an overview of Revelation it can be seen that dominating the second half of the book is the rise, dominion and judgement of the beast. This beast is best understood as representing the Antichrist (the great opponent of Christ who would come in the last days), and his dominion in the world. Thus, the second half of the book of Revelation has as its major theme the rise, dominion and judgement of the Antichrist. Furthermore, this figure can now be identified as the pope of Rome *(see 'Antichrist Revealed', 2017, by the same author)*. Therefore, it follows that the papacy will be a focus throughout the interpretation of the second half of the book. Moreover, this links naturally with a prior concern with events to do with the Roman Empire, because the emergence of the papal dominion was inseparably and crucially linked with the demise of the Roman Empire. Thus, an interpretation that is concerned first with matters to do with the Roman Empire, and then with the progress of the papal dominion, is one that forms a unified and continuous whole.

Thirdly, an interpretation of Revelation that has this focus is also in harmony with the revelation given to Daniel (found in Daniel chapter 7) concerning the time until Christ's return. Towards the end of the Jewish exile, the prophet Daniel was given revelation concerning the four great powers/Empires that were to dominate the world of God's people from his time until the establishing of the kingdom of God. From history and

Scripture, these can now be identified as Babylonia, Medo-Persia, Greece and Rome. He was also shown a certain power arising from the fourth, Roman power/Empire, which would be destroyed at the final establishing of Christ's kingdom (ie, at Christ's return). From history, and from the New Testament teaching concerning the Antichrist, this power arising from the Roman power/Empire can now be identified as the Antichrist of the New Testament, who is the pope of Rome *(see 'Antichrist Revealed' for a discussion of this)*. So, the revelation given to Daniel shows the Roman power — first as imperial Rome and then as papal Rome — to be, from its rise until the return of Christ, the final power of significance as far as the people of God are concerned. And this is of relevance when we come to interpret the prophecy of Revelation, which was received by John in the days of the Roman Empire, and which concerns the time until Christ's return. It is strongly supportive of an understanding of Revelation which focuses first on events to do with the Roman Empire and then on the papacy.

So, history and Scripture together indicate that the prophecy of Revelation should be interpreted with a focus on the progress of the Roman Empire and the papacy, and the church's relationship with these.

The arrangement of the prophecy — As will be seen, while in the book there is a progressive unfolding of events, there is also a grouping together of events with other material interspersed. Therefore, before going on it will be helpful to outline the arrangement of the prophecy.

Essentially, the unfolding of events is centred on and divided between the opening of the seven seals, the sounding of the seven trumpets, and the pouring out of the seven bowls of God's wrath (see chapters 6, 8–9, 15–16). Specifically, as interpreted here, the seals concern events to do with the pagan Roman Empire; and they cover the time from John's day until the reign of the Emperor Constantine in the fourth century, when the Empire became a Christian Empire. The trumpets cover the time from when the Empire became a Christian Empire to just before the Reformation in the sixteenth century — a time notable for the fall of the Roman Empire, and the rise and ascendancy of the papacy and its dominion. The seven bowls of God's wrath deal with God's judgement of the whole papal system and its adherents, and they cover the time from the Reformation onwards.

In addition, in between and following the seals and trumpets and bowls are other visions (chapters 7, 10–14, 17–20), which serve two main purposes. Some of these picture the safety and blessedness of the church in the midst of all the events signified; others go back over the time previously covered, but with a slightly different focus. The book then ends with visions of the church's blessed future (chapters 21–22).

This basic arrangement of all that follows needs to be kept in view as we go forward. *(A summary of Revelation can be found following Chapter 22, which may assist seeing the overall arrangement of the book.)*

Finally, it would be helpful to say something about the importance to us of the earlier historical chapters of Revelation. At the beginning of this work it was stated that this study of Revelation has been written with the objective of helping the people of God to understand the time in which we live. Given this, as we go on to consider the things that John was shown concerning the things to come, some people may question why the earlier historical chapters (which concern events that for us are long past and seem to have little immediate relevance to today) have been followed through in some detail. This has been done because it is only by progressively following through the events prophesied that we can discern with confidence which part or parts of Revelation refer specifically to the time in which we live, and that we can make full sense of these portions of the book.

We come, then, to consider the section of Revelation that speaks of the things that were to come.

The opening of the first four seals (6:1–8)

Having received the scroll from God the Father, Christ then proceeded to open the seals. As already noted, this represents the revealing and executing of God's preordained purposes for this age. First they were to be revealed, and in their time they would most certainly be accomplished.

For John, as Christ opened the seals, there would have been a new vision for him to take in and record as each was opened. However, on viewing them all, it can be seen that the first four seals form a group, and have certain things in common. Therefore, we will consider these four seals together, looking first at the things they have in common, before going on to look at each seal in detail. This will assist us in understanding what these seals are depicting.

The first thing that is notable about the first four seals is that the opening of each is followed by the coming forth of a horse and rider — each horse being a different colour. This bears some similarity to two visions seen by the prophet Zechariah (see Zech 1:8–11; 6:1–8). In the first vision, Zechariah saw a rider on a coloured horse, and behind him horses of three varying colours; in the second vision, Zechariah saw four chariots with horses, each team of horses having a different colour. These are portrayed as envoys of God that are sent by him to patrol the earth; and they are shown reporting on the state of the earth (Zech 1:11), and playing a part in God's activity in the world (Zech 6:8). Essentially, therefore, their symbolism has to do with God's sovereignty over the Gentile nations, and the working out of his sovereign purposes in the world. Similarly, the four horses and riders seen by John, which went forth from heaven when Christ opened the first four seals, represent the execution of God's sovereign purposes in the pagan or unbelieving world.

Also common to the first four seals is that, with the opening of each seal, one of the four living creatures summons John to "Come and see" (or, some versions have them calling "Come", making this a summons to the horses and riders to come forth).

This association of the living creatures with the unveiling or execution of the first four seals — which, in the main, depict trouble in the world — indicates that these purposes of God in the world are not incompatible with God's gracious and merciful purpose to save men. And this is important to note because very often we view the troubles and upheavals that God sends upon this world purely as judgements of God. In fact, however, they can also serve a saving purpose, which is to unsettle men. Here it is notable that in the first of Zechariah's visions referred to, the nations are described as resting quietly (at ease). This is the condition of the generality of mankind — men rest secure in their worldly existence and are unconcerned about the things of God. However, in his mercy, God acts to disturb people at ease, and often uses this as a means of softening people's hearts to the gospel.

This, then, is the general significance of the first four seals. And this needs to be kept in view as we now go on to consider each of these seals in more detail.

v1,2. First, John saw Christ (the Lamb) open one of the seals; and he heard one of the four living creatures saying with a loud voice, "Come and see". In response to this summons, John looked and he saw a white horse. And the one who sat on it "had a bow; and a crown was given to him, and he went out conquering and to conquer". This is a picture of conquest by a great power. Moreover, his power to conquer is given by God (a crown was given to him), and conquest is his determined goal (he went out to conquer). This is understood by many to signify the Lord Jesus Christ going out conquering souls and establishing his kingdom (which he does through the gospel, by his Spirit). Certainly, it would seem fitting to begin with this; and certainly, since his exaltation, Christ has been conquering the hearts of men, and establishing his kingdom. However, the first four seals seem to form a related group, dealing with actual events and upheavals happening in the world. Therefore, it would seem better to view this first horse and rider as portraying actual conquest in the earth by a great power.

v3,4. Christ then opened the second seal. As before, John was summoned by one of the living creatures to "Come and see"; and he saw going forth from heaven a fiery red horse. And to the one who sat on this horse, it was granted "to take peace from the earth, and that people should kill one another; and there was given to him a great sword". This pictures peace ending, and war and bloodshed breaking out. This results from man's action (men kill one another); however, it is also sent by God (it was granted to the rider to take peace from the earth, and he was given a great sword).

v5,6. Christ then opened the third seal, and again John was summoned to "Come and see". So John looked, and he saw a black horse; and the one who sat on this horse "had a pair of scales in his hand". Also, John heard a voice saying, "A quart of wheat for a denarius, and three quarts of barley for a denarius; and do not harm the oil and the wine." This pictures a situation of inflated prices (a denarius was a typical day's wage — see Mt 20:1–2), and one in which the basic necessities of life (wheat and barley) are costly to obtain, while luxuries (oil and wine) are unaffected. It portrays a situation of privation for the ordinary person while the rich person continues to live in luxury. This represents economic crisis or scarcity/famine, again sent from God.

v7,8. Christ then opened the fourth seal, and again John was summoned to "Come and see". So John looked, and he saw a pale horse. And the one who sat on this horse was named "Death, and Hades followed with him" (Hades is the abode of the dead). And to these, power was given over a fourth of the earth "to kill with sword, with hunger, with death [probably pestilence], and by the beasts of the earth". This portrays Death and Hades making great conquests, again in the sovereign purpose of God (they were given this power to kill). Moreover, the causes of death listed are the four agents of death spoken of by Ezekiel which he calls four severe judgements (see Ezek 14:21). These can stand separately but often go together. War draws scarcity and famine after it, pestilence often follows, and wild animals become a threat when a place is devastated — all of which bring death. Of course, death is always with us; but this represents death, and the threat of death, being present to an unusual degree. However, all of this is in God's control and is limited by him (they were given power over a fourth of the earth only).

So, these first four seals depict conquest by a great power, war breaking out in the earth, economic crisis or scarcity/famine, and death coming to many people.

We come, then, to the fulfilment of the first four seals. To see this, we need to remember that these seals represent the execution of God's sovereign purposes in the pagan or unbelieving world (see discussion above); also, viewing Revelation historically, they concern things happening during and immediately following John's day (these are the first things John was shown concerning the things to come). From this, it follows that these seals concern events happening in the pagan Roman Empire, which was the world of John's day, and which continued to be the world of the early church until Christianity became the religion of the Empire in the fourth century. And, looking back to the pagan Empire during those centuries, we can see the fulfilment of these first four seals.

Firstly, we can see the fulfilment of the first seal (depicting conquest by a great power) in the conquest of the ancient world by Rome. Of course, at the time of John, Rome had been conquering and was already in the ascendancy. However, the Roman Empire was still expanding (it was not at the height of its power), and for some years, under several great emperors, there was continued conquest and expansion (the maximum size was reached in the second century). With Rome's ascendancy, the peoples of the Empire enjoyed peace and good government under the dominion of the Roman power. (NB: The vast Empire, with its good organisation and peace, provided the ideal environment for the rapid spread of the gospel; and, in God's providence, this was a significant factor in the rapid growth and spread of the church in the world.)

Following this, however, there was a period of crisis, which we can see signified under the next three seals (which depict war and bloodshed, economic crisis/famine, and death). At the end of the second century, war and fighting broke out in many parts of the Empire, and it was indeed a case of peace being taken from the earth. There were civil wars in the Empire; there were wars with Persia; and from about 220 onwards there were raids on the northern frontier by barbarian tribes. In addition, in the third century there was also great economic crisis. Taxes were heavy, inflation and prices were high and, as a result, throughout the Empire people were ruined and impoverished. Moreover, during this time of crisis in the Empire, death and the threat of death were present to an increased degree, with pestilence also contributing to this. All of this marked the beginning of the Empire's decline.

So, in God's preordained, sovereign purpose, for a time Rome continued to increase in power and prospered. However, as its power reached a great height, God did not allow it to be at ease in its pride and seeming security and invincibility; rather, God brought a time of crisis marked by war, a failing economy, pestilence and death. And as these events unfolded, this portion of Revelation would have been a great encouragement to the church by assuring the church of God's sovereignty over the power of Rome, and his sovereignty over the unsettling things that were happening in the Empire.

However, while these seals have a specific fulfilment in relation to the pagan Roman Empire, they also picture things that have occurred, and will occur, in the world throughout the gospel age. Thus they also lend themselves to a more general application; they help us, in our own time, to keep sight of God's sovereignty over the rise and fall of great powers, and over all the distressing things (wars, economic crises, famines, plagues etc) happening in the world today. These things will continue throughout the gospel age, preventing man from becoming complacent and at ease in this fallen world which is under God's judgement. The believer, however, should not be alarmed or dismayed by these things, knowing that they are happening in the sovereign purpose of God.

The opening of the fifth seal (6:9–11)

v9–10. Christ then opened the fifth seal; and John saw a scene depicting the souls of martyred saints in heaven — the souls of those who had been put to death for their faithful testimony to the Lord Jesus Christ. These are pictured under the altar (at the foot of the altar). Also, they are said to be crying out to God to know how long it would be until he judged and avenged their blood on those who dwell on the earth.

Here, the altar would seem to be a reference to the altar of incense in the tabernacle. Notably, this altar was sited just before the Most Holy Place, near to the presence of God (see Ex 30:1-10). Moreover, the incense burnt on this altar symbolised the offering up of prayer (an association between incense and the prayers of God's people is seen in 8:3–4; also Ps 141:2; Lk 1:8–10). Thus, this altar is a fitting place to picture those who are crying out to God. However, we must not imagine from the cry of these martyrs, that the martyrs now in heaven are literally calling out to God for justice (of note is that the incense which symbolises prayer is absent from the imagery, suggesting that literal prayer is not in view here). Rather, we can understand this as showing us that, in a sense, the death of the martyrs constantly cries out for justice — it is set before God and noted by God, and in due time will be avenged by God, who is holy and true.

v11. Then the martyrs were each given a white robe, which is a symbol of the holiness and blessing that is the reward of those who die for their faith. Also they were told to rest a little while longer, until the full number of believers destined for martyrdom were killed. There were going to be more martyrs, and it was when the number was completed that God would avenge their blood.

Thus, with the opening of this seal, the focus moves from events happening in the unbelieving world, to the church and the persecution of God's people. However, this is portrayed through a scene that contains much by way of encouragement and comfort, especially for believers going through a time of severe persecution.

First, the opening of this seal, and the ensuing scene of the martyrs crying out in heaven, sets before us a stark reminder that the church is appointed to suffer times of severe persecution, and that in following Christ we may be called upon to lay down our lives for him. At the same time, however, it also shows us, for our comfort, that even persecution to death is in the preordained purpose of God; he determines times of persecution and, indeed, who among his people will be called upon to lay down their lives for Christ. Moreover, it assures us that though men may be able to destroy our bodies, they cannot harm our souls; also, God, who is just, will avenge the death of his people. And so, while we must forgive our enemies and bless those who persecute us, we are to know that there will be a day when God will avenge the blood of his saints.

However, while there is much by way of general encouragement here, within the historical framework of Revelation this seal also has a more specific fulfilment. And, particularly, it concerns the death of the saints at the hands of pagan Rome which, like the other things already seen, was in the preordained purpose of God. To a large extent Rome was tolerant of the church, and in the earlier years there were only some localised persecutions. However, in the second half of the third century and beginning of the fourth century there were some periods of very severe, general persecution. There were large, well-organised persecutions under the Emperors Decius and Valerian (in the years 250–251, 257–260). Then severe persecution broke out under Diocletian, who was set on uprooting Christianity completely (this broke out in 303 and lasted for nearly ten years). It is probably these persecutions that are particularly in view here.

Moreover, it is notable that part of the reason for these severe persecutions was the crisis that arose in the Empire, seen under the second to fourth seals. It was felt, at that time, that the Empire's safety lay in a revival of the old values and ways of the Roman people; consequently, while trying to restore the Empire out of the chaos into which it had fallen, attempts were made to rid the Empire of Christians, who were perceived to be disloyal and a disturbing element. So, many were killed. However, the souls of such martyrs are pictured in a place of safety and blessedness with God, receiving assurance that their death will be avenged. They are also shown awaiting further martyrs — which may refer to the remainder to be killed by Imperial Rome, or it may refer to all the martyrs (and perhaps especially those who later would die at the hands of the papacy).

So, this seal concerns the persecution of God's people; and, more specifically, at this point in Revelation it concerns the persecution of the early church by Rome. It is notable, however, that what we have here is not imagery depicting the church's actual persecution, but imagery depicting the safety and blessedness of the persecuted. Thus this is a vision especially intended to give reassurance and comfort; and, undoubtedly, it would have been a source of great strengthening to those who were called to endure Rome's persecution — as, indeed, it can be to all who are called to endure severe persecution for Christ's sake.

The opening of the sixth seal (6:12–17)

v12–14. Following this, Christ opened the sixth seal; and John looked, and he saw a scene of great upheaval and disturbance in the earth and heavens (sky), like the end of the world. This picture of the whole order of things being shaken is symbolic of a day of judgement; consequently, it immediately makes us think of the final dissolution of all things at Christ's return. However, in Scripture we also find this type of imagery in passages predicting a day of judgement to come for some particular people, society or system (eg, for Babylon — Is 13:1,10,13, and for Egypt — Ezek 32:2,6–8). Thus, there is warrant for such an interpretation here.

v15–17. John also saw people of all stations of society crying out to be hidden from God and even crushed out of existence, because the day of his wrath had come and no one was able to stand before him. This pictures men in great terror at the anger of God, and it shows this day of judgement to be a day of terrible reckoning for the wicked. And again, while this imagery makes us think of the final day of reckoning, in Scripture it is found in other contexts (see, for example, Hos 10:7–8 which concerns judgement on Samaria, and Lk 23:29–30 which concerns the fall of Jerusalem). Thus, again, there is warrant to relate this to a specific judgement in history.

So, this sixth seal depicts some great coming day of judgement. And, taking into account the point we have reached in the unfolding of events, the common historicist understanding is that the fulfilment of this can be found in the downfall of paganism in the Roman Empire — the time when heathen government fell and paganism was removed from the Empire. This happened in the fourth century when, following the conversion to Christianity of the Emperor Constantine (in 312), the Empire became a Christian empire under Christian emperors.

Prior to this, and during all the time of the church, the Empire had been a pagan empire under pagan emperors. Following the conversion of Constantine, however, all of this changed as the emperor became Christian and as Christianity became first the favoured, and then the official religion of the Empire (laws were also passed against paganism at this time). So, pagan government and religion was swept away. And, in terms of biblical language, the imagery used here is quite appropriate for depicting this. The fall of pagan government and religion was a time of great upheaval in the Empire, when the whole order of things was shaken. Moreover, it was also a time of great judgement and reckoning for the pagan Roman world, which was corrupt and wicked, and was cruelly persecuting the church.

Also notable, however, is that this time of great change in the Empire also marked a significant turning point for the church. Essentially, the church found itself in a whole new situation — its world was no longer a pagan empire headed by pagan emperors, but a Christian empire with Christian emperors. And this brought great change for the church. On the more positive side, it brought an end to the severe persecution the church had been suffering at the hands of Rome. At the same time, however, it also marked the time when there began to be a large number of nominal Christians in the church; also it brought the beginning of state involvement in church affairs, and much greater organisation. In view of this, there are many who would regard the Empire becoming Christian as a development that was not favourable for the church. Whatever we make of this development, however, we must remain clear that the fall of paganism in the Empire happened according to the preordained purpose of God, as a judgement of God on the pagan Roman world.

So, viewing Revelation historically, the opening of the first six seals unfolds a continuous series of events happening in the pagan Roman Empire, between the time of John and the reign of the Emperor Constantine in the fourth century, when the Empire became a Christian empire. First the Empire reached the height of its conquest and power; then it suffered a time of chaos, experiencing war, and economic chaos and other trouble; this gave rise to severe persecution of the church — until God intervened and judged paganism, and it was brought down.

Chapter 7
The church kept and blessed

Having seen Christ open six of the seals, John may have expected to then see the opening of the seventh seal. However, this did not happen immediately, but first John was given two visions concerning the church.

The sealing of the 144,000 (7:1–8)

v1. After seeing the scene of great upheaval and distress associated with the opening of the sixth seal, John saw four angels standing at the four corners of the earth, holding the four winds of the earth. These four winds are portrayed as destructive agents of God (they have power to harm the earth, the sea and the trees), and they represent great judgements of God to come in the earth. However, these judgements are depicted as being held back (the angels who are tasked to inflict these judgements are holding the winds "that the wind should not blow on the earth, on the sea, or on any tree").

v2,3. John then saw another angel ascending from the east, having the seal of the living God. And this angel cried out to the four angels not to harm the earth, the sea, or the trees until the servants of God had been sealed on their foreheads.

So, the coming judgements of God were not to be let loose until God's servants were sealed. This reminds us of a vision seen by Ezekiel (Ezek 9:1–6), which showed the faithful Jews, who mourned over the abominations done in Jerusalem, being marked on their foreheads before judgement fell on the city. And both in Ezekiel and here, the sealing or marking of God's faithful people prior to judgement being released, depicts these faithful ones being plainly distinguished as belonging to God, and being marked out for safety in the midst of God's judgements.

v4–8. John then heard the number of those who were sealed. The number was one hundred and forty-four thousand of all the tribes of the children of Israel, twelve thousand out of each tribe.

This might seem like a plain reference to the people of Israel. However, the list of twelve tribes given in these verses is unusual: Dan is missing altogether; Levi is included (the Levites had a distinct calling and no allotment of land, and are often absent from lists of the tribes); and Joseph and one of his sons, Manasseh, are listed, whereas more usually Joseph is not named and his two sons, Manasseh and Ephraim, are included. This suggests that the reference here to the tribes of the children of Israel is not to be taken literally; rather, it is symbolic of something else. And interpreting this in context, here "all the tribes of the children of Israel" would seem to represent the outward professing Christian church; and the one hundred and forty-four thousand who were sealed would seem to represent the true and faithful believers in the midst of this church.

So, the imagery here depicts the true people of God being distinguished in the midst of the professing church, and being marked out for safety prior to judgement falling upon the earth. Moreover, the listing of the tribes, and the number sealed from each, indicates completeness — all the faithful were marked, none were missed. (Some commentators suggest that the significance of the omission of Dan and Ephraim from the list lies in the fact that these tribes were greatly given to idolatry; so, their omission teaches that if Christians are unfaithful, they cannot expect any special protection from God in a day of trial or evil.)

This vision offers great comfort to God's people in a situation of widespread nominalism, or in one of apostasy (in which the church has fallen away from the true faith). It is a wonderful assurance that God knows who are his, and that God will keep his people safe (ie, keep them from spiritual harm) through any judgements he may see fit to bring upon the professing church, or upon the Christian world.

However, while there is general encouragement to be gained from this vision, within the historical framework of Revelation it has a specific significance. This significance becomes clear when we note the point that has been reached in Christ's revealing of things. Looking back, John has just seen the opening of the sixth seal, which was understood to concern the downfall of paganism in the Empire, when the Empire became Christian. And, as already noted, this transition from a pagan empire to a Christian empire marked the beginning of there being a large number of nominal Christians in the church (essentially, it brought a change from the church being principally made up of true believers, to the true believers being a minority in the total professing church). Looking forward, John is about to be shown the opening of the seventh seal which, as we will see, ushers in a series of judgements on the Roman world, now nominally Christian. It is in this context that we must understand this vision of the sealing/distinguishing of the true believers amongst the professing church before judgement is released in the earth. It shows us that, in the midst of the Christianized world, God knew who were his people, and he would keep them safe from harm (spiritual harm) through the judgements that were to come.

The multitude from the great tribulation (7:9–17)

v9,10. After seeing the sealing of God's people on earth, John was then shown a scene depicting God's people as they will be in heaven, after passing through the tribulation of this world.

John looked, and he saw a vast multitude from all peoples and nations, standing before the throne and before the Lamb. This vast multitude reminds us that although, at any one time, the number of true believers in the world, and even in the professing church, is relatively small, in heaven we will find ourselves part of a vast number saved out of all the peoples of the earth. And this multitude was "clothed with white robes". Here, the word used for 'robe' is one more suited to describing a stately robe than an ordinary garment; moreover, it seems to be used in Revelation when the glorified saints are especially in view (it is also used in 6:11). So, this depicts the saints perfected and glorified in heaven. Also, this multitude had in their hands palm branches, which are associated with joy and rejoicing (see Lev 23:40), and they were crying out with a loud voice, saying, "Salvation belongs to our God who sits on the throne, and to the Lamb!" So, the glorified saints are shown joyfully praising God and the Lamb, giving God and Christ all the glory for their salvation.

v11,12. John also saw all the angels standing around the throne and the elders and the four living creatures. And these fell on their faces and worshipped God: first, by affirming the praise of the saints (with an "Amen"); then by adding their own praise, in which they declare that all the glory and honour belongs to God, and is due to him through all eternity. This worship of the angels, that they add to that of the saints, reminds us that the redeemed people of God, glorified and dwelling in his presence, will eternally be a testimony to the glory, wisdom and power of God; and it reminds us that through all eternity, God's work of salvation will be to his praise and glory.

v13,14. Then, to assist John's understanding, one of the elders questions John concerning the identity of the multitude in heaven arrayed in white robes (who they are, and where they came from). And, when John confesses his ignorance, the elder explains that these are "the ones who come out of the great tribulation" — the glorified, rejoicing saints John saw in heaven are ones having passed through and emerged from a great trial. He also informs John that they "washed their robes and made them white in the blood of the Lamb" — they had come through a great trial, but their salvation and victory was through Christ and his saving work alone.

v15–17. The elder also describes the resultant blessedness of those coming through the great tribulation. Theirs is the blessing of dwelling eternally in God's presence, where they enjoy communion with him, and worship him and live for him ("they are before the throne of God, and serve Him day and night in His temple"; and "He...dwell among them"). Also they will experience no more want ("they shall neither hunger anymore nor thirst anymore"), and no more trials and struggles ("the sun shall not strike them, nor any heat"); but they will know full life and satisfaction ("the Lamb...shepherd them and lead them to living fountains of waters"). And God will comfort them and relieve them of all affliction and grief ("God will wipe away every tear from their eyes").

This scene of the vast multitude in heaven is, therefore, a picture of the glorified saints, and the eternal blessedness of those who have endured great tribulation for Christ's sake and, by God's grace, have overcome. It is a picture of Christians as they will be in their heavenly home, after passing through the tribulation of this world. Therefore, this vision provides comfort and encouragement for the church of all times. All Christians are called to endure much trouble in this world as they live for Christ and serve him (Jn 16:33; Acts 14:22). And this vision, setting before us our heavenly destiny and blessedness, is a great encouragement to press on through all the trials of this life, knowing that ahead lies relief from all struggles and hardship, and a life of full satisfaction dwelling in God's presence forever. Moreover, by setting before us the fact that our salvation is through Christ's saving work alone, this vision also provides reassurance that we can and will stand in all the trials of this life, and endure to the end. Salvation is from God; and on that day when we stand in God's presence, we will know that we endured and have reached our heavenly destiny not because of any power in ourselves, but because Christ saved us and gave us the victory.

Especially, however, this vision is an encouragement for those having to endure a time of particularly great trial or opposition; and this, it would seem, is the special significance of this vision at this point in Revelation. During the centuries after the Empire became Christian, there was to come for the church a time of great trial in the form of terrible apostasy, followed by great persecution. This vision shows that God's people, by God's grace, would overcome; and it sets forth the great and eternal blessedness they would know in God's presence, after they had suffered a little while. It also serves as a reminder that the true destiny and glory of the Christian is not a Christianized world, but heaven. This is the believer's destiny and true habitation.

So, before the opening of the seventh seal, John was shown two visions holding great comfort for the church: first, a vision showing God's keeping power; and then a vision of the heavenly destiny of the church. And, within the historical framework of Revelation, they would seem to relate particularly to the time after the Empire became Christian. As such, they show that in the midst of the Christianized world, God knew who were his people, and that through the judgements to come and the great trial ahead, God would keep his people safe, he would give them power to overcome, and he would bring them to their heavenly home — where all the trials and sufferings of this life are past, and there is blessedness in God's presence forever.

Chapter 8
The sounding of the trumpets

The opening of the seventh seal (8:1–6)

v1. After seeing the sealing of God's people, and the great multitude in heaven who come out of the great tribulation, John then saw Christ open the seventh seal. And when he opened this seal "there was silence in heaven for about half an hour". This silent pause before John was shown the events ushered in by the opening of the seventh seal, could indicate that there was going to be a lapse of time between the events associated with the sixth seal, and the events that were now to unfold. Alternatively, and perhaps preferably, this can be understood as a dramatic pause — a silence of expectation and anticipation of what is to come (see Zech 2:13). As such, it conveys a sense of waiting with awe for what God will do. With the opening of the sixth seal John had beheld a scene of great upheaval in the earth and sky, causing terror among men; so there could only be a sense of wonder in anticipation of God's further deeds.

v2. Then John saw "the seven angels who stand before God, and to them were given seven trumpets". The opening of the seventh seal is to usher in a further group of events, revealed under the sounding of seven trumpets; and in preparation for this, John saw the trumpets being given to the angels who were to sound them.

In Scripture, we read of trumpet sounds accompanying great interventions of God (see Mt 24:31; 1 Cor 15:51–52); and it is probably in this sense that we are to interpret the sounding of these trumpets — as heralding and signifying interventions of God in the world which, as we will see, in this case are a group of judgements. These judgements are included under the seals (they come with the opening of the seventh seal), and therefore they are part of the preordained purposes of God for this age, but they also form a distinct group of interventions of God in judgement.

v3,4. John then saw another angel, holding a golden censer, who came and stood at the golden altar which was before the throne of God; and the angel was given much incense, that he should offer it with the prayers of all the saints upon the altar. And John saw the smoke of the incense, with the prayers of all the saints, ascending before God.

Here we again have a reference to the altar of incense in the tabernacle, which was sited just before the veil to the Most Holy Place. As already noted (in the comments on 6:9,10), the incense burnt on this altar symbolised the offering up of prayer. Moreover, the coupling here of the symbol (incense) with the reality (the prayers of the saints) would seem to indicate that, unlike in 6:9,10 (where incense is not depicted accompanying the cry of the martyrs), it is actual prayer that is in view here — prayer being offered up to God by his people.

v5. Then the angel who had offered the incense upon the golden altar took the censer, filled it with fire from the altar, and threw it to the earth. And there followed noises, thunderings, lightnings, and an earthquake.

These noises, thunderings, etc, represent judgements of God breaking out in the earth. And, notably, the imagery here connects these judgements with the prayers of the saints ascending before God — showing that the prayers of God's people play a part in ushering in the judgements of God. This is not to say that God's people should pray for God's judgement on the world; rather, we can understand this to mean that, as God's people pray for the coming of his kingdom, for the furthering of his saving purposes, for protection from their enemies, and for God to be glorified, these prayers play a part not only in God performing his works of salvation, but also in him performing his acts of judgement. Certainly, here the prayers of the saints are shown preceding and playing a part in the judgements to come under the sounding of the trumpets.

v6. With this, "the seven angels who had the seven trumpets prepared themselves to sound" — upon hearing the noises, thunderings, etc, they made themselves ready to sound out these judgements of God.

We come, then, to the trumpet judgements. These, as we will see, concern great judgements of God that fell upon the Roman Empire and Christian world between the time when the Empire became a Christian empire in the fourth century, and the Reformation in the sixteenth century — a span of time notable for the fall of the Roman Empire and the rise of the papacy and its dominion. They concern things that in and of themselves were significant judgements of God, but that were also important to the papacy's rise to power. Therefore, although the papacy is not depicted here (this comes into focus later), as we consider these trumpet judgements, something will also be said about the significance to the papacy of the events depicted.

The sounding of the first four trumpets (8:7–13)

As with the first four seals, the first four trumpets have certain things in common and form a related group. Therefore, they will be considered together.

The common features in the first four trumpets are that in each case the imagery is of judgement on a certain aspect of the physical creation (the earth and vegetation, the sea, the rivers, the heavenly bodies); also, in each case it is one third of the various parts of the physical creation that is judged (so, these judgements are limited in their scope). Moreover, the imagery employed is, on the whole, a combination of imagery used in the Old Testament to depict God's judgement of Babylon (which he brought down completely), and imagery that reminds us of the plagues of Egypt (by which God judged all that the Egyptians worshipped and depended on for life and comfort).

In view of this, and taking into account the point we have reached in the unfolding of events, the natural conclusion is that these four trumpet judgements concern the fall of the Roman Empire. More specifically, they depict God judging the Roman world and bringing down the Roman Empire and civilisation. (By 'Roman Empire' is meant the western Empire centred on Rome as distinct from the eastern part of the Empire centred on Constantinople, which continued for a considerable time after the fall of the Empire in the west, and was later termed the Byzantine Empire.)

With this general understanding in view, we come to a more detailed look at these first four trumpet judgements.

v7. Having prepared themselves to sound the seven trumpets, the first of the angels then sounded his trumpet. And with this, "hail and fire followed, mingled with blood, and they were thrown to the earth". And "a third of the trees were burned up, and all the green grass was burned up" (cf. Ex 9:23–25 — the plague of hail that fell upon Egypt).

Taking this to concern the Roman Empire, this picture of a great destroying and consuming storm falling upon the earth is imagery depicting God's judgement falling upon the Roman world, and the Roman world being consumed. Concerning the nature of this judgement, of note is that in Isaiah 28:2 similar imagery is used for judgement by an invading force (this is part of a prophecy of judgement on the northern kingdom of Israel, which was judged at the hands of the Assyrians who invaded Israel and took the land). Also of note is that here in Revelation the hail and fire is said to be mingled with blood, suggesting that this judgement involves bloodshed. Given all of this, it would seem that the judgement depicted here was fulfilled in the overrunning and overtaking of the Roman world by barbarian tribes, who were the instrument of God's judgement upon the Roman Empire. At the very end of the fourth century, barbarian peoples both inside and outside the Empire began to conquer the Roman lands, until nearly all the Roman world was under barbarian domination.

v8,9. Then the second angel sounded his trumpet. And with this, "something like a great mountain burning with fire was thrown into the sea". And "a third of the sea became blood. A third of the living creatures in the sea died, and a third of the ships were destroyed".

The imagery of a burning mountain being thrown down is similar to imagery used by the prophet Jeremiah to describe God's judgement of Babylon (see Jeremiah 51:24–26, where Babylon is described as a destroying mountain, and God says he will roll it down and make it a burnt mountain). Moreover, the striking of the sea and it becoming blood reminds us of the first plague of Egypt (see Ex 7:19–21). From this it would seem that what is being depicted here is both God judging Rome (the seat of the Empire) and bringing down its power over the peoples, and God judging the life of the Roman world. Again, the instrument of this was the barbarian peoples, who overran and took the city.

v10,11. Then the third angel sounded his trumpet. And with this, "a great star fell from heaven, burning like a torch, and it fell on a third of the rivers and on the springs of water". And we are told that the name of the star is "Wormwood" (which is a bitter and injurious plant); "and a third of the waters became wormwood, and many men died from the water, because it was made bitter".

The description of a brilliant star falling from heaven is similar to a description in Isaiah of the fall of the king of Babylon, where he is termed Lucifer (shining one or "Day Star") (see Is 14:4,12). This indicates that this depicts God bringing down the Roman emperor — it depicts the emperor falling from power. Moreover, the striking of the waters and them becoming bitter would seem to depict God judging the Roman culture — judging everything that was to the people a source of life and refreshment. And again, all this happened as part of the barbarian conquest of the Empire.

v12. Then the fourth angel sounded his trumpet. And with this, a third of the sun and moon and stars was struck, "so that a third of them were darkened". And so, a "third of the day did not shine, and likewise the night".

Again, this is similar to language used by Isaiah when speaking of God's judgement of Babylon (see Is 13:1,10); likewise, it is similar to language used by Ezekiel in relation to God's judgement of Pharaoh and Egypt (see Ezek 32:2,7–8). It also reminds us of the plague of darkness in Egypt (see Ex 10:21-22). This striking of the heavenly bodies, bringing darkness to the earth, is imagery of great and fearful judgement, like the end of the world; and with reference to the Roman Empire, it would seem to depict the Roman Empire (imperial Rome) being brought to a complete end. When God judges great powers he does not always bring them down completely, but the Roman Empire's fall was complete: the sphere of Rome's power was progressively diminished until, in 476, the last Roman emperor was deposed; and with this the Roman Empire came to a complete and final end.

So, understanding Revelation historically, we conclude that these first four trumpet judgements concern the fall of the Roman Empire; they depict God's judgement falling upon the Roman world, and the Roman Empire and way of life being judged and brought down. All of this happened through the conquering of the Empire by the barbarian peoples who, in God's purpose, brought an end to the Roman Empire and civilisation. This, of course, was a just judgement of God — it fell upon an Empire that had devoured and trampled the nations, and that, in pride, thought it was invincible and would never end. The fall of the Roman Empire was also of great significance to the rise of the papal dominion. While the Roman emperor and Empire existed they stood in the way of the establishing of the papal dominion (the Roman Empire is the restrainer Paul speaks of in

2 Thes 2:6–7 — see 'Antichrist Revealed', 2017, by the same author, for a discussion of this). Conversely, the fall of the Roman Empire opened up the way for the bishop of Rome to rise up and establish his dominion from Rome.

v13. Having witnessed the sounding of the first four trumpets, John then looked, and he heard an angel flying through heaven crying, "Woe, woe, woe to the inhabitants of the earth, because of the remaining blasts of the trumpet of the three angels who are about to sound!" This is a solemn warning that the three trumpet judgements still to come were to be terrible judgements, even worse than those that had gone before. So, this shows us that while the fall of the Roman Empire was a terrible judgement of God (it might have seemed that nothing could be worse), the three judgements to follow are much more terrible.

Chapter 9
The sounding of the trumpets (cont.)

The sounding of the fifth trumpet (9:1–12)

v1. Then the fifth angel sounded his trumpet. With the sounding of this trumpet, we are to see the release of some terrible evil into the world.

First John saw "a star fallen from heaven to the earth". Who or what this fallen star represents, is difficult to decide. However, taking into account the context, and the point we have reached in the unfolding of events, one strong possibility is that it represents the fall of Christian ministry (the leaders of the churches were symbolised as stars in 1:20), or the fall of an eminent Christian leader (possibly the bishop of Rome).

And "to him was given the key to the bottomless pit" (or abyss) — the abode of demons (see Lk 8:31). So, this fallen one is shown being permitted by God (the key was given to him) to release some great evil of demonic origin upon the earth, as a terrible judgement of God. And, as we will see, the following imagery strongly indicates that this is some powerful demonic deception (notable is that Paul warns about deceiving spirits and doctrines of demons — 1 Tim 4:1).

v2. And he opened the bottomless pit, and from the pit came smoke, which is likened to "the smoke of a great furnace"; so "the sun and the air were darkened because of the smoke". This pictures dense smoke billowing out of the pit and filling the whole atmosphere so that it blots out the light and brings dense darkness on the earth. So, here is something originating from the demonic realm, that robs the world of light and brings darkness to men; and so we have the first indication that some powerful deception is in view here — one that robs the world of gospel light.

v3,4. Then out of the darkening smoke locusts came upon the earth. And these locusts were given power "as the scorpions of the earth have power" (that is, power to sting men). And they were commanded not to harm the grass, or any vegetation, or any tree, but "only those men who do not have the seal of God on their foreheads".

The specific command not to harm the grass, etc, would seem to show that these stinging locusts that come upon the earth do not concern some form of political judgement, or something that physically overtakes the earth (cf. 8:7, where the striking of the trees and grass concerned God judging the Roman Empire). Rather, these locusts concern something that overtakes the people and harms men personally. However, those who the locusts may harm are only those who do not have the seal of God on their foreheads. This is a reference to the vision John saw, recorded in 7:1–8, which concerned the true people of God being distinguished in the midst of the Christianized world, and being kept safe through the coming judgements of God. So these locusts were permitted only to harm unbelievers or the nominally Christian, but not the true people of God.

v5,6. And these locusts "were not given authority to kill them, but to torment them for five months" (the time period is commented on under v7–10); and the torment they could cause was very severe (it is likened to the sting of a scorpion, which is very painful). So it is made clear that these locusts do not concern something with power to kill men — to physically destroy them; rather, they concern something that causes men great torment — that causes them great inner hurt and distress. Moreover, the severity of the hurt these locusts could cause is further highlighted by the fact that men would rather die than endure it, but death eludes them. This is something that causes men unbearable suffering, but from which people cannot escape — it holds them captive.

So these locusts represent something demonic, with power to cause great hurt and harm to men's souls, and to rob them of peace. However, this harm was to be inflicted only on the unbelieving, and not on God's people. And again, this points to this being some terrible deception (deception harms men's souls), which will overtake the unbelieving world, but from which God will keep his people safe.

v7–10. John then gives a detailed description of the locusts. "The shape of the locusts was like horses prepared for battle" — these locusts were like a well-organised and equipped army. "On their heads were crowns of something like gold" — they had the appearance of having great authority; and "their faces were like the faces of men" — they had the appearance of possessing great wisdom (man, being unique in intelligence amongst God's creatures, typifies intelligence and wisdom).

"They had hair like women's hair" — they had a seductive power, and an appearance of gentleness; and "their teeth were like lion's teeth" — although appearing gentle, they were, in fact, ferocious and devouring.

"And they had breastplates like breastplates of iron" — they were or seemed to be strong and invincible; and "the sound of their wings was like the sound of chariots with many horses running into battle" — they made rapid progress and were overwhelming.

"They had tails like scorpions, and there were stings in their tails" — it is with these they inflict their tormenting harm on men. And they had power "to hurt men five months" (see also v5) — this time period may indicate that the time of their influence was determined and limited by God; or, more probably, it indicates that these locusts were totally given to the task of causing men hurt (desert locusts have a lifespan of around 3–5 months).

This detailed description of the locusts shows the characteristics of the great demonic evil that these locusts represent. It is something extremely powerful and overwhelming and hard to resist; it is something seeming to have great authority and wisdom; and it is something seductive (very attractive to men and seemingly good). However, it in fact consumes men's lives and does them great harm. Again, all of this is true of deception. Deception is powerful and hard to resist; it seems to carry authority and wisdom; and it is very appealing to men and seemingly good. However, really it destroys men's lives, darkening their minds and harming their souls. So, it would seem that these stinging locusts, coming out of the bottomless pit, represent deceiving spirits that bring upon the earth some great deception.

v11. Lastly, we are told that these locusts "had as king over them the angel of the bottomless pit", whose name is "Abaddon" or "Apollyon" — which mean 'destruction' and 'destroyer'. So, this great army has a king or commander over them, who would seem to be Satan — the leader of the demonic hoards, and the deceiver of men and corrupter of men's souls. This, then, is Satan's army; but it is also God's instrument to execute his judgement on the unbelieving world.

We come then to consider what this trumpet judgement concerns. Some who interpret Revelation historically view this trumpet (along with the sixth trumpet) as concerning the Islamic hordes that swept across the Mediterranean world following the rise of Islam in the seventh century. In some respects this fits the imagery here, because these hordes brought with them the spiritual darkness and deception that is Islam. However, they were also an invading force that physically overtook much of the Christian world — and the demonic power represented here is not such a thing (see comment on v4). Thus, such an understanding of this trumpet is not favoured here. Rather, taking into account both the imagery, and the time we have reached in the unfolding events, it would seem that what this trumpet concerns is the powerful deception that overtook the church and Christian world during the centuries after the Empire became Christian — deception which robbed the world of gospel light, and which gave rise to the Roman Catholic religion and

Church. (*See the note at the end of this chapter for more detail on the Roman Catholic apostasy.)

Of course, prior to this, the church was not without false teaching and false teachers. However, during the Middle Ages the church became engulfed in error, and fell away from the faith. Essentially, the church began to absorb pagan beliefs and practices, which it Christianized and presented as the true faith; also, it developed a way of salvation dependent not on faith in Christ alone, but on works. So the true gospel was eclipsed, and the church and Christian world was overtaken by a religion of works, idolatry and superstition, masquerading as true Christianity. And this was a powerful deception, that both compelled men to believe it (as it was presented as the true faith and only way of salvation), while it also held great attraction to men (a religion of works, idolatry and superstition is very appealing to natural man). Its effect, however, was only to bring great harm, as it darkened men's minds, corrupted their lives, and brought not peace and joy but only great anguish of soul (a religion of works leads to great discomfort of soul, as it awakens men to their sin but then provides no sure remedy).

Furthermore, this great deception that overtook the church and Christian world was a great judgement of God on the Christian world for its resistance to the true gospel. By the time we are concerned with here, the gospel had gone forth but many had not believed it (the vast majority in the Christian world were merely nominally Christian). So in judgement God gave them over to this powerful deception, which was of the devil, but was, first of all, a judgment sent by God on those who refused to believe the truth of Christ. All of this, however, was according to the preordained purpose of God (see 2 Thes 2:3,9–12 where, writing about the revealing of the man of sin/Antichrist, Paul speaks of the same falling away, and speaks of those who do not love the truth being sent strong delusion by God). God's people, however, were kept safe from deception in the midst of this terrible judgement. Throughout the time of the church being engulfed in error and falling away from the faith, there was a faithful remnant.

Finally, inseparable from this was a departure by the churches' leaders from the true faith, and from their true office (during this time the churches' leaders took on the role of priests, mediating between God and the people). Moreover, it was in the midst of this great deception, that the bishops of Rome raised themselves up, claiming and endeavouring to exercise supreme authority over the church and over Christendom. So, this great deception and the emergence of the false office of the papacy went hand in hand (see again 2 Thes 2:3, where Paul associates the revealing of the man of sin/Antichrist, who is the pope of Rome, with the great falling away).

So, this trumpet judgement concerns the flood of deception that overtook the church and Christian world in the centuries after the Empire became Christian, and that gave rise to the Roman Catholic religion and Church.

(Of note here is that, in recent times, in the West there has been a marked increase in the prestige and influence of the papacy and the Roman Catholic Church. When we consider this in the light of this trumpet judgement, and in the light of the way that the western nations and churches have been turning from true biblical Christianity, we see that God is still using the Roman Catholic error as an instrument of his judgement. However, this trumpet also assures us that in the midst of all that God allows to happen, he will not let his true people be overtaken by deception, but he will preserve his people from falling away.)

v12. The end of the first woe is then announced (the fifth trumpet was the first woe — see 8:13). From this we see that this powerful deception engulfing the Christian world was a much worse judgement of God than God's judgements on the Roman Empire, which resulted in the end of the Roman Empire and civilisation. From this we need to learn that God's spiritual judgements (God giving people over to some powerful deception, and to idolatry and wickedness) are much more to be feared than any of God's judgements that affect us politically, materially, or even physically.

So this is the first woe, and two more are to come.

The sounding of the sixth trumpet (9:13–21)

v13,14. Then the sixth angel sounded his trumpet. With the sounding of this trumpet, we are to see the release of a great destroying army. This begins with the release of four angels who are bound at the river Euphrates.

First, John heard "a voice from the four horns of the golden altar which is before God" telling the angel who had the trumpet, "Release the four angels who are bound at the great river Euphrates." Of note here is that these angels are bound and then released. This shows us that this is all in God's control — this is a judgement from God. Also notable is that the voice commanding the release of this judgement is said to come from the golden altar which is before God. This reminds us of the scene shown to John, prior to these judgements, of the prayers of the saints ascending before God (see 8:3–5). So, it reminds us of the part played by the prayers of God's people in this judgement; and it helps us to remember that even in a hard and threatening providence, such as we have here, God is carrying forward his saving purposes and working for the good of his people.

Also significant is the site of these bound angels, which are described as at the river Euphrates. This tells us something important about this judgement. The river Euphrates marked the extreme eastern boundary of the ideal promised land (see Ex 23:31; Josh 1:3–4). It was also the barrier between the people of God and their classic enemies, Assyria and Babylon, who, significantly, were not only enemies of Israel, but were also used by God to judge apostate Israel and Judah. This indicates that this is a judgement coming from outside the church/ Christendom, to judge apostate Christendom.

v15. So the four angels were released. These are said to have "been prepared for the hour and day and month and year". This shows that God had predetermined the exact time of this judgement. In all things God is acting to an exact, predetermined timetable, and he sets his purposes in motion at his appointed time. It is also said that these angels "were released to kill a third of mankind". So we see that this judgement, unlike the locust judgement, was to involve physical harm and death. And this was to fall on a third of mankind — which should not be taken literally, but should be regarded either as indicating that this judgement was to fall on a significant portion but not the entirety of mankind, or as indicating that, just as God had predetermined the exact time of this judgement, he also had predetermined its extent. Again we see how everything has been preordained by God and is in his control.

v16. John then, without any introduction, switches to describing a vast advancing army. The angels were released to execute the judgement, and this is now depicted as an army of horsemen, vast in size (John heard the number which was two hundred million). This is an overwhelming force, impossible to stop.

v17–19. John then describes the horses he saw in the vision (John's reference to this as a vision reminds us that this is all highly symbolic, and not to be understood literally). John tells us, "those who sat on them [the horses] had breastplates of fiery red, hyacinth blue, and sulphur yellow" — they were clad in brightly coloured armour, making them very impressive. And "the heads of the horses were like the heads of lions" — they were fierce and devouring; and "out of their mouths came fire, smoke, and brimstone", and "by these three plagues a third of mankind was killed". The fire and brimstone reminds us of God's judgement on Sodom and Gomorrah (Gen 19:24), and so it is imagery of sudden judgement on the wicked.

Moreover, these horses did not only have power in their mouths to kill men, but also power in their tails; their tails were "like serpents, having heads; and with them they do harm". Since serpents (or snakes) harm men by means of injecting a poison into them, we should probably understand that the harm these horses inflict with their tails is a poisoning of men's souls. So, this army has a double power — the horses have both power to inflict upon men physical harm and death (they kill men with the plagues coming out of their mouths), and power to harm men's souls (they harm men with their serpent-like tails).

v20,21. Finally, we are told that those who were not killed by these plagues did not repent of their idolatries and wickedness. The mention here that the people did not repent, suggests that this judgement was sent by God not purely as a judgement, but also to cause people to consider their ways and turn back to him (it provided an opportunity for reflection and repentance). However, people's hearts were so hardened against God, that even this terrible judgement did not cause them to repent.

We come then to consider what all of this represents. What we see here is some terrible judgement of God coming from outside the Christian world, to judge apostate Christendom. Moreover, this is depicted as an overwhelming force that has power both to kill men and to do harm to their souls. And at this point in the unfolding of events, there is really only one thing that this can represent — which is the great flood of Islam that in the Middle Ages overwhelmed much of the Christian world, and was a terrible judgement of God on Christendom, which had become full of idolatry and wickedness.

Islam arose in the seventh century in Arabia, and from the outset was a militant religious and political movement intent on imposing Islam on the world. In pursuit of this goal, in the mid-seventh century, the followers of Islam began to sweep across the Christian world, conquering the people and spreading the deception that is Islam; and for many centuries Islam was Christendom's greatest enemy. First, Islamic armies swept out of Arabia and overran the lands of the Eastern Empire (ie, the eastern part of the old Roman Empire, which was centred on Constantinople, and which had continued after the fall of Rome and the Empire in the west). They also conquered North Africa and Spain, and then tried to push into the heart of Europe, but were repelled. The Eastern Empire survived this onslaught but lost much of its territory. Moreover, wherever the Islamic armies conquered, much of the church was wiped out.

Eventually, however, the Arab power began to decline; but it was followed, in the eleventh century, by the rise of Turkish power (first the Seljuk Turks and then, later, the Ottoman Turks), and some take the view that it is especially the Turkish expansion that is depicted here. Certainly, the Turks were a vast and formidable force. From the region of the Euphrates they spread westward, conquering the peoples and spreading the religion of Islam. The Turkish offensives further diminished the eastern church. They were also instrumental in bringing the final end of the Empire in the east (this can be counted as ending in 1453 when Constantinople fell).

The conquering by Islam of much of Christendom was a great judgement of God on the church and Christian world for its idolatry and wickedness. However, those who were not conquered did not repent. The hardness of people's hearts was such that even this terrible judgement did not cause the people to turn from their idolatrous and superstitious ways. Rather, the church and Christian world continued in its false religion, which held great attraction to people, but also bound them in terrible darkness.

Finally, also of note is that, although these events were not of direct relevance to the rise of the papacy (as were the fall of the Roman Empire in the west and the great falling away/apostasy of the church), they were of significance. As the papacy sought to claim and exercise supreme power over the church and over Christendom, these claims were never accepted or yielded to by the churches in the east. Moreover, it was the emperor who stood supreme over eastern Christendom. However, the diminution of the eastern church and the demise of the Empire in the east, brought about by Islam, removed this major challenge to the pope's supremacy in Christendom.

(Of course, Islam continues to be very powerful and militant in our own time, and it is still a great threat to the nations of the West. Not only that, Islam is currently making great inroads into the West through people from the Islamic nations taking up residence in the West, and through Westerners converting to Islam. When we consider this in the light of this trumpet judgement, and in the light of the way that the western nations have been turning from Christianity, it would seem that God is continuing to use Islam as an instrument of his judgement. So, while this trumpet primarily concerns the overrunning of apostate Christendom by Islam in the Middle Ages, it also helps us to rightly assess developments in our own time.)

So, as interpreted here, the first six trumpet judgements concern: the fall of the Roman Empire, which came to an end during the fifth century (the first four trumpets); the great flood of deception that overtook the church and Christian world during the centuries after the Empire became Christian (the fifth trumpet); and God's judgement of apostate Christendom by means of the Islamic conquests (which also brought an end to the Empire in the east) (the sixth trumpet). Thus, these trumpets concern things happening between the time of the Empire becoming Christian in the fourth century and the Reformation in the sixteenth century. Moreover, they cover the time of the rise and ascendancy of the papacy and papal dominion — and although the papacy itself is not depicted here, significantly they concern developments important to the papacy's rise to power.

Note on the Roman Catholic apostasy: First, it must be said that the Roman Catholic Church teaches many things that are orthodox and that make it appear orthodox. Particularly, it teaches that God is one, but also three persons (the Trinity); it teaches the full deity and humanity of Christ; and it teaches the doctrines of the virgin birth, the death of Christ for men's sins, the bodily resurrection of Christ, Christ's ascension and rule, and his second coming. However, along with this, the Roman Catholic Church also teaches many other doctrines that contradict and deny the truth about Christ and the salvation that we have in him, and which make the Roman Catholic Church one that has departed fundamentally from the faith.

Foundational to the development and propagation of its erroneous doctrines has been a false view of authority in the church. The Catholic Church does not regard Scripture as the church's sole and sufficient authority for all matters of faith and conduct; rather, it counts tradition (the teaching handed down by the Church) as being of equal authority with Scripture. Moreover, with this it holds that the Church is the divinely appointed custodian and interpreter of the Bible, and a person must accept the Church's interpretation of Scripture. It is this different approach to revelation and authority that, from an early date, enabled false beliefs and practices to be propagated and to overtake the church.

The erroneous beliefs and practices of the Roman Catholic Church developed over many centuries. Of course, from the beginning, the church was troubled by false teachers promoting teachings that were contrary to the apostolic faith. However, the centuries after the Empire became Christian saw a whole series of changes in the faith and practice of the church — changes that moved the church of the Middle Ages further and further away from the faith and practice of the New Testament church and that gave rise to the Roman Catholic religion.

The long period from the Christianization of the Empire to the Reformation saw such changes as: growing belief in baptismal regeneration (ie, that a person is born again through baptism with water); growing belief in the priestly role of ministers as mediators between God and the people, and a growing wrong distinction between 'the clergy' (ministers) and 'the laity' (the other believers); growing belief that the bread and wine of the Lord's Supper actually become the body and blood of Christ (transubstantiation), together with the notion of the re-offering of Christ's sacrifice on an altar; an increased emphasis on liturgical worship and ritual, with candles, incense, robes and vestments being used in worship; growth in the practice of venerating and praying to Mary and the saints, and a growing interest in relics; confession to a priest becoming an established practice; and growing belief in the doctrine of purgatory, which led to the practices of saying Masses for the dead and of selling indulgences.

Thus, gradually and progressively there came into the church a whole array of beliefs and practices that were not founded in Scripture (and, in many instances, were Christianized pagan beliefs and practices). Furthermore, with the passage of time, these beliefs and practices became more firmly and formally established, eventually to form a whole system of beliefs and practices that the church presented as the true faith and way of salvation. In fact, however, it was a system that denied the finished work of Christ, that made salvation dependent on the ministry of the Church (the clergy) and on man's works, and that led the people into idolatry and superstition. So, the church was overtaken by erroneous beliefs and practices. Moreover, with this, the simple gospel of salvation by grace alone through faith alone was eclipsed, and men were consigned to follow a religion of superstition and works, leading only to bondage and death.

Chapter 10
The little book

Having witnessed the sounding of the first six trumpets, John may have been expecting the seventh angel to sound his trumpet. However, as with the opening of the seals, the sixth trumpet is not immediately followed by the sounding of the seventh (this comes in 11:15); rather, certain other visions intervene.

The angel with the little book (10:1–11)

First, John was made ready to receive and pass on the visions which were to follow the sounding of the seventh trumpet — visions which, as will be seen, involve terrible things to happen in the earth.

v1. John tells us he saw "another mighty angel coming down from heaven". Here, some commentators take this angel to represent the Lord Jesus Christ, while others see this as a straightforward reference to an angel. Whichever it is, of note is that up to this point little has been said about the appearance of the angels that John saw; in this case, however, the angel is described in detail, and each of the things mentioned has some connection with God and Christ. We are told he was "clothed with a cloud", and he had "feet like pillars of fire" — which remind us of the pillar of cloud and pillar of fire in the wilderness, in which God was present with his people, and which were also instruments of God to guide and protect his people (see Ex 13:21–22; 14:19–20). Also, "a rainbow was on his head" — which reminds us of God's covenant with his people in Christ (see 4:3). And "his face was like the sun" — which reminds us of the glory of Christ, and of his purity and splendour (see 1:16).

Thus the appearance of this angel displays God's saving mercy and faithfulness, and his care and protection of his people. And, the fact that this is displayed at this point would seem to be significant. Following the sounding of the seventh trumpet, we are to be shown disturbing things; and the reminder here of the salvation we have in Christ, and of God's faithfulness and care, suggests that these are things God wants us to be assured of as we look at all that unfolds once the seventh trumpet sounds. So, these are things to keep in sight as we study the following chapters, and the troubling things they contain.

v2. John also tells us that the angel "had a little book open in his hand". Previously, John had seen a sealed scroll (which can also be termed a book) in the right hand of God, and a strong (or mighty) angel crying out concerning the opening of the scroll (see 5:1–2). Now, John sees a mighty angel with a little book open in his hand. This book, as with the scroll seen earlier, signifies the preordained purposes of God. However, this book is a little book, indicating that it does not signify the purposes of God for the whole gospel age, but only a part of these — that is, the things John was to be shown following the sounding of the seventh trumpet. Moreover, this book is open, because the sounding of the seventh trumpet marks the point at which the hidden purposes of God are finally revealed and brought to a close (see v7).

And this angel coming down from heaven with the book "set his right foot on the sea and his left foot on the land". The placing, by this mighty angel, of one foot on the sea and one foot on the land probably indicates his mastery over both spheres; so it shows that his coming to earth with the little book, and therefore the message associated with the book, is of universal significance and affects the whole world.

v3,4. And the angel cried out with a loud voice; and when he did, "seven thunders uttered their voices". But, as John was about to write down the messages conveyed by the seven thunders (just as he had recorded everything else he had seen or heard), he heard a voice from heaven telling him to keep these things hidden (to seal them up) and not to reveal them (not to write them).

These seven thunders could represent another group of judgements of God, which it is not God's purpose for us to know. If so, this is a reminder that God has not made known to us all that he has purposed for this gospel age; also, it serves as a warning against making detailed timetables of events. Alternatively, these thunders could simply signify the voice of God speaking to John, and thus concern things that were for John alone (just as Paul heard things that he could not utter — see 2 Cor 12:3–4). If so, this reminds us that it is God's prerogative to reveal things to his people, and in his sovereign purpose God shows some people more than others. (Even in this day when revelation is complete, the knowledge and experience of himself that God gives his people varies greatly.) Whichever it is, however, there is no point in engaging in speculation concerning precisely what was conveyed to John by these thunders since it is clearly not God's purpose for us to know.

v5–7. Then the angel "raised up his hand to heaven"; and he swore an oath by God "that there should be delay no longer, but in the days of the sounding of the seventh angel...mystery of God would be finished, as He declared to His servants the prophets". Here God is described in terms that portray him as the eternal God and creator of all things. He is the one who is over all, and who will certainly fulfil what he has planned. And by this one, the angel swears that with the sounding of the seventh trumpet, the hidden purposes of God for this world, which had been announced to the prophets of old (but at that time were still not understood), would be finally revealed and accomplished/completed.

As we will see, the sounding of the seventh trumpet (see 11:15–19) is followed first by a series of visions which concern the origins, rise and identity of the Antichrist, and then by the pouring out of the seven bowls of God's wrath — which concern the final events of the gospel age, and especially God's judgement of the Antichrist and his dominion. So, the sounding of the seventh trumpet marks the point of the Antichrist being revealed and then swiftly judged. And, with this, the hidden purposes of God for this age will be finally known and will come to an end.

v8–10. Then the voice which John heard from heaven (v4) spoke to him again, telling him to take the little book which was open in the hand of the angel. So, John went to the angel and asked for the book; and the angel told him to take and eat it, and it would make his stomach bitter, but it would be as sweet as honey in his mouth.

Imagery similar to this is found in Ezekiel and Jeremiah (see Ezek 2:9–3:3,10; also Jer 15:16) where it concerns God's prophet receiving God's message, and really digesting it and being affected by it before he speaks it. So, John was shown that he was to really take in, and meditate upon the revelation he was to receive following the sounding of the seventh trumpet. Also, he was shown that it would be pleasant to him (the receiving of God's word is always pleasing to a believer, whatever its content may be), but as he really took it in and was affected by it, it would be unpleasant to know. John was to be shown disturbing things happening in the world, and while this increased knowledge of God's purpose would be gratifying to him, it would also cause him great anguish and distress. However, John was ready to receive all that God had to show him, and willingly he took the book out of the angel's hand and ate it; and, indeed, it was as sweet as honey in his mouth, but when he had eaten it his stomach became bitter.

v11. John was then told he "must prophesy again about many peoples, nations, tongues, and kings". John was to tell the churches all he was to be shown concerning what was to happen in the world (as with the rest of this prophecy, John did this by writing down all he saw and heard and sending it to the churches). So, at this point in Christ's revealing of things, John's commission to receive and pass on the revelation of Christ was renewed.

Thus, John was made ready to receive and pass on the things he was to be shown following the sounding of the seventh trumpet — things it would be unpleasant and painful to know. And here there is a challenge for us. As we study all that is revealed in the following chapters, we must not be content for these things simply to inform our minds, but our goal must be that they really affect our hearts. And the key to this will be giving time to considering these things, asking God that we may truly take in and be affected by all that he is showing us. Moreover, God would want us to do this knowing it will cause us anguish, but willing to have our hearts touched by truths that are unpleasant and painful. All of this is important if we are to rightly respond to all that is to be revealed, and especially if we are to be equipped to share it with others.

Chapter 11
The true witnessing church

The two witnesses (11:1–14)

v1,2. Following the renewing of his commission to receive and pass on the revelation of Christ, John was then given "a reed like a measuring rod"; and he was told to rise and measure "the temple [or sanctuary] of God, the altar, and those who worship there", but to leave out and not measure "the court which is outside the temple".

This reminds us of the vision Ezekiel saw of the new temple, in which he saw a man with a measuring rod who measured the temple and showed him its design (see Ezek 40:3ff). This vision looked forward to the building of the new covenant church of Christ (a spiritual temple) which God was to establish according to his design. Similarly, John's vision also concerns the church. In this case, however, the vision would not seem to concern the building of the church. Rather, the measuring that John was tasked to do (or not do) would seem to be concerned with distinguishing the true church of God (that God has established, and that measures up to his word and standards), and the false church (that does not bear measuring by God's word and standards).

So, here the temple (or sanctuary) John was to measure represents the true church, with its life ordered by God's ways and standards. The altar represents true worship as God has ordained and desires. The worshippers represent the true believers who worship and live as God has prescribed. In short, the temple, the altar and the worshippers, which John was to measure, represent the true church of God, established, ordered and kept by him.

In contrast, the court outside the temple, which John was not to measure, represents the false church. This court, which we are told "has been given to the Gentiles", very probably is a reference to the outer court of the Jerusalem temple, which was added by Herod (it was not part of God's original design), and which the Gentiles were allowed to use. So, it represents that part of the visible church which does not conform to God's design, and which consists of those who are not members of God's covenant community but are merely nominal Christians.

And John was further told that the Gentiles "will tread the holy city [another figure for the church] underfoot for forty-two months". This treading of the holy city depicts the non-believers bringing into the church their pagan ceremonies and customs (their idolatrous religious practices) and worshipping God in a false way (see Is 1:12ff; also Dan 8:13, for similar imagery). Moreover, forty-two months is the same time as the reign of the beast (see 13:5), ie, the reign of the Antichrist (in Revelation the beast is a figure for the Antichrist). Thus, this indicates that this treading of the holy city happens during Antichrist's reign.

So, John was shown that, in God's purpose and for a time preordained by him, the unbelieving world would be permitted to overrun the church with its godless religious practices and godless ways; he was also shown that, along with the true church, there would be a false, apostate church comprised of those who were not true believers, but were merely nominal Christians. It was further revealed to John that the time of the church being overrun was the time of the reign of the Antichrist — who can now be identified as the pope of Rome.

Understood in a more general sense, the imagery here reminds us of the constant danger the church faces of being polluted by worldly beliefs and ways. However, at this point in Revelation, particularly in view would seem to be the long period from when the Empire became a Christian Empire up until the Reformation, during which the church became largely a church of nominal believers, and it progressively absorbed and Christianized pagan beliefs and practices and fell away into idolatry, superstition and error. All of this happened in the preordained purpose of God. *(*See the note at the end of this chapter for a discussion of which period of papal history equates with Revelation's reign of the beast/Antichrist.)*

v3. After being told of the treading of the holy city, John was then shown that there would be a true witness during all that time.

First, John was told that God would give power to his two witnesses, and they would "prophesy one thousand two hundred and sixty days [the same time period as the forty-two months in v2], clothed in sackcloth". This depicts a true witness being sustained by God, and being made by his people, during all the time of the treading of the holy city. Moreover, the symbolism of two witnesses depicts this being a small but adequate witness, which leaves people without excuse (two witnesses were needed for a testimony to be established — see Deut 19:15; hence Jesus sent out his disciples in twos — see Mk 6:7; Lk 10:1). Furthermore, the sackcloth depicts these witnesses not only proclaiming the gospel, but also recognising the terrible state of the church and mourning over it. So, this portrays the true believers, who were small in number compared with the total professing church, making a powerful witness to the truth throughout the time when the church absorbed pagan beliefs and practices and fell away from the faith.

v4. These two witnesses are further described as "the two olive trees and the two lampstands standing before the God of the earth". This reminds us of Zechariah's vision of a lampstand and two olive trees (see Zech 4:2ff); and it is a further portrayal of the true, witnessing church — the lampstands depicting God's witnesses as bringing light (God's truth) to the world, and the olive trees depicting them witnessing by the power of the Holy Spirit supplied by God.

v5. Moreover, John was told that if anyone wants to harm these witnesses, "fire proceeds from their mouth and devours their enemies". This reminds us of Elijah, and the fire that at his word came down from heaven and consumed those who came to seize him (see 2 Kgs 1:10,12). It also reminds us of God's word to Jeremiah, "I will make my words in your mouth fire, and this people wood, and it shall devour them" (see Jer 5:14). Thus this would seem to portray God's defence and preservation of his witnessing church throughout the time in view here.

v6. These witnesses are also said to "have power to shut heaven, so that no rain falls in the days of their prophecy"; and "power over waters to turn them to blood, and to strike the earth with all plagues". This is a clear reference first to Elijah, who prophesied and prayed that it would not rain on the land and it did not rain (see 1 Kgs 17:1; Jas 5:17), and then to Moses, who was God's instrument to release his plagues on Egypt (see Exodus chapters 7–12). Thus, this would seem to depict the faithful witness of the true believers (which left people without excuse), together with their mourning over the state of the church, playing a part in God's judgements falling upon the Christian world (cf. 8:4–5).

So, John was shown that during all the time of the unbelieving world overrunning the church with its godless religious practices and ways, there would be true believers who, sustained and empowered by God's Spirit, would make a powerful witness that left people without excuse. He was also shown that this witness would be kept and preserved by God, and that it would play a part in God's judgements falling on the Christian world. And looking back to the Middle Ages, we can see that throughout that time, when the church absorbed pagan beliefs and practices and fell away from the faith, there were groups of true believers (both within and outside the church), who sought to witness to the truth and to challenge the falsehood and corruption in the church. These varied in the amount of light they had (some were more orthodox than others), and their prominence and influence waxed and waned, but still there was a witness throughout all that time.

v7. John was then told that when the witnesses finish their testimony (or, as some commentators render it, 'when they are about to finish their testimony'), "the beast that ascends out of the bottomless pit will make war against them, overcome them, and kill them". This is the first reference to the beast, which is central to much of the remainder of the book; and it is notable that, from the outset, the evil origin of the beast is made clear — it is said to ascend out of the bottomless pit (or abyss), showing it to be associated with evil forces and to be an instrument of Satan (notably, it also has the same origin as the great deception of the fifth trumpet — 9:1). Particularly, however, here we are told that, when the witnesses reach the end of their testimony (ie, as the time of the trampling of the holy city draws to a close), the beast will make war against them, overcome them and kill them — it will launch a great persecution against the true, witnessing believers, and will be allowed by God to overcome and destroy them.

As already noted, the beast is a figure for the Antichrist, who can now be identified as the pope of Rome. So here, for the first time, the papacy comes into view; and, historically, what we see depicted here is the great persecution that the papacy launched against the true believers towards the end of the Middle Ages. This was not the beginning of persecution by the Roman Church. Looking back to the Middle Ages, we can see that during all that time there was opposition to those who made a stand for the truth, and who sought to give witness to the true gospel. However, in the centuries just prior to the Reformation this was especially severe. The papacy's opposition to the true believers began in earnest in the thirteenth century with the foundation of the Inquisition, which was an agent of persecution, torture and death. This then continued into the fourteenth and fifteenth centuries, and many true believers were tortured and killed. All of this was a determined effort on the part of the papacy to silence and extinguish the true, witnessing church.

v8. We are further told that the dead bodies of the witnesses "will lie in the street of the great city which spiritually is called Sodom and Egypt, where also our Lord was crucified". The great city in Revelation is Babylon (see 14:8; 16:19); and, as will become clear (especially from chapter 17), this represents papal Rome (which, as the seat of the Church of Rome, can also stand for the Church of Rome itself). So here, for the first time, the Church of Rome comes into view.

And here, the great city, in which the bodies of the witnesses lie, is likened spiritually to Sodom, which is a symbol for great wickedness, and to Egypt, which is a symbol for oppression. It is also described as the city where Christ was crucified. This of course was Jerusalem, but here this symbolises the seat of false religion which opposes Christ. So, the Church of Rome is depicted as being full of wickedness, as being the oppressor of God's people, and as being the seat of false religion which persecutes the true church. And this is an apt description of the Church of Rome. By the end of the Middle Ages it was full of idolatry, superstition and immorality. And the bodies of the witnesses did, in a sense, lie in its streets — it was the Church of Rome (as an institution) that opposed and sought to extinguish all those who held to and proclaimed God's truth.

v9,10. We are then given a description of the response of all the peoples to this. We are told they will see (will look upon) the dead bodies of the witnesses three and a half days, and not allow their dead bodies to be buried. Also, they will rejoice over and celebrate the death of the two witnesses (here termed prophets) because these two prophets tormented them.

This shows us that, while it was the Church of Rome that killed the witnesses, the peoples took notice of this. It also depicts great malice and contempt being felt towards the true believers (the people would not allow the bodies of the witnesses to be buried, but they left them on display). Also we see great smugness and pleasure being displayed at their destruction (the people celebrated the death of the witnesses/prophets, as if a great victory had been won). And we are told the reason for this — it was because the witness of the true believers troubled their consciences (the witnesses tormented them). Silenced, however, they could torment them no longer. So we see here that, while it was the Church of Rome that sought to extinguish the witness, the peoples approved of this and shared the Church's animosity towards the true believers, because their witness to the truth troubled the consciences of men.

(Here, it is not easy to decide what the three and a half days signifies. One suggestion is that it reminds us of the time that elapsed before either Lazarus or Jesus was raised from the dead. Whatever it signifies, however, it shows us that for a time it seemed to the people that the witness had been extinguished.)

v11. However, when it seemed as if the witness had been extinguished, after the three and a half days "the breath of life from God entered them, and they stood on their feet, and great fear fell on those who saw them". This depicts God, following the terrible persecution which seemed to have extinguished the true church, raising it up to witness once more — that is, establishing once more a church of true believers, witnessing to Christ. And, within the historical framework of Revelation, this can only refer to the Reformation. As already noted, prior to the Reformation the papacy made a determined effort to eliminate the true believers, with considerable success. However, into a situation in which it seemed as if the true church had once and for all been silenced and eliminated, God intervened; and, in a relatively short space of time, there was raised up by God a large, faithful church, witnessing to the true gospel. And here this is depicted as causing great fear to fall on those who saw this. At the Reformation, that which the Church of Rome had sought to destroy suddenly sprang up again and spread with greater impact than before; and this was a reviving of the true church of such staggering proportions that it could only strike great consternation into the hearts of those who detested the believers and the truth they proclaimed.

v12. These witnesses are then portrayed being called up to heaven, and ascending to heaven in a cloud in the sight of their enemies. Although the description here reminds us of Christ's ascension into heaven (see Acts 1:9), in this context this should not be taken to represent the church actually going to heaven. We must remember that the resurrection of the witnesses represents the raising up by God of a true witnessing church (the church rising again in her successors), and this church necessarily must exist on earth. Taking this into account, the ascending of the witnesses to heaven would seem to portray the true church being bestowed with heavenly honour and blessing. And this was seen by her enemies — by this, the true church was vindicated by God in the sight of those who hated her.

v13. We are then told, "In the same hour there was a great earthquake, and a tenth of the city fell. In the earthquake seven thousand people were killed, and the rest were afraid and gave glory to the God of heaven." Here, the raising up of the witnessing church is shown to be accompanied by part of the city (the Church of Rome) falling. This further depicts what happened at the Reformation. At that time, the raising up by God of a true church proclaiming the true gospel, went hand in hand with a significant, although not crippling, part of the Church of Rome falling. This happened as many were won out of the Roman Church and whole areas of Europe became Protestant. And so the Church of Rome lost a great deal of ground both spiritually and temporally (which fittingly is depicted as an earthquake causing a tenth of the city to fall).

Moreover, in the great upheaval of the Reformation people were killed — there was actual fighting and bloodshed as the Church of Rome sought to hold on to and reclaim the ground it was losing. Also, men did fear and give glory to God. The loss of ground by the Church of Rome was accomplished by the powerful working of God's Spirit, by whom people were convicted of their idolatrous and sinful ways. As a result many believed in Christ. Moreover, so great was the upheaval at that time, that all would have had to acknowledge that something of immense significance was happening in the world.

So here in verses 1–13, and prior to the sounding of the seventh trumpet, we have seen: the great apostasy of the Middle Ages (when the church absorbed and Christianized pagan beliefs and practices, and fell into idolatry, superstition and error); the presence and witness of the true church of God during all that time; the terrible persecution of the true believers at the hands of the papacy and the Roman Church prior to the Reformation (which seemed virtually to eliminate God's true church); and the raising up of the true church at the Reformation, which was a mighty blow to the Church of Rome, and was accompanied by it losing a great deal of ground both spiritually and temporally.

Moreover, it follows that the period of time covered here corresponds to the time of the fifth and sixth trumpet judgments, but with a different focus. When considering these judgements (Chapter 9) we saw that the fifth trumpet judgement concerned the great flood of deception that overtook the church and Christian world during the centuries after the Empire became Christian; and the sixth trumpet concerned the Islamic conquest of apostate Christendom, and particularly the Turkish expansion in the centuries just prior to the Reformation. Thus these judgements spanned the time from the Empire becoming Christian to the Reformation. And, in this chapter, this same time has been in view, but now with a focus on the true church: on the presence, witness and preservation of the true church during this time; on the attempt by the papacy and Roman Church to destroy the true church; and on the restoration of the true church at the Reformation.

v14. John was then told, "The second woe is past. Behold, the third woe is coming quickly." The second woe was the sixth trumpet judgement, and the third woe is the seventh trumpet judgement (see 8:13; 9:12). Thus, this warning returns us to the trumpet judgements, and it prepares us for the sounding of the seventh trumpet, which now follows.

The sounding of the seventh trumpet (11:15–19)

v15. Then the seventh angel sounded his trumpet. When this happened, John might have expected to see a scene depicting some terrible judgement. Instead, however, the first thing he saw was a scene of praise in heaven.

As this unfolded, first John heard loud voices in heaven declaring the establishment of the eternal kingdom of God. Here, the past tense in this declaration ("have become") should not be taken to mean that this great event has happened; rather, it is expressing the certainty of this happening — it is as good as having occurred. Christ will reign, and his enemies will be put under his feet. It is fitting for this to be announced at this point when the seventh trumpet is about to sound (see 10:7). This trumpet ushers in the final events of the gospel age, which concern God's judgements on Christ's enemies, and lead to Christ's return and the final establishing of his kingdom.

v16–18. At this acclamation of the establishing of God's kingdom, John then saw the twenty-four elders (who represent the whole church of God) fall down and worship God. Moreover, he heard them, in an outburst of thanksgiving to the almighty and eternal God, proclaiming the climax of all things when God's reign is over all, when his enemies are finally judged, and his people receive their reward. Of course, Christ's final victory is something believers should always have in view, and it should be a constant cause of thanksgiving and ground of hope. However, it would seem that this is specially set before us here because Christ's final victory is what the events associated with the sounding of the seventh trumpet will lead to; not only that, it is something we need to keep in view as the troubling events associated with the seventh trumpet unfold.

v19. Following this, John then tells us "the temple of God was opened in heaven, and the ark of His covenant was seen in His temple". The opening of the temple reminds us of those times in the history of the Jews when, after a time of apostasy and neglect of the temple, the temple was opened and the true worship of God was restored (see 2 Kgs 23:1ff, and 2 Chr 29:3). Moreover, the disclosing of the ark portrays the way into God's presence being made open (the ark of the covenant is a symbol of God's presence with his people). And at this point, when the Reformation has just been depicted, this reminds us of the regaining of the true gospel and of true worship at the Reformation. Prior to this, the church had fallen away from the true worship of God; also, it had, in a sense, shut up the way back to God by making salvation dependent on man's works and on the mediation of the priesthood. At the Reformation, however, the true worship of God was restored, and the truth of the free and direct access of the sinner to God through Christ was regained. And the opening of the temple in heaven and disclosing of the ark reminds us of this.

John also tells us that when the temple was opened and the ark disclosed, "there were lightnings, noises, thunderings, an earthquake, and great hail". These are symbols of the awesome power of God and of judgement coming from the presence of God, and here they point to the judgements to come associated with the sounding of the seventh trumpet. The blessing of the Reformation was accompanied and followed by terrible judgements of God in the earth.

Note on the time of Antichrist's reign: Those who regard the Antichrist as a figure still to come, naturally regard his reign as still future. However, understanding the Antichrist to be the pope of Rome, one must conclude that the reign of the Antichrist has already come, and that it relates to the time of the papacy holding sway over the nations. However, while that much is clear, there are differences of view regarding exactly which portion of papal history equates with Revelation's reign of the beast/Antichrist. This is because, as tends to happen with earthly powers, neither the rise nor the decline of papal power have happened suddenly, but both have taken place over a *period of time. Moreover, when we trace the rise and decline of papal power, a number of events stand out as particularly significant.* This has led to different conclusions being reached regarding where, historically, the time of papal power corresponding to Revelation's reign of the beast/Antichrist, begins and ends.

However, an answer does present itself if we consider history and Revelation together, and especially this chapter (chapter 11). Importantly, this chapter describes two other things happening during the reign of the beast/Antichrist (during the 42 months when it is granted to the beast to exercise authority — see 13:5). The first is the treading of the holy city by the Gentiles (v2). And, as discussed above, this relates to the long period from when the Empire became a Christian Empire up until the Reformation, during which the church became largely a church of nominal believers, and it absorbed and Christianized pagan beliefs and practices and fell away into idolatry, superstition and error. The second is the prophesying of the two witnesses (v3), which depicts the true believers making a powerful witness during the time of the treading of the holy city, when the church became largely an apostate church, right up until the Reformation.

All of this indicates that Revelation's reign of the beast/Antichrist spans the time from when the Empire became a Christian Empire in the fourth century, to the Reformation in the sixteenth century. And the period of papal history which equates with this begins when the bishop of Rome began to rise to power (following the Empire becoming Christian); it covers the time when the bishop of Rome elevated himself, and first claimed and then exercised great dominion over the nations (the period of the Middle Ages); and it ends when papal power began to decline (at the Reformation). In other words, it corresponds to the period of time when God allowed the papacy to rise up and exercise dominion over the nations — up until the time when God's judgement of the papacy begins (which we will *see unfolding with the sounding of the seventh trumpet and pouring out of the bowls of God's wrath).*

Moreover, this conclusion is compatible with what Revelation tells us about the length of Antichrist's reign. In 13:5 this is said to be 42 months. Elsewhere, where this same period is in view, it is designated as 42 months (11:2); 1260 days (11:3; 12:6); and 3½ years (see 12:14). Traditionally, when interpreting this, historicist commentators have followed the principle that one day in prophecy stands for one year in history; thus it has been understood that these time periods signify a reign of the Antichrist of 1260 years. There are biblical grounds for this approach. In Scripture, there are two clear examples of God appointing one day to represent a year (see Num 14:33–34; Ezek 4:4–6). Also, we know that the seventy weeks (490 days) prophecy of Daniel (Dan 9:23–27) had its fulfilment over a timescale of 490 years. Thus the 42 months of Antichrist's reign (or 1260 days — a month was counted as 30 days) can be taken to signify a reign of 1260 years. And this is helpful because, while it does not resolve all the difficulties associated with determining exactly the years in papal history that correspond to the reign of the beast/Antichrist, it does show us the magnitude of the length of time we are concerned with. And it is notable that the period from the Empire becoming a Christian Empire (which took place during the fourth century) to the Reformation (which took place during the sixteenth century) has a timescale in the region of 1260 years.

Chapter 12
War with the dragon

Introduction to chapters 12–14

Having seen the sounding of the seventh trumpet, and witnessed the lightnings, noises and so on, John might have expected then to see the judgements associated with the seventh trumpet. However, before being shown these judgements, John was first shown a series of visions (recorded in chapters 12–14) which take us back over the time already covered — as if Christ, having shown John the future up to the Reformation, at this point has him review that same time. These visions, however, are not a straightforward recapping of what has already been revealed, but they cover the same time with a different focus. Particularly they bring into view Satan's activity. Also they bring into view the Antichrist (ie, the pope of Rome) and his dominion, which was only touched on in the earlier chapters.

[In the previous chapters we have covered developments in the pagan Roman Empire, the persecution of the church by pagan Rome, and the fall of pagan Rome (the first six seals — chapter 6). Also, we have covered the time of the papal dominion, and seen events and developments important to the papacy's rise to power (the trumpet judgements — chapters 8 and 9). And we have had mention of the beast (a figure for the pope and his dominion) and seen his persecution of the church prior to the Reformation (see 11:7). However, up to this point, we have not been shown Satan's part in all this. Nor have we been shown in any concrete form, the rise, identity and reign of the papacy. Now, however, these things come into view, before we see the papacy's judgement. And it is not without significance that it was at this point in Christ's revealing of things that John was shown this. We have just had the Reformation portrayed; and it was particularly at that time that the papacy was identified as the Antichrist of Scripture, and a new perspective was gained on the past history of the church. Thus it is very fitting at this point, when Christ's revelation has reached the time of the Reformation, that there is a reviewing of the time gone before, and especially a depiction of the Antichrist/the pope and his dominion.]

The woman and the dragon (12:1–6)

First, John was shown a vision depicting Satan's design to destroy the church as soon as it began.

v1,2. John records that "a great sign appeared in heaven". All that John was shown was in the form of signs — symbols that represented and pointed to something else. However, John's description of what he saw here as a "great sign", indicates that it struck John as having special importance and significance. And this great sign was "a woman clothed with the sun, with the moon under her feet, and on her head a garland of twelve stars". In the book of Revelation the symbolism of a woman is used to represent the church (both the true church and the apostate church); and here this glorious woman represents the church of Christ (later we will see the harlot, who represents the apostate church of Antichrist, ie, the Church of Rome — see 17:3–5). And this woman was clothed with the sun — which depicts the glory the church has in Christ, and perhaps especially the righteousness she has in him (see Mal 4:2). Also, she had the moon under her feet — which would seem to show her standing above this world or dwelling in the heavens, and thus to depict the church as belonging not to this world but to heaven. And, she had on her head a garland of twelve stars — which would seem to represent the twelve apostles, and thus the true gospel that they laid down and by which the church triumphs.

John then tells us, "being with child, she [the woman] cried out in labour and in pain to give birth". Some understand this to represent Israel travailing to give birth to Christ (to the Messiah, who was long promised). However, in Isaiah 66:7–8 similar imagery is used to depict the bringing forth of God's people (see also Gal 4:19). Thus there is scriptural ground for taking the imagery here to represent the church travailing to bring forth a people for Christ; and in this context, this would seem to be the better interpretation. So, as this vision unfolded, John was taken back to the earliest days of the New Testament church, and to its beginning in this world.

v3,4. Then John saw another sign appear in heaven, "a great, fiery red dragon having seven heads and ten horns, and seven diadems on his heads". The imagery here of a fiery red dragon shows this to be a fierce and frightening foe of the church. Moreover, later in this chapter, this dragon is identified with Satan (see v9) — who is, of course, the great enemy of God and his people. However, while Satan is in view here, the symbolism of heads and horns suggests that more than just Satan is being depicted. As we will see, heads and horns in Scripture are imagery for governments and kings (see 17:9–10,12); moreover, throughout the book of Revelation, the imagery of seven heads and ten horns depicts a power centred on Rome (the city on seven hills — see 17:9). So, it would seem that this dragon does not simply represent Satan, but Satan ruling and acting through the Roman power. Moreover, it would seem that, specifically, it is pagan Rome that is in view here, which, when the church began, was Satan's great instrument by which he held sway over the peoples and sought to destroy the church (in Chapter 13 we will see similar imagery used in connection with papal Rome, and the significance of the heads and horns and diadems will be discussed more fully there).

John then tells us that the dragon's tail "drew a third of the stars of heaven and threw them to the earth". Here, it is difficult to decide what this signifies; however, in this context, it very possibly represents Satan attacking and bringing down a proportion of the leaders of the church (the leaders of the churches are depicted as stars in 1:20). Certainly, one of Satan's main tactics against the church is to endeavour to cause its leaders to fall or become ineffective.

We are also told that the dragon stood before the woman to devour her child as soon as it was born. Understanding this woman and child as indicated above, this shows Satan intent on destroying the church as soon as it appeared, so as to prevent its growth and continuance in the world. Moreover, it shows him ready to do this through pagan Rome, which was his great instrument of power at that time.

v5. John then tells us that the woman "bore a male child who was to rule all nations with a rod of iron". This portrays the bringing forth of a church of true believers (who form the spiritual body of Christ). And these were to rule all nations with a rod of iron. We have already seen a similar thing said of the church in Christ's message to the church in Thyatira (see 2:26-27); and here, in this context, this would seem to refer to the church judging men and sealing their destiny (the church does this by its preaching, which makes known to men their sinfulness and God's salvation, and results in men either believing in Christ unto salvation, or rejecting the truth and being confirmed in their condemnation).

Immediately, however, John saw this child being "caught up to God and His throne". This is a picture of the church being snatched away from Satan, who was ready to devour it, and being taken immediately into the special protection of God. It is a symbol of God's care and protection of the church from its infancy, and it shows God preserving the church from Satan's attempt, through pagan Rome, to destroy it.

So, here John was taken back to the earliest days of the church. And he was shown Satan's intent, by means of pagan Rome, to destroy the infant church, and the church's protection and preservation by God. And, as already noted when considering the fifth seal (6:9–11), we know from history that in the days of the pagan Empire, the emperors did persecute the church and attempt to destroy it (especially in the years just prior to the Empire becoming a Christian Empire). However, God preserved his church, and did not allow his church to be completely destroyed.

v6. Following this, we are told, "the woman fled into the wilderness, where she has a place prepared by God, that they should feed her there one thousand two hundred and sixty days". We encountered this time period in chapter 11 (see v2–3), where we saw that it had to do with the time of the church's great apostasy and the reign of the Antichrist (the pope of Rome). In that chapter, the true church was depicted making a powerful witness during all that time. Now, here, the true church is depicted taking refuge in a place (the wilderness) where she is sustained by God. This is pictured again in verse 14, after the judgement of the dragon is described, and will be discussed more fully at that point.

Defeat of the dragon (12:7–12)

Having been shown Satan's design to destroy the early church, and God's protection and preservation of the church, John was then shown a vision of a great battle, culminating in Satan being judged.

v7. John saw war break out in heaven, between Michael and his angels and the dragon and his angels. Here, some understand Michael to be a chief angel (see Jude v9); others take this to mean Christ (Michael also appears in Daniel as the prince and guardian of God's people, and many understand this to be a figure for Christ — see Dan 10:13,21; 12:1). In either case, what we see pictured here is a great battle between Christ and his heavenly forces, and Satan and his heavenly forces. We must not imagine from this, however, that there was a literal war in heaven. Rather, this is simply a picture of great conflict between Christ and Satan, and in this context is best understood as depicting the spiritual battle that was behind the persecution of the early church by pagan Rome. This persecution was part of the great battle that exists between Christ and Satan (which, of course, is the case for the struggles of the church at all times).

v8,9. However, in this great battle the dragon and his angels did not prevail, and they were cast out of heaven to the earth. This signifies Satan failing to win in his conflict with Christ, and being judged. And on an earthly level this has to do with Satan not being allowed to succeed in his design to destroy the early church by means of pagan Rome, and him being judged in the fall of paganism in the Roman Empire (as noted earlier, this was brought about when the Empire became Christian, with which pagan government and pagan religion were swept away, and an end was brought to the terrible persecution the church had been suffering). So, Satan's attempt to destroy the early church through pagan Rome was unsuccessful, and ended when paganism was brought down.

Moreover, it is here that the great dragon is identified with Satan: we are told he is called "the Devil" (which means accuser or slanderer — see also v10), and "Satan" (which means adversary). Particularly, however, he is identified with "that serpent of old...deceives the whole world". The "serpent of old" is a reference to the serpent in the garden of Eden, through which Satan deceived Eve and brought about the fall of man (see Gen 3:1ff). Thus it reminds us of Satan's cunning, and that one of the primary means used by Satan to bring men under his sway is deception. Moreover, in this context, his deceiving of the whole world would seem to refer especially to Satan's deceiving of the nations through the falsehood of paganism (with all its idolatry and superstition). Satan had deceived the world with idolatrous paganism, and through pagan Rome had sought to destroy the church; however, he was not permitted to succeed against the church, and was judged by paganism being swept away from the Empire.

v10,11. After seeing the dragon cast down, John then heard a loud voice in heaven triumphantly proclaiming the victory of Christ over Satan. In this proclamation, Satan's judgement in the fall of paganism is depicted as a great deliverance for the church, in which God showed himself to be a mighty God, and Christ showed himself to be a mighty Lord and Saviour. It is also described as the accuser of the brethren, who accused them before God day and night, being cast down. This shows his judgement in the fall of paganism, quashing all his indictments against the church and vindicating God's people.

John also heard the victory of the church (the persecuted brethren) being proclaimed. They overcame him "by the blood of the Lamb" — Christ's death destroyed the power of Satan over God's people. Also they overcame him "by the word of their testimony" — by their faithful confession of and witness to Christ, in which they stood firm. And "they did not love their lives to the death" — they showed courage, and love and loyalty to Christ, and did not shrink back from dying for their faith. In all these ways the saints (by Christ's power) overcame in the battle with Satan. They stood firm and kept the faith, even to death; and when they had done this for a while and had the victory, God judged Satan.

v12. Lastly, John heard a call for the heavens and those who dwell in them to rejoice. The downfall of paganism and end of persecution was a cause of great rejoicing for the church, and indeed for all of heaven.

Also, however, he heard a cry of, "Woe to the inhabitants of the earth and the sea! For the devil has come down to you, having great wrath, because he knows that he has a short time." This is a solemn warning that Satan's judgement in the fall of paganism would have dire consequences for the world, because it has enraged him, because he knows he has a little time. To understand this we need to remember that from earliest times after the fall, the devil had deceived the world with idolatrous paganism — this was his master deception and means by which he held sway over the nations. Consequently, the downfall of pagan government and religion in the Empire, when the Empire became Christian, was a major defeat and a great setback in his evil design to hold the nations under his power. So the devil is shown filled with rage and indignation — his defeat has fuelled his evil intent towards mankind. And this will be of dire consequence to the inhabitants of the earth.

The dragon's renewed persecution of the woman (12:13–17)

v13. Having been warned of the devil's great anger at being cast down, John was then shown what this would mean for the church (later, in Chapter 13, we will see what this meant for the world).

John tells us, "when the dragon saw that he had been cast to the earth, he persecuted the woman who gave birth to the male child". This depicts Satan's renewed and unrelenting malicious persecution of the church. His downfall in the fall of paganism did not stop him, but only reinforced him in his design to destroy the church.

v14. Again, however, John saw the church experiencing God's protection — he saw the woman finding safety in the wilderness. This takes us back to verse 6 where, after Satan's failed attempt to destroy the early church by means of pagan Rome, the woman was said to flee into the wilderness, where she has a place prepared by God and is fed for one thousand two hundred and sixty days (the time of the church's great apostasy and the reign of the Antichrist/the pope of Rome). Now, referring to the same thing, the woman is said to be given eagle's wings "that she might fly into the wilderness to her place, where she is nourished for a time and times and half a time [three and a half years], from the presence of the serpent".

This imagery reminds us of the people of God being taken out of Egypt, away from all the idolatry and oppression of Egypt, into the wilderness where they had divine nourishment and protection (see Ex 19:4). It depicts God protecting and sustaining his church throughout the time of the church's great apostasy and the papacy's reign. We will see from chapter 13 that it was by means of the apostate church and the papacy that Satan, defeated in the downfall of paganism, renewed his deception of the world and opposition to the true church; and what is depicted here is God protecting and providing for his people in the midst of this. It is also notable, however, that while the woman is given the eagle's wings, she must fly into the wilderness. This reminds us that while God protects and sustains his church in the midst of apostasy and persecution, it is the church's responsibility to keep herself in God's care by keeping apart from false religion. This is the place where the church will be safe and fed.

v15,16. Then "the serpent spewed water out of his mouth like a flood after the woman, that he might cause her to be carried away by the flood". This depicts some attempt by Satan to sweep away and destroy the church; and, most likely, it depicts him trying to bring the church down with a flood of heresies (this water spews from the serpent's mouth — from the mouth of the one who deceives — see v9). Certainly, heresy is the other major means, along with persecution, that Satan uses to destroy the church. And certainly, immediately after the Empire became Christian there were some serious heresies that threatened the church — most notably the Arian heresy, which became rampant in the church and nearly wiped out true Christianity (Arianism denied the deity of the Son and of the Holy Spirit).

However, we are told "the earth helped the woman, and the earth opened its mouth and swallowed up the flood". This would seem to depict the world in some way helping the church, which did happen in the case of the church's battle against Arianism. In this great controversy, the Emperor and authorities supported the true doctrine, and this played an important part in saving the church from being totally swept away by this error. So, again, Satan was not allowed to destroy the church.

v17. Finally, we are told "the dragon was enraged with the woman, and he went to make war with the rest of her offspring". This further depicts Satan's unremitting hostility towards the church, and it looks ahead to his renewed persecution of God's people by means of the Roman Church and papacy. And here God's people are described as those "who keep the commandments of God and have the testimony of Jesus Christ" — who hold to the truth and live godly lives and bear witness to Christ. This is the outward evidence that a person truly belongs to Christ; and this is what brings the hostility of Satan.

So, in this chapter we have had portrayed Satan's intense and relentless hostility towards the church, and his unwavering intent to destroy the church. Particularly, we have seen Satan's attempt by means of pagan Rome to destroy the infant church; his failure in this intent and his judgement (which involved the bringing down of paganism in the Empire); and his great rage in the face of this defeat. In the next chapter we will see depicted Satan's new instrument, the papal power, by which he renews his purpose to deceive the world and destroy the church. Before this, however, we have also seen God's protection of and provision for his true church during all the time of the church's great apostasy and the papacy's reign — and we need to keep this in view as we consider the next chapter.

Chapter 13
The two beasts

The beast from the sea (13:1–10)

For Satan, the fall of pagan Rome, when the Empire became Christian, was a crushing defeat, as it robbed him of his great instrument by which he held sway over the nations and persecuted the church. However, we saw in the last chapter that, rather than this defeat stopping him, its effect was to enrage him, with dire consequences for the world (see 12:12). Now we will see Satan's malicious and cunning response, which was to raise up another instrument — this time a great pseudo-Christian power — by which to gain power over the nations and destroy the church of God.

v1. First, as a new vision opened up, John found himself standing on the seashore; and he saw "a beast rising up out of the sea". In Scripture, beasts are symbolic of world powers in opposition to God, and they represent both kings (or rulers) and their kingdoms (or dominions) (see Dan 7:17,23). Moreover, the emerging of great powers from the sea portrays them as mysterious, evil and threatening (the beasts Daniel saw also came from the sea — see Dan 7:2–3). So, this beast represents a great and awe-inspiring world power (one that will evoke both devotion and dread); and, specifically, it depicts Satan's new instrument by which, after his defeat in the fall of paganism in the Empire, he pursued afresh his goals of ruling over the nations and destroying the church.

We have, of course, already encountered the beast in chapter 11 (v7), where it was said to ascend out of the bottomless pit (showing it to be associated with evil forces and to be an instrument of Satan), and where it was shown persecuting God's witnesses (the true believers). And, historically what this beast represents is the papacy and its dominion which, following the fall of paganism in the Empire, emerged as Satan's great instrument. Moreover, what is especially depicted here is the papacy during the time of its rise and reign in the Middle Ages, when the bishops of Rome elevated themselves and held increasing and great sway over the Christian nations of Europe. (Of course, Satan has many means by which he rules over people and persecutes the church; but this depicts his supreme instrument which he raised up following the downfall of paganism in the Empire. We must keep in sight, however, that even this was in the preordained purpose of God and ultimately served his wise and just purposes.)

Moreover, describing the beast that he saw, John tells us it had "seven heads and ten horns, and on his horns ten crowns [or diadems], and on his heads a blasphemous name". In this, there is much similarity with the dragon, which also was depicted as having seven heads and ten horns, and crowns (or diadems) (see 12:3). However, with respect to this imagery, there is also a significant difference between this beast and the dragon. In the case of the dragon, the kingly diadems or crowns are on the seven heads (which signify Rome — see 17:9), and the ten horns are uncrowned; thus the imagery is depicting the Roman Empire which had an imperial power at Rome, and which was divided into various provinces (the ten horns). In the case of the beast, however, the seven heads (signifying Rome) have a blasphemous name, and the crowns or diadems are on the horns. Thus the imagery depicts a blasphemous power seated at Rome, while the lands that comprised the Roman Empire consist of various kingdoms; and this indicates that, historically, what this beast symbolises is the papal dominion. History records that during the century following the fall of paganism in the Roman Empire, the Roman Empire itself fell and became divided into various kingdoms. It also records how, following this, the bishop of Rome, by means of false and even blasphemous claims (see comments on v6), began increasingly to exert authority over the peoples. And so there was seated at Rome a blasphemous power, while the lands of the old Empire were comprised of various kingdoms.

v2. Then, further describing the beast that he saw, John tells us it "was like a leopard, his feet were like the feet of a bear, and his mouth like the mouth of a lion". In this respect, this beast combines the features of the first three beasts Daniel saw — the first like a lion, the second like a bear, and the third like a leopard (see Dan 7:3–6). These three beasts represent the Babylonian, Medo-Persian and Greek powers, which were three of the four great world powers that held sway over the Jewish people from the time of the exile. (The fourth was the Roman power, which Daniel saw depicted as a fourth terrible beast.) Thus the beast John saw is a kind of composition of the first three beasts Daniel saw, with the fierceness, strength and swiftness of them all; it is a great power in which is concentrated all the frightfulness of its predecessors that dominated the world and held sway over the people of God. And, since it is the papal power that is represented here, we must consider this to be a true depiction of the papal power and let it inform our assessment of the papacy, no matter how much the outward face of the papacy might belie this.

John also tells us, "the dragon gave him his power, his throne, and great authority". In the previous chapter, the dragon represented Satan, and Satan acting and ruling through pagan Rome. So, this beast was to exercise Satan's power, rule and authority — it is Satan's instrument, set up by him to do his work and to promote his interest. Also, the power of pagan Rome was, in a sense, transferred to this beast — all that Satan had sought to do through the pagan Roman emperors and Empire, he was now endeavouring to achieve through this beast. Again, we must accept this as a true depiction of the papacy and its dominion.

v3. John also notes that one of the beast's heads was "as if it had been mortally wounded, and his deadly wound was healed". This shows that this beast represents a power which had suffered a seemingly fatal blow, but which in fact had recovered and survived. This accurately depicts the appearance of the papal dominion, which rose up in and occupied the place of the Roman emperors and Empire. The fall of the Roman Empire in the fifth century meant the end of a great empire that had been considered to be unassailable and eternal. Following this, however, there emerged in its place the papal dominion, with the popes, seated at Rome, first claiming and then exercising great power over the Christian kings and nations of Europe. So, in a sense, the Roman Empire, which had been brought down, was revived in and continued in the papacy and its dominion.

Then, having described the beast that he saw, John tells us "all the world marvelled and followed the beast" (or "wondered after the beast" — AV); all the world was filled with wonder and was drawn after this beast. Certainly, this was the case with the papacy. When this great power appeared in the world, the unbelieving world was moved to follow with undue devotion. (It will be helpful at this point to reiterate that what is being depicted here is the papacy during the Middle Ages, when the pope elevated himself and held sway over the Christian nations of Europe; of course, today the pope still draws great devotion from his followers, but this is not what is specifically in view here.)

v4. John then adds, "so they worshipped the dragon who gave authority to the beast". In following the beast, the unbelieving world in fact worshipped Satan who was the power behind the beast (they paid honour to and subjected themselves to Satan). Again, we must accept this as being the case with the papacy — in showing devotion to the pope, the unbelieving world, in fact, paid honour to and subjected itself to Satan.

Also, they worshipped the beast, saying, "Who is like the beast? Who is able to make war with him?" The unbelieving world was in awe of the beast and found his power irresistible. And, certainly, this was the effect the papacy had. By means of the spiritual and temporal power the popes both claimed and exercised, and the bewitching false religion they headed, they exercised a great hold over the peoples so that the peoples could not resist honouring and subjecting themselves to the papacy.

v5. Then the beast "was given a mouth speaking great things and blasphemies" — he was given a mouth making great boasts and claims, and uttering things that deny and dishonour God. The boasting and blasphemy of the beast was, of course, from Satan, the power behind the beast. However, his blasphemy was also permitted by God, who ultimately ordained all that this beast would do.

Also, the beast "was given authority to continue for forty-two months". This is not the time of the beast's (ie, the papacy's) existence, but the time ordained and given by God for him to conquer and rule over the nations before his judgement (it is the time he is permitted to exercise authority and to raise himself up and prevail). And, as already discussed *(see the note at the end of Chapter 11)*, this corresponds to the long period from when the Empire became a Christian Empire in the fourth century, to the Reformation in the sixteenth century. This period saw the bishop of Rome first claim, and then exercise more and more spiritual and temporal authority over the kings and nations of Christian Europe, with him eventually succeeding in exercising supreme control (it is widely agreed that it was in the thirteenth century that the effective sovereignty of the pope over Christendom reached its height).

v6. Then, having been permitted to utter blasphemies and to rise up and rule, the beast "opened his mouth in blasphemy against God". He blasphemed "His name" — that is the titles and nature of God. Also he blasphemed "His tabernacle" — this could refer to the Lord Jesus Christ, by whom God dwelt among men, or to the church on earth. And he blasphemed "those who dwell in heaven" — this could refer to the glorified saints or to all the church. Essentially, this shows the beast speaking things contemptuous of God and Christ and the church, and certainly this describes the papacy. As the popes elevated themselves, they took to themselves the titles of Christ and claimed for themselves the power and authority of Christ. Also they vehemently denied the true gospel of Christ, and classed as heretics those who proclaimed the true gospel. All of this is the worst kind of blasphemy. It also played an important part in the popes gaining sway over the peoples.

v7. Moreover, it was also granted to the beast "to make war with the saints and to overcome them" — he was permitted by God to persecute the church and to kill God's people. And, certainly, this is something that the papacy did, especially in the centuries just prior to the Reformation. At that time, many true believers were persecuted, tortured and killed, especially through the notorious Inquisition.

Also, "authority was given him over every tribe, tongue, and nation" — in God's purpose the beast was permitted to exercise rule over all the peoples. Again, we can see this fulfilled in the papacy's subjection of and rule over Christian Europe during the Middle Ages. As noted above, beginning as early as the fourth century, the bishops of Rome pursued this power, first claiming and then exercising more and more spiritual and temporal power over the nations of Europe, until by the thirteenth century they were exercising supreme control. It might seem that this cannot be a fulfilment of the beast being given authority over every tribe, tongue and nation. However, we need to see that the great powers signified in Daniel — Babylonia, Persia, Greece, and Rome — are described in terms of having power over all peoples and all the earth (see Dan 2:37–39; 7:23; also Ezra 1:2), and yet these empires were not literally worldwide. Rather, these were the great powers which, in turn, were granted by God power to rise up and dominate the world of his people in the periods concerned. Hence, from a scriptural point of view, it is quite valid to hold that the beast's reign over the nations was fulfilled in the papacy's subjection of and rule over Christian Europe during the Middle Ages.

v8. We are then told, "all who dwell on the earth will worship him [the beast], whose names have not been written in the Book of Life of the Lamb slain from the foundation of the world". This again expresses the great dominion of the beast — he was given authority over all peoples, and all would honour him and subject themselves to him. However, importantly, the statement here is also qualified — all will worship the beast, except those who God has ordained for life and salvation in Christ (all except true Christians). This encourages us to know that those belonging to Christ would not worship the beast; rather, they would be kept by God and would not follow this godless power. And in the time of the rise and ascendancy of the papacy, the peoples were led away to honour and subjugate themselves to the pope. However, God preserved his true church and kept his people safe. They are the ones depicted elsewhere being protected and provided for by God, during the time of the papacy's reign (see 12:6,14).

v9. Having had this detailed description of the beast and its power, there is then a call to hear: "If anyone has an ear, let him hear." This call emphasises the importance of heeding all that is said here about the beast. This beast depicts Satan's great instrument to deceive the world and rule over the peoples. Moreover, here the church's supreme enemy is revealed. Thus it is vital that careful attention is paid to this.

[Although the time of papal power depicted here is now past (we are now in the time of the papacy's judgement), in a day when few recognise the pope of Rome as the Antichrist of Scripture, we need especially to renew the call for people to pay attention to and understand what is written here. And, in fact, in this call there is encouragement that true believers will understand. When studying Christ's messages to the seven churches it was noted that the true believer is the one who has ears to hear. Therefore there can be hope that, as this portion of Scripture is studied afresh, God's people will identify the beast as the papacy and its dominion.]

v10. Finally, come words of great comfort and strengthening for the church, in a promise of judgement for those who persecute God's people: those who oppress and kill will be oppressed and killed — they will be judged. Moreover, we are told, "Here is the patience [or perseverance] and the faith of the saints." Knowing the eventual judgement of those who oppose God and seek to destroy the church, is a great encouragement to persevering through all opposition and pressing on in faith towards the heavenly hope.

So, in conclusion, what we see depicted here, under the symbolism of this beast, is the papacy and its dominion, by which Satan, following his defeat in the fall of paganism in the Empire, renewed his purpose to rule the nations and destroy the church. Moreover, what is especially depicted here is the papacy during the time of its rise and reign in the Middle Ages, when it rose up and held sway over the Christian nations of Europe, and cruelly persecuted the true church.

The beast from the earth (13:11–18)

v11,12. Following this, John then saw another beast, in this case "coming up out of the earth" — which may indicate that this beast is less mysterious and threatening than the first beast, or it may indicate that its emergence in the world was less perceptible. Moreover, describing this beast, John tells us "he had two horns like a lamb and spoke like a dragon". This depicts an imitation of Christ or Christianity. It depicts a great, pseudo-Christian power — a power that gives all the appearance of being truly Christian, but really it is false. Moreover, it is its speaking, which is like that of a dragon, that exposes this great power; what it says and how it speaks show its true nature.

John also tells us that this beast "exercises all the authority of the first beast in his presence [thus they exist together], and causes the earth and those who dwell in it to worship the first beast, whose deadly wound was healed" (see v3). This makes clear that this pseudo-Christian beast has a oneness and equality with the first beast (he has the same authority as the first beast); but it also shows that he is serving not his own interests, but the goals and interests of the first beast (he causes all the inhabitants of the earth to worship the first beast). So, this lamb-like beast is shown to be inseparably linked with the first beast — the power, time and objective of both beasts are all the same.

Taking this into account, it is the view of many that this pseudo-Christian beast is not an entirely different power from the first beast; rather, it also depicts the papacy, portraying this using a different image and from a different perspective. So, in the first, frightening beast, we saw the papacy in its political or temporal power (having rule over the nations). Now, here, in this more benign-looking pseudo-Christian beast, we see the papacy in its ecclesiastical guise and power. In other words, what is in view here is the religious face and religious power of the papacy — a power which the popes exercise through the claim to be the Vicar of Christ (ie, Christ's representative on earth) and through the power of the Roman Church (ie, the ecclesiastical system) which the pope heads, and which exerts a hold over people by means of the false religion (Roman Catholicism) it teaches and administers. (Here it is notable that, just as the fallen Roman Empire was, in a sense, revived in the papal dominion, so paganism was, in a sense, revived in the Roman Catholic religion — which essentially is a mixture of Christianity and paganism. And in this we see more of the cunning of the evil one — after paganism was suppressed in the Empire, Satan, in essence, devised no new deception, but simply revived paganism in a Christianized form.)

Moreover, if we view both of these beasts as depicting the papacy, then the relationship between these two beasts shows us something very important about the way the papacy pursues its goals; it shows us that it does this under the guise of religion and of doing good to men's souls. In the relationship between the two beasts, the more benign-looking religious beast is promoting the goals and interests of the more terrifying political beast; and fundamentally, it was as a religious figure (the so-called 'Vicar of Christ') and through the religious system they headed (the institution of the Roman Church) that the popes achieved dominion over the peoples and caused the peoples to honour and subject themselves to the papacy.

v13,14. We are then told that this lamb-like beast "performs great signs, so that he even makes fire come down from heaven on the earth in the sight of men". And we are told the effect of this — "he deceives those who dwell on the earth by those signs which he was granted to do in the sight of the beast, telling those who dwell on the earth to make an image to the beast who was wounded by the sword and lived". The fire from heaven reminds us of Elijah calling down fire from heaven to burn up his sacrifice — which he did to show the people that the Lord was God in Israel and he was his prophet, and to turn the people back to God (to worship and serve him) (see 1 Kgs 18:36–39). And here, this pseudo-Christian beast performing great signs, and making fire come down from heaven, similarly depicts him authenticating the first beast, and causing the peoples to worship him. In contrast with Elijah, however, in this case the people are deceived and are led away into idolatrous worship of the beast.

And again, this portrays the working of the papacy. It was as a religious figure, the so-called 'Vicar of Christ', that the popes justified their rule over the nations and attracted the devotion of the peoples. Also, it was the Roman Church (by which is meant here the ecclesiastical system) that supported the claims of the popes and led the peoples into subjection to them. Not only that, associated with the Roman Church were miracles and pretended miracles, which served as lying signs; and these played a part in the people being deceived into believing that the Roman Church was the true church, and thus being led away to honour and obey the pope. Moreover, we need to recognise that the devotion to the pope that the world was led into was nothing short of idolatry. In fact, there is a sense in which the pope is the image of the beast. His office embodies all that the beast stands for, and honour of and subjection to him is the grossest form of idolatry.

v15. We are further told that this lamb-like beast "was granted power to give breath to the image of the beast, that the image of the beast should both speak and cause as many as would not worship the image of the beast to be killed". This depicts this pseudo-Christian beast enabling the first beast to make pronouncements against any who will not submit to him, and to have them killed. And it was in their ecclesiastical power (as the so-called 'Vicar of Christ', with the support of the Roman Church) that the popes were enabled to make pronouncements against the true believers and all who would not honour or be subject to them, and have them excommunicated or killed. This was a further means by which the papacy gained power over the peoples.

v16,17. Lastly, this lamb-like beast is said to cause all, of every station in life, "to receive a mark on their right hand or on their foreheads, and that no one may buy or sell except one who has the mark or the name of the beast, or the number of his name". Here, the mark and the name and the number essentially concern the same thing. They depict an open sign of allegiance to, identification with, and subjection to the beast. And only those who display this allegiance may buy or sell. So, this pseudo-Christian beast is depicted as causing the people to show allegiance to the first beast on the basis that without this they cannot obtain what they need to live. And, as the so-called 'Vicar of Christ', with the support of the Roman Church, the popes claimed there was no salvation outside the Roman Church, and that subjection to the pope was necessary for salvation (for the receipt of saving grace); and this was another means by which the people were brought into subjection to the papacy. (It is also possible that literal buying and selling is in view here; there was a time, during the papacy of Martin V, 1417–31, when trading with 'heretics' was prohibited, thus making allegiance to the papacy necessary for the buying or selling of goods.)

v18. Finally comes wisdom, and something for those with understanding (true believers) to discern — the identity of the beast. This can be known from the number of the beast, "for it is the number of a man: His number is 666".

Unsurprisingly, this number has been interpreted in various ways, even by those who see the papacy depicted here. One line of reasoning is that six is a number suggesting imperfection (it falls short of seven, the number of completeness or perfection), and when used in connection with man, indicates fallenness; so 666 as the number of a man denotes some especially wicked man, even a man deified (triune 6). Thus, it follows that 666 as the number of the beast indicates that the beast represents a power where such a man is prominent. And this, of course, is fulfilled in the papacy, which takes to itself the titles of Christ, and receives to itself the honour and devotion due to Christ alone. So, in short, by this line of reasoning, 666 denotes the blasphemous office of the pope — fallen man deified.

In summary: At the beginning of this chapter we noted that, for Satan, the fall of pagan Rome was a great blow, as it robbed him of his great instrument by which he held sway over the nations and sought to destroy the church. In this chapter, we have seen the new instrument that he raised up — the papal dominion, here depicted under the imagery of two beasts. In the first, fierce beast, we saw the papacy in its political or temporal power, exercising dominion over the nations (specifically in the Middle Ages). Then, in the lamb-like beast, we saw the papacy in its religious or ecclesiastical guise and power. And this is the face that the papacy presents to the world. Moreover, it was by means of their religious persona and power (as the so-called 'Vicar of Christ' and through the Roman Church) that the popes came to rule over the nations and receive the honour of the peoples, and that they persecuted the true people of God. All of this, however, happened in the preordained purpose of God, and ultimately served his wise and just purposes.

Chapter 14
Salvation and judgement

The Lamb and the 144,000 (14:1–5)

The two beasts described in chapter 13 must have been for John a disturbing sight, and they concern disturbing things. As already noted, they depict Satan's new instrument by which, following his defeat in the fall of paganism in the Empire, he renewed his purpose to rule over the nations and destroy the true church of Christ. Moreover, historically, they concern the papal dominion, and especially the papacy's rule over Christendom in the Middle Ages when, by means of its religious power, the papacy rose up to hold sway over the nations. However, after seeing these disturbing things, John was then shown by way of contrast, and as an encouragement and comfort, a vision of Christ and his true kingdom and church.

v1. First, as a new vision opened up, John looked and he saw "a Lamb standing on Mount Zion". This Lamb, of course, depicts the Lord Jesus Christ, the true Saviour and Lord of the church; moreover, the imagery of him standing on Mount Zion (on the mount of the city of God), depicts Christ at the head of and present with his church (it also contrasts with the lamb-like beast of the previous chapter, which concerned the papacy and its dominion over Christendom).

Moreover, John tells us that with him were "one hundred and forty-four thousand, having His Father's name written on their foreheads". These one hundred and forty-four thousand have been mentioned before in chapter 7. There they were shown being sealed on their foreheads, and they represented the true believers being distinguished in the midst of the outward professing church, and set apart for safety in the midst of God's judgements in the earth. Moreover, historically, this was understood as bearing particular reference to the true believers being kept safe during the time after the Empire became Christian (when they were a minority in the total professing church); especially, it concerned them being kept in the midst of the great flood of deception that was to overtake the church and lead to its apostasy (see the fifth trumpet, especially 9:3–4). Now, this one hundred and forty-four thousand appear again, this time pictured with the Lamb on Mount Zion, and shown having Christ's Father's name on their foreheads. And, at this point in the history, it would seem they are picturing the true believers in Christ who belonged to God, and who were kept by him and were loyal to him during the time of the beast's/papacy's reign (ie, during the time of the rise and ascendancy of the papacy and the Roman Church in the Middle Ages).

v2,3. John also relates that he heard "a voice from heaven, like the voice of many waters, and like the voice of loud thunder"; and he heard "the sound of harpists playing their harps" (see 5:8 and 19:6 for similar imagery). This describes a loud but melodious song being sung in heaven, and would seem to depict the praise of the hundred and forty-four thousand. And, we are told that they sang "a new song before the throne, before the four living creatures, and the elders". So, the worship of the one hundred and forty-four thousand is shown to be at God's throne in heaven, which shows it to be true worship of God. Moreover, the song they sang is described as a "new song"; also, we are told "no one could learn that song except the one hundred and forty-four thousand who were redeemed from the earth". This is a song of salvation in Christ, sung with reality, in the way that only those who are truly saved can do (others may sing the words of the song, but only the redeemed can sing it truly, with true meaning and feeling). So, these true believers during the time of the reign of the papacy are shown offering true worship to God and Christ; and this stands in contrast to the world's worship of the pope.

v4,5. The hundred and forty-four thousand are then described in terms which express their faithfulness to Christ, and which distinguish them from the rest of mankind who showed allegiance to the pope. First, they are described as "the ones who were not defiled with women, for they are virgins" — these are the ones who kept themselves pure from false religion for Christ (see 2 Cor 11:2–4). They are also described as "the ones who follow the Lamb wherever He goes" — these are the ones who are Christ's disciples, who are loyal to him and do his will, and who are ready to suffer for his sake. So these are the true followers of Christ, who were faithful to him during the time of the papacy's reign.

Moreover, we are told these "were redeemed from among men, being firstfruits to God and to the Lamb". At great cost, these were saved by God out of mankind and out of this world and, by grace, are choice ones who belong to God and Christ (the firstfruits were the first part of the harvest that was holy, and in a special sense belonged to God — see Deut 26:1–2,9–10). So, it was redeeming grace that made these ones Christ's, and made them loyal to him.

Lastly, we are told, "in their mouth was found no deceit [or guile], for they are without fault before the throne of God". Their Christian profession was sincere; freely saved by God's grace in Christ, their hearts were right with God, and they walked with sincere devotion to him in the midst of a wicked world.

So, here we see depicted the true church of Jesus Christ during the time of the reign of the beast — that is, during the time of the rise and ascendancy of the papacy and the Roman Church in the Middle Ages. And this church is portrayed offering true worship to God, and being truly devoted to Christ — standing in contrast to nominal Christendom which gave honour to and showed allegiance to the pope.

The proclamations of the three angels (14:6–13)

v6,7. Following this, John tells us he saw "another angel flying in the midst of heaven, having the everlasting gospel to preach to those who dwell on the earth". The description of the gospel as everlasting reminds us that God's saving purpose in Christ is from eternity, that it never changes, and that it brings everlasting fruit. This gospel is, of course, always to be preached. Moreover, we have seen that throughout the reign of the beast (the papacy), there were true, witnessing believers (chapter 11). However, within the historical framework of Revelation, this angel having the gospel to preach would seem especially to mark the recovery of the gospel at the Reformation, when the everlasting gospel began to be truly and widely proclaimed once more.

Particularly, however, this angel with the gospel is said to be sounding out a call and a warning to men, saying with a loud voice, "Fear God and give glory to Him, for the hour of his judgement has come; and worship Him who made heaven and earth, the sea and springs of water." Of course, the gospel should always include a warning of judgement and a call for men to honour God. Here, however, the angel's call and warning is a special call to men to fear and honour and worship God, because the time of God's judgement of Babylon, that great city, has come (see v8 below). Essentially, this is a call to men to abandon the Roman antichristian system, with its devotion to the pope, and instead to believe the true gospel which gives glory to God; and it is a call to do this not only so that God receives the glory and worship that is his due, but also in view of his judgement — because the papacy and Roman Church is to be judged, and anyone who continues to share in its sins, will also share in its judgement.

v8. After seeing this, John then tells us that another angel followed, announcing the fall of Babylon, that great city. The great city has been mentioned before as the place where the witnesses were put to death (see 11:8). Also, a tenth of the city was said to fall when the witnesses were resurrected (see 11:13). Now, for the first time, it is named 'Babylon'. Babylon is a symbol of human rebellion against God and of false religion (see

Gen 11:1ff — the building of Babel), and of pride and idolatry (these characterised the city and empire of Babylon). Moreover, as can be seen from elsewhere (especially chapter 17), specifically, 'Babylon' is a figure for papal Rome which, as the seat of the Church of Rome, can also stand for the Church of Rome itself (which is characterised by false religion, idolatry and pride).

And here, this second angel is announcing Babylon's fall, notably in words that echo Isaiah's proclamation of the fall of literal Babylon (see Is 21:9). In both of these cases the fall of Babylon does not refer to its wickedness, but to its judgement. Moreover, the past tense (fallen) does not mean its judgement has happened (Isaiah was prophesying a considerable time before Babylon fell); rather, it expresses that it will most certainly take place (it is as good as done). So, this angel is proclaiming the coming, certain judgement of Babylon — of the Church of Rome. Moreover, the reason for Babylon's judgement is given — it is "because she has made all nations drink of the wine of the wrath of her fornication" (see Jer 51:6–8). This combines two thoughts: by all her impurity and idolatry she has seduced and intoxicated the peoples, and has corrupted them; and this brings the wrath of God. This certainly is true of the Church of Rome, which seduced the nations into false religion away from God. And for this God is judging her.

v9–11. Then a third angel followed, loudly proclaiming, "If anyone worships the beast and his image, and receives his mark...himself shall also drink of the wine of the wrath of God, which is poured out full strength into the cup of his indignation." Thus this angel gives a clear and solemn warning that any who continue to honour and be loyal to the pope and the papal system will also experience God's judgement, meted out in full measure and without mitigation (see Ps 75:8). Moreover, the angel then goes on to describe what such a person will suffer (v10b–11) — here using graphic imagery which expresses a state of great and everlasting misery and destruction, and which points towards the final judgement. Essentially, therefore, what we have here is a solemn warning that all who continue to honour and be loyal to the papacy, will suffer eternal condemnation and punishment.

So, in the proclamations of the three angels, we have: a call for people to believe the true gospel, and to honour and worship God, because the time of his judgement (his judgement of the Roman Church) has come; an announcement of the coming, certain judgement of the Roman Church; and a warning of eternal punishment for those who do not take heed but continue to honour and show allegiance to the papacy. And all of this is very relevant to the time of the Reformation. The recovery of the true gospel at the Reformation went hand in hand with the pope being identified as the Antichrist of Scripture, and the Roman Church being identified as Babylon. And at that time, not only were people called to simple trust in Christ for salvation, but they were also urged to recognise the antichristian nature of the papal system and to turn away from the erroneous beliefs and practices of Rome. Moreover, the Reformation also marked the time of the beginning of God's judgement of the papacy and Roman Church, which is still ongoing and is yet to reach a climax (we will see this judgement depicted under the pouring out of the seven bowls of God's wrath — chapter 16). So, the pronouncements of the three angels mark the point of the Reformation, and were relevant to that time.

Moreover, the pronouncements of these angels have also been relevant ever since, and will be to the end of time. Ever since the Reformation, as well as preaching the gospel, the church should have been calling people out of the Roman Catholic Church (see 18:4), and warning those who will not heed this that they are in danger of being eternally lost. Moreover, in these days of ecumenism, those churches that are uniting themselves with the Church of Rome need to realise that they are entering into communion with a body that is under God's judgement, and that this cannot be without consequence for them.

v12. John was then told, "here is the patience [or perseverance] of the saints". The knowledge of God's judgement of this antichristian system is, for the true people of God, a help to enduring and remaining faithful to the end. Moreover, the saints are then described as "those who keep the commandments of God and the faith of Jesus" — who walk in obedience to God and trust in the Lord Jesus Christ in all things. This is what characterises the true people of God; and this is the key to remaining steadfast in the midst of all persecution and error.

v13. Lastly, John heard a voice from heaven telling him to write, "Blessed are the dead who die in the Lord from now on." Moreover, he heard this being affirmed by the Spirit. Of course, all who die in Christ are blessed — they enter their eternal rest and reward. However, in this context, this would seem to refer especially to those who died at the time of the Reformation for proclaiming and defending the truth of Christ, and to those who have similarly died since. These are especially blessed in dying for two reasons. Firstly, death brings them "rest from their labours" — it brings a happy relief from the toil and trials and suffering they have endured for the sake of proclaiming and defending the true faith. Also, "their works follow them" — which could mean that in heaven their service and suffering will bring reward, or it could mean that the effect of their work continues in the earth after they have gone. Certainly, those at the Reformation who laboured and suffered much to proclaim the true gospel, and to deliver people from the false religion of Rome, brought truth and freedom not only to their own generation but to the generations that followed.

The reaping of the earth (14:14–20)

v14–16. Then, as another vision opened up, John tells us he looked, and he saw "a white cloud, and on the cloud sat One like the Son of Man, having on His head a golden crown, and in His hand a sharp sickle". This represents the Lord Jesus Christ, portrayed as the Son of God incarnate and the Lord over all (the

Lord and Saviour), ready to reap the harvest of the earth. John then tells us that another angel came out of the temple, crying with a loud voice to Him who sat on the cloud, "Thrust in Your sickle and reap, for the time has come for You to reap, for the harvest of the earth is ripe." Since it would not seem fitting for an angel to command the Lord Jesus Christ, we should probably view the apparent command of this angel as an announcement that the time has come to reap the harvest, because it is ready. And so, the time to reap having come, "He who sat on the cloud [the Lord Jesus Christ] thrust in His sickle on the earth, and the earth was reaped".

In Scripture, the imagery of harvest can have to do with salvation or with judgement. All of the following are described in terms of harvest: Christ gathering in the lost via his labourers (see Mt 9:37–38; also Jn 4:35–38); the gathering in of the fruit of God's kingdom (see Mk 4:26–29); the gathering and separating of the righteous and the wicked at the end of the age (see Mt 13:24–30,36–43); and judgement of the wicked (see Jer 51:33, where the imagery of threshing is included). Consequently, the harvest pictured here is understood variously, with some taking it to be a symbol of judgement. However, in view of the fact that a clear image of judgement follows (see v17–20), it would seem most fitting to regard this as a picture of Christ gathering in those he is saving. As such, this harvest could be seen as a picture of Christ gathering in his people at the end of the age. However, in this context (when the Reformation has been in view), it would seem better to see it as having reference to the Reformation and depicting Christ saving people out of apostate Christendom. Certainly, the recovery and preaching of the true gospel at the Reformation resulted in a great number being saved and, in a sense, being gathered out of the apostate world. Not only that, the Reformation paved the way for a great harvest of souls in the generations to come.

v17–20. John then tells us, "another angel came out of the temple which is in heaven, he also having a sharp sickle"; and then another angel came out from the altar, who "had power over fire". And this angel cried out, "Thrust in your sharp sickle and gather the clusters of the vine of the earth, for her grapes are fully ripe." Again, as above, it is probably best to understand this apparent command as an announcement that the time has come to reap the harvest, because it is ready. And so, "the angel thrust in his sickle into the earth and gathered the vine of the earth, and threw it into the great winepress of the wrath of God".

This picture of the ripe grapes being gathered, and then thrown into the winepress of the wrath of God, is clearly imagery of judgement on the wicked when their sins have reached full measure (see Is 63:2–4; Joel 3:13). Moreover, the imagery of the call to reap being sounded by an angel who comes out from the altar, and has power over fire, indicates that the prayers of the saints have played a part in this judgement coming upon the earth (see 8:3–5). So, having had a picture of salvation, we now have a picture of judgement.

John then adds, "the winepress was trampled outside the city"; and he describes the vast amount of blood that flowed out of the winepress — it came "up to the horses' bridles, for one thousand six hundred furlongs" (literal translation, one thousand six hundred 'stadia', a distance equivalent to about 184 miles). This trampling of the winepress outside the city reminds us of the Lord Jesus Christ being crucified outside the city (see Heb 13:12), and thus prompts a comparison between the two: Christ was the sinless one who bore the punishment for the sin of his people; the wicked bear their own punishment, and are justly punished. Moreover, the vast amount of blood indicates a great slaughter, and thus the judgement of a vast number.

So this depicts a time of great judgement, and, as a result, is understood by some to depict the final judgement. Certainly, the imagery is appropriate for this. However, in this context, it would again seem more fitting to relate this to the Reformation, and to see it as depicting God's judgement falling upon apostate Christendom. By the time of the Reformation, apostate Christendom was full of idolatry and wickedness and was ripe for judgement; and at that time, not only were many saved out of apostate Christendom, but God's judgement fell upon the apostate world (the nature of this judgement will be seen in chapter 16).

Thus, in these two images of reaping, we have a picture of salvation, together with a picture of judgement — which, within the historical framework of Revelation, would seem to be a picture of souls being saved out of apostate Christendom, and a picture of apostate Christendom being judged. Often in God's working, salvation and judgement come together (eg, Ex 14:26-30), and this is what happened at the time of the Reformation.

Chapter 15
Prelude to the bowl judgements

Introduction

The visions recorded in chapters 12 to 14 form an interlude between the sounding of the seventh trumpet (which is the third woe — see 11:14–19; also 8:13–9:1; 9:12–13), and the judgements ushered in by this — which are now to be depicted under the pouring out of the seven bowls of God's wrath. These intervening visions followed a depiction of the Reformation (see 11:7–13), and they covered again the time from John's day to the Reformation. They showed: the devil seeking to destroy the early church through pagan Rome, and the devil's defeat in the downfall of paganism in the Empire (chapter 12); the devil's new great instrument, the papacy (with its political and religious power), and the papacy's reign during the Middle Ages (chapter 13); the true church during the time of the rise and ascendancy of the papacy and Roman Church (14:1–5); the call for men to honour and worship God, and the announcement of God's judgement of the Roman Church (14:6–13); and the saving of people out of apostate Christendom and the judgement of apostate Christendom at the time of the Reformation (14:14–20). Now we have the introduction to the pouring out of the seven bowls of God's wrath which, as we will see, primarily concern God's judgement upon the papacy and the Roman Church.

The angels receive the bowls of God's wrath (15:1–8)

v1. After seeing the gathering and treading of the grapes, John then saw another sign in heaven, which he describes as "great and marvellous" — it was something of great importance in the history of the world, and something causing wonder and amazement. And what he saw was "seven angels having the seven last plagues". Plagues stand for great calamities or catastrophes, and they denote severe judgements of God. Moreover, these are the "last" plagues, "for in them the wrath of God is complete". These are the climactic and most severe judgements of God, in which God's wrath reaches its full measure. Taking into account the point we have reached in the unfolding of events, and the fact that these judgements feature both the beast and Babylon, it has to be concluded that, primarily, these plagues concern God's judgements to be visited upon the papacy and the Roman Church. Its sin had reached a fullness, and God's wrath was now to be poured out in fullness, bringing its ruin and final end.

v2–4. Having seen the seven angels with the seven last plagues, John then saw a scene of encouragement — he saw those who have the victory over the beast singing a song of victory.

These ones here who "have the victory over the beast, over his image and over his mark and over the number of his name", clearly represent those who have been kept from or delivered from allegiance to the pope and his antichristian system; and, in this context, they would seem particularly to represent those who were saved out of this at the time of the Reformation. And these ones are standing on what John describes as "something like a sea of glass mingled with fire" — which would seem to portray that these ones have been cleansed and purified by Christ (cf. 4:6). They are also said to have "harps of God". These harps accompany their victory song; and, their description as harps 'of God' would seem to indicate that these overcomers sing their victory song only because of what God has done for them and in them (their victory is through God and Christ alone, and they sing out of new hearts given by God and created to be instruments of his praise).

We are then told "they sing the song of Moses, the servant of God, and the song of the Lamb" — the song they sing is a song of deliverance (the song of Moses refers to the song Moses and the children of Israel sang following their deliverance through the

Red Sea — see Ex 15:1–18). And in their song, these ones extol the greatness of God's works, and the justice and truth of his ways — an acclamation which, in this context, would seem to refer especially to the deliverance of the Reformation, together with God's judgement of apostate Christendom (these were great works of God that manifested his justice and truth). Moreover, they do this hailing God as the "Lord God Almighty" (he is the one who is all-powerful over all the world), and hailing him as "King of the saints" (this stands in contrast to the papacy's dominion over the world). Then, in view of this, they ask the rhetorical question, "Who shall not fear You, O Lord, and glorify Your name? For You alone are holy. For all nations shall come and worship before You, for Your judgements have been manifested." When our holy God intervenes in the affairs of men, and his acts of salvation or judgement appear in the earth, men worship him. And at the Reformation, God's great and holy and just works of deliverance and judgement appeared in the earth, which was a cause for the peoples to fear and glorify God.

v5,6. After hearing this great song of deliverance, John then tells us that he looked, and "the temple [or sanctuary] of the tabernacle of the testimony in heaven was opened". This picture of the tabernacle of the testimony being opened takes us back to the sounding of the seventh trumpet (see 11:15,19); and so it reminds us that what is to follow (ie, the pouring out of the seven bowls of God's wrath) is, in fact, the judgement associated with the sounding of the seventh trumpet. And, in both places, what we have is an allusion to the Most Holy Place of the Jewish tabernacle or temple, where the ark of the covenant (containing the ten commandments) was situated, and where God dwelt amongst his people.

Then, having seen the temple (or sanctuary) opened, John tells us, "out of the temple came the seven angels having the seven plagues"; and he describes these angels as "clothed in pure bright linen, and having their chests girded with golden bands" (which resembles the clothing of the high priest). The emergence of these angels from the temple (from the temple of the tabernacle of testimony in heaven) depicts them coming from God's presence, and shows that the judgements associated with them are to be poured out with God's sanction. It also shows that God is to be vindicated in these judgements — these judgements will give testimony to the justice and truth of God. Moreover, the apparel of these angels adds to the gravity of the scene — it speaks of purity and dignity, and so further reinforces the pure and grave nature of these judgements.

v7,8. John then saw one of the four living creatures give to the seven angels "seven golden bowls full of the wrath of God who lives forever and ever". These bowls convey the last plagues — the terrible judgements of God to be visited upon the papacy and Roman Church, and upon all the enemies of God. And of note is that it is one of the four living creatures that gives these bowls to the angels. The involvement of one of these creatures (whose symbolism concerns God's merciful purpose to save men — see comments on 4:6–8) sets before us the inseparable link between God's saving purposes and his judgements; these go hand in hand and are in no way incompatible with one another.

John then tells us, "the temple was filled with smoke from the glory of God and from his power, and no one was able to enter the temple till the seven plagues of the seven angels were completed". This reminds us of the occasions when the glory of God filled the tabernacle and the temple (see Ex 40:34–35; 1 Kgs 8:10–11; also Ezek 44:4). And, in this context, it stresses the inevitability of these judgements — these judgements of God had been long delayed, but once they had begun they would proceed with swiftness until they were completed. Moreover, there is also a suggestion here (in the fact that no one could enter the temple until the plagues were completed) that these judgements could not be interrupted or turned away by the intercession of the church. Once begun they would surely all be poured out. All of this warns us against looking for a reprieve for the papacy and the Roman Church. Such a thing will not occur.

Their judgement is certain, and our concern should not be to pray for God to save the Roman Catholic Church (as an institution), but to call people out of it.

Chapter 16
The bowls of God's wrath

The command to pour out the bowls (16:1)

v1. Having seen the seven angels be given the seven bowls of God's wrath, John then heard a loud voice from the temple saying to the seven angels, "Go and pour out the bowls of the wrath of God on the earth." Since no one was able to enter the temple until the plagues were completed (15:8), it would seem that this voice is the voice of God commanding the angels to pour out his judgements. And, as we will see below, at God's command, immediately the bowls are poured out, one after another, including the seventh bowl.

This pouring out of bowls full of God's wrath is imagery of swift and full and final judgement. These are the seven last plagues, in which the wrath of God is complete (see 15:1) — these are to bring the ruin and final end of the whole Roman antichristian system. With the pouring out of the seven bowls we will see depicted both God's judgement of the followers of the pope and the Roman Catholic religion, and his judgement of the papacy and the Roman Church itself (as an institution). Both are justly judged — the followers of the Roman Catholic religion for rejecting the truth of Christ and following the false religion of the papacy, and the papacy and Roman Church for leading the world astray and persecuting the saints.

So we come to look in detail at these great final judgements of God to be poured out on the earth.

The pouring out of the first four bowls (16:2–9)

As with the first four seals and trumpets, the first four bowl judgements form an associated group and therefore will be considered together. At the outset, however, it must be acknowledged that interpreting these first four bowl judgements is not easy, and even amongst those who view Revelation historically, there are differences of approach.

One approach has been to interpret these bowls primarily in political terms, and to relate them to the struggles that broke out across Europe following the Reformation. Certainly, the centuries after the Reformation were a time of great turmoil in Europe when there were international and civil conflicts between Roman Catholic and Protestant peoples, and much resistance to the Roman Church's authority. Consequently, if the fulfilment of these bowl judgements is looked for in historical events happening in the Christian world during the post-Reformation years, then these are the events that stand out. However, another approach has been to interpret these first four bowls more in spiritual terms — to concern spiritual judgements upon the whole Roman antichristian system and its adherents. And this would seem to be a better way of interpreting the imagery here, as discussed below.

First of all, the imagery of the first four bowls of wrath is clear imagery of judgement. Moreover, there are certain similarities between these bowls and the first four trumpet judgements, which concerned the fall of the Roman Empire (see 8:7–12). Particularly, in both we see the various parts of the physical world being struck (the earth, the sea, the rivers and springs, the heavenly bodies); and both involve imagery that reminds us of the plagues of Egypt.

At the same time, however, there are also some significant differences. Firstly, the first four trumpets do not picture the direct infliction of suffering on the actual bodies of men, whereas these bowl judgements contain such imagery (see v2,8–9). This indicates that these bowl judgements represent something much more terrible and severe. Also, in the case of the trumpet judgements only a third of each part of the physical world was struck, whereas with these bowl judgements there is no limitation. This again indicates much more severe judgement, and the climactic judging of all that is evil.

Moreover, when considering the imagery of the first four trumpet judgements, we saw that the scenes showing the various parts of the physical world being struck included imagery used in the Old Testament for the fall of ancient Babylon; thus the imagery depicted not merely God judging the Roman world and way of life, but also him bringing down the Roman Empire. In the case of the first four bowl judgements, however, no Old Testament imagery used to depict the fall of Babylon (or any other power) is involved; rather, we simply see the various parts of the physical world being struck, with great emphasis being placed on the effect on the lives of men. This indicates that they do not concern the fall (in the sense of demise and final end) of the papal Roman power (the imagery for this is lacking); rather, they merely depict God in some way striking the whole Roman Catholic domain or system, with terrible effects on its followers.

We come then to look at the first four bowl judgements.

v2. Following God's command to the seven angels to go and pour out the bowls of God's wrath, the first angel poured out his bowl. And this was poured "upon the earth". And, with this, "a foul and loathsome sore came upon the men who had the mark of the beast and those who worshipped his image" (ie, upon the followers of the beast).

This depicts God's judgement falling upon the Roman Catholic world, and those loyal to the pope and his antichristian system being afflicted with some evil and grievous open wound. Thus it would seem to portray those who showed allegiance to the pope and his system being given by God to bear some unwholesome condition that causes great harm. And, certainly, those who follow the pope and his religion, which is a religion of idolatry, superstition and works, are given to something which for them is unwholesome and harmful.

v3. Then next, the second angel poured out his bowl. And this was poured "on the sea". And, with this, "it [the sea] became blood as of a dead man; and every living creature in the sea died".

This depicts God's judgement falling upon the Roman Catholic world or domain, and it being struck with a deadliness that causes death. Thus, it would seem to portray the whole Roman Catholic system being consigned by God to be only of a deadly nature, so that it brings only death to men.

v4–7. Then the third angel poured out his bowl. And this was poured "on the rivers and springs of water". And, with this, "they [the rivers and springs] became blood".

This depicts God's judgement falling upon the Roman Catholic world or system, and everything that is to the people a source of life and refreshment becoming polluted and deadly. Thus, this would seem to portray the whole Roman Catholic system — all its dogmas, rites and ordinances — being consigned by God to minister only harm and death to those who seek life from it. Thus, from this point in time, those who continued in this apostate system would drink only from polluted and deadly streams, finding in its dogmas, rites and ordinances no spiritual life and refreshment, but only corruption and death.

Upon seeing this, John then heard "the angel of the waters" extolling the righteousness of God in this judgement. Those affected by this judgement "shed the blood of saints and prophets" (they shed the blood of God's people); thus it is just that God has "given them blood to drink" — that they are punished with death. So we see that by his judgement of the Roman Catholic system, God is not only judging its false religion, but he is also avenging the persecution of his people (persecution that was carried out by the Roman Church but was approved of by the people — see 11:8–10). Moreover, we see that the punishment fits the crime. They shed blood and so they will drink blood — they will be given over to the deadly religion of Rome.

And John then heard "another from the altar" affirming the declaration of the angel, and further proclaiming God true and righteous in his judgements. In the face of God's judgements on the Roman Catholic system and its followers, we must take care to keep in sight and affirm God's justice in this. And this we will do when we rightly recognise the nature of Roman Catholicism.

v8–9. Then the fourth angel poured out his bowl. And this was poured "on the sun". And, with this, "power was given to him to scorch men with fire".

Here, some understand the sun to represent some eminent earthly ruler who in some way does harm to the papacy and its interest. However, in this context, it would seem better to understand this to represent the pope himself (who usurps the place of Christ, the true Sun of righteousness who brings light and healing to men — see Mal 4:2); in which case, this depicts God's judgement falling upon the Roman Catholic world in that the papacy becomes only a source of great hurt to men. So, those showing allegiance to the papacy would, under its dominion and decrees, suffer only great harm.

We are then told, "men were scorched with great heat, and they blasphemed the name of God who has power over these plagues; and they did not repent and give Him glory". This shows the people suffering greatly as a result of their continued allegiance to the papacy; but it also shows them continuing to resist God and reject his true way. So we see further the very final nature of these judgements. (It should not be assumed from the imagery here, and in v10b–11, that the followers of the beast/papacy are necessarily sensible of the hurt they are suffering or that they are overtly railing against God. It must be remembered that this is a revelation or unveiling of things otherwise unseen; thus the imagery is showing spiritual realities, and not necessarily what is sensibly felt or overtly done.)

So, as understood here, these first four bowl judgements depict the whole Roman Catholic sphere — the Roman Catholic system and its adherents — being judged. And, essentially, they would seem to concern the whole Roman Catholic system being consigned by God to be nothing but harmful and deadly, and those who remain in the system being given over and abandoned to a system (to dogmas, rites, ordinances and leadership) which brings them only hurt and death. This is a terrible judgement on any church, and it would seem that this is what happened to the Roman Church and its adherents at the time of the Reformation.

Prior to the Reformation, although the Roman Church was an apostate church, there were still true spiritual reforming movements within the Church (eg, the movements associated with Wyclif and Hus); thus there was life within the Church. The Reformation, however, marked a turning point. At this point in his purposes God showed many the true faith; and at this time there was powerful preaching of the true gospel and a clear call for people to recognise the falsehood and evils of the Roman Catholic religion and to turn from it. However, many people would not believe the true gospel or heed the warnings. Moreover, the Roman Church itself resisted all fundamental reform; in fact, it anathematised (pronounced accursed) all who embraced the true faith, and it reaffirmed its apostate position (particularly important in this was the Council of Trent, held by the Roman Church during the years 1545–63). The result of this was a clear division of the church in Europe into, on the one hand the Roman Catholic Church, and on the other hand the Protestant churches that arose out of the various reforming movements that sprang up across Europe at that time.

Thus, at the time of the Reformation, there was a physical separation; and these bowl judgements indicate that this marked the point of God giving the Roman Church over, totally and irreversibly, to its corrupting and deadly religion, so that it ministered only harm and death to its followers. From that point onwards God has saved many out of the Roman Catholic Church and religion. However, since then the Roman Church has stood under these judgements of God and there has been in it (as a system) no light or life, but it has been only a source of darkness and death to those who have been loyal to it (in fact, since then the Roman Church has promulgated further false doctrines, especially in relation to Mary; also the papacy has added to its blasphemous claims that of papal infallibility).

The dreadfulness of this judgement cannot be over-emphasised. To be consigned by God to spiritual darkness and death is the worst judgement that can befall a system or people; and the imagery of these first four bowls indicates that this is the judgement that has fallen upon the Roman Catholic Church. Accepting this may not be easy for some; however, doing this is important because it can only make us see more clearly, and feel more urgently, the need to call people out of this deadly system, which is irreversibly under God's judgement.

The pouring out of the fifth bowl (16:10–11)

As discussed above, the first four bowl judgements concern God's judgement of the whole Roman Catholic system and its adherents. Now, with the pouring out of the fifth bowl, we turn to God's judgement of the papacy, and of the Roman Church itself (as an institution), which is the subject of the last three bowl judgements.

v10–11. Then the fifth angel poured out his bowl. And this was poured "on the throne of the beast". And, with this, "his kingdom became full of darkness".

This depicts God's judgement being visited upon the seat of authority or rule of the beast, and his rule or kingdom being brought down (in this context, the imagery of darkness would not seem to depict the absence of gospel light, but the kingdom of the beast suffering great trouble and distress, and the beast's power in the world being extinguished — see comments on 8:12). Thus this represents God, in judgement, bringing down the pope's dominion in this world — which may have reference to his political power over the nations in general, or it could refer more specifically to his rule over Rome and the Papal States, which were his actual lands. The pope lost his dominion over both of these spheres during the centuries following the Reformation.

Prior to the Reformation, the pope had become an actual sovereign ruler over Rome and the Papal States (these were territories in the Italian peninsula that were under the direct rule of the pope). Also, by means of his claim to be the Vicar of Christ, the pope had risen to a place of exercising supreme authority over the rulers and nations of Europe. At the time of the Reformation, however, the pope lost control over those nations and states that became Protestant. Also, in the centuries following this, the growing nationalistic spirit in Europe resulted in even the Roman Catholic rulers and peoples revolting against the pope's jurisdiction over their national affairs. Moreover, in the nineteenth century, the pope also lost his sovereign rule over Rome and the Papal States (this was finally lost when Italy became a unified kingdom; at that time, first the Papal States were taken in 1861, and then Rome in 1870). So, by the end of the nineteenth century, the papacy's political power and temporal dominion had been brought down. This is not to say that the pope was left with no influence; he still exercised supreme spiritual power in the Roman Catholic Church, and he could still exert political influence through faithful Roman Catholics in high positions. However, he no longer exercised over the rulers and nations the power he once had done, and he had lost his own lands. This loss of political influence and temporal power was part of God's judgement on the papacy, which proudly and blasphemously had claimed and endeavoured to exercise supreme power over the nations.

We are then told, "they [those already referred to above, who were in allegiance to the papal system] gnawed their tongues because of the pain". Also, they "blasphemed the God of heaven because of their pains and their sores, and did not repent of their deeds". This shows the harm that resulted from the first four bowl judgements continuing to be experienced by the adherents of Roman Catholicism: at the Reformation God judged the whole Roman Catholic system with terrible effects on its followers, and the effects have been experienced by all the followers of Roman Catholicism ever since. This also shows the hardening of people's hearts continuing — it shows the people, in spite of the harmful nature of these judgements, continuing to resist God and reject his true way.

The pouring out of the sixth bowl (16:12–16)

With the sixth bowl judgement we are coming very near to the end, and to the climax of God's judgement of his enemies; and, as will be seen, this sixth bowl judgement is very much preparatory to this. Moreover, it is of special significance to us because the events of recent years indicate that we are, in our own time, seeing the fulfilment of the judgement depicted here. In view of this, more space will be devoted to discussing this bowl. However, while it is possible to comment to some degree on the actual historical developments represented here, these comments can only be tentative and partial. We will not know the full and precise fulfilment of what is depicted here until the events concerned are past.

v12. Next, the sixth angel poured out his bowl. And this was poured "on the great river Euphrates". And, with this, "its water was dried up, so that the way of the kings from the east might be prepared".

In this imagery we see some parallel with that of the sixth trumpet judgement. There, the river Euphrates was the place from where a great judgement was released on apostate Christendom (see 9:13–16); and this judgement was understood to concern the overrunning of apostate Christendom by the followers of Islam, and perhaps especially the Turkish invasion which brought an end to the Empire in the east. Now, in this sixth bowl judgement, the river Euphrates is depicted as being dried up, so that the way of the kings from the east might be prepared. This parallel with the sixth trumpet has led many in the past, who have understood Revelation historically, to interpret this as God judging the Turkish power and bringing it down (and thus, in essence, bringing down the power of Islam); they then see this as paving the way for a gathering of the scattered Jews, or those of the eastern nations (and perhaps especially Muslims) into the church (see Is 11:15–16 & Zech 10:10–11 for similar imagery).

In many ways, it is understandable that this has been a common interpretation of this verse. When discussing the sixth trumpet it was noted that the Turks were a great and formidable power, intent on conquest; moreover, their conquests eventually led to the Turks coming to rule over a vast Islamic Empire, often called the Ottoman Empire (at its height in the sixteenth century, this controlled much of south-east Europe, western Asia and northern Africa). However, as tends to happen with earthly empires, there was an eventual decline in Turkish power and break-up of the Empire, until it finally came to an end when Turkey became a republic in the early 1920s. In view of this history, and the parallel with the sixth trumpet, it is understandable that the drying up of the Euphrates has been interpreted as God judging the Turkish power and bringing it down (and thus God judging Islam and breaking its power).

However, while it is the case that the Turkish Empire did break up, and now no longer exists, we can now see that this has in no way meant the end of the Islamic peoples and nations; nor has it meant the end of Islamic militancy and threat. Rather, as was noted when discussing the sixth trumpet, Islam continues to be very powerful in our own time and, notably, is currently both making great inroads into the West, and being a great threat to the nations of the West (thus the judgement of the sixth trumpet would seem to be ongoing). Therefore, the understanding that the drying up of the Euphrates concerns God judging the Turkish Empire, and bringing about the demise of Islamic power, is questionable.

Moreover, also questionable is the view that the imagery of the way of the kings from the east being prepared concerns a way being made for people to be gathered into the church. This is because the drying up of the Euphrates to prepare the way of the kings from the east would seem to be connected with and playing a part in the great gathering of the nations to Armageddon (ie, to the final great battle and to judgement) described in the following verses (see v13–16, discussed below). Thus it would not seem to concern people being gathered into the church.

Given all of this, how then should we understand this verse? Firstly, the drying up of the Euphrates could still be understood as depicting the demise of the Turkish Empire, without it also being understood in terms of God judging and diminishing Islam as a whole (which, plainly, is still widespread, powerful and militant). Furthermore, the break-up of the Turkish Empire into independent nations could be seen as removing an obstacle to and facilitating the gathering of those nations with the rest of the peoples to the final great battle.

However, there is an alternative way of understanding the imagery of this verse, which would seem to fit the context better. As already noted when discussing the sixth trumpet, the river Euphrates marked the extreme eastern boundary of the ideal promised land. It was also the barrier between the people of God and their classic enemies, Assyria and Babylon. Thus, another way of understanding this verse is that it is depicting God, in judgement, removing the boundary or barrier between the Christian world and the non-Christian world (both the Islamic nations and the other eastern nations with their own religions, such as Buddhism, Hinduism etc) — the purpose of this being to prepare the way for the non-Christian nations or peoples to be gathered, along with the traditionally Christian nations, to Armageddon (to the final great battle).

Understood like this, this verse, depicting God in judgement drying up the Euphrates, essentially has to do with all the opponents of God and his people being gathered to the final great battle and to judgement. And, the particular importance of what we see here would seem to be that it shows us, while it is God's opponents (the dragon, beast and false prophet) that are instrumental in this gathering (see v13–14), ultimately it happens in the will and purpose of God, as part of his judgement of his enemies (it is God who initiates and ultimately brings this gathering about). This will be discussed further below.

v13,14. Having seen the drying up of the Euphrates, John then saw the gathering that this drying of the Euphrates assists. John says he saw "three unclean spirits like frogs coming out of the mouth of the dragon, out of the mouth of the beast, and out of the mouth of the false prophet". And he tells us "they are spirits of demons, performing signs, which go out to the kings of the earth and of the whole world, to gather them to the battle of that great day of God Almighty".

We have already seen that the dragon represented Satan (that serpent of old) (see 12:9) and Satan acting through pagan Rome (by which he held sway over the peoples before the Empire adopted Christianity as its religion) (see 12:3). We have also seen that the beast represented the papacy and its dominion (Satan's new instrument by which he held sway over the peoples after the fall of pagan Rome) (see 13:1–4). Here, the false prophet is the same entity as the beast from the earth (which causes the people to worship the first beast — see 13:11ff; also 19:20); so it represents the papacy in its religious or ecclesiastical power (a power that the papacy exercises through the whole ecclesiastical system of the Roman Church, which the pope heads). Thus, what is depicted here is Satan (represented by a symbol that also concerns heathen empire) and the papacy (expressed in its political and religious power) exerting an influence over the kings of the earth and of the whole world (over those with the power and the rule). Moreover, we are told that this is for the purpose of gathering them (and thus their people also) to the battle of that great day of God Almighty — ie, gathering them together in some kind of collective opposition to God, to the final great battle and the great day of God's judgement.

From this, it is possible to highlight some important features of this gathering; highlighting these will help us to see the true nature of this gathering and its relevance to today.

Features of the gathering

(a) First of all, the gathering of the nations/peoples pictured here concerns some form of collective rebellion against or opposition to God. Of course, rebellion and opposition to God have been with us since the fall — these are basic to the nature of fallen man. But what is particular about the opposition we see here is the collective and comprehensive nature of it: it is orchestrated by the great enemies of God — the dragon, the beast and the false prophet (the devil, the papacy and the Roman Church); and it involves a gathering and uniting of the peoples in some shared and collective conflict with or opposition to God. (Notably, we see a similar gathering in Acts 4:27–28, where we read how Herod and Pilate, with the Gentiles and Jews, gathered together against the Lord Jesus.)

(b) Secondly, this gathering is a worldwide gathering that catches up both the Christian and non-Christian nations. This is indicated by the fact it is described as a gathering of "the kings of the earth and of the whole world". This clearly indicates that it involves all the nations and peoples. Moreover, the fact that mention is made of both the kings "of the earth" and "of the whole world", would seem to be significant: most probably, it indicates that this gathering includes both the leaders of the Christian world and the leaders of the non-Christian world. That said, it is the case that some manuscripts do not include here "the kings of the earth", but merely say "the kings of the whole world". However, the mention of both would make sense in this context, especially if we understand the drying up of the Euphrates as being the removal of the barrier between the Christian world and non-Christian world to prepare the way for this gathering (see comments on v12 above): it makes clear and highlights that this worldwide gathering/rebellion involves some kind of association or alliance between the traditionally Christian peoples and the non-Christian peoples — something which would not normally have been engaged in. (Again, we see something similar in Acts

4:27–28, where we find people who would not normally act together uniting in common opposition to Christ.)

(c) Thirdly, this gathering is achieved through great deception. In the imagery we see that the kings are gathered by unclean spirits which come from the mouths of the dragon, the beast and the false prophet, and which are spirits of demons, performing signs. This reminds us of the incident recorded in the Old Testament, in which a lying spirit was placed in the mouth of the prophets to persuade Ahab to go into battle and to disaster, as a judgement upon him (see 1 Kgs 22:19–23). In that case, by false prophecy, one man was enticed to battle and thus to judgement. These spirits, by worldly policy and religious deception, with lying signs, gather the whole world to the battle of that great day of God Almighty. Moreover, it is notable that it is the kings that are influenced — it is first of all by the deception of leaders that all the peoples are gathered to the final great battle and great day of reckoning. This, of course, is what we might expect; it is leaders (those with the power and influence) who ultimately determine the direction taken by the people they lead.

(d) Finally, ultimately this gathering is happening in God's purpose, as part of his judgement. We see this in the fact that it is depicted under the sixth bowl of God's wrath, and thus it is part of God's judgement upon the papacy and upon all his enemies. Moreover, it is a gathering "to the battle of that great day of God Almighty" — a description which makes clear that the gathering and rebellion depicted here is to culminate not in a great victory for God's enemies, but in a day of God's judgement (that great day of God Almighty). So, while this gathering to battle is orchestrated by the enemies of God (the dragon, beast and false prophet), it is happening in God's purpose, to bring his enemies and this godless world to a day of judgement (again, see the gathering in Acts 4:27–28, where we also see God's enemies bringing about God's preordained will).

[NB: The actual battle and judgement that this gathering culminates in is depicted later (in 19:17–21 and 20:7–10), and will be discussed then. However, at this point it will be helpful to make reference to the second passage because it adds to our understanding of this bowl judgement. This second passage prompts us to look back to the account of the judgement of Gog found in Ezek 38:1–39:10, which describes a gathering similar to that depicted here. In these chapters we are told that God is against Gog, and so he is going to lead him out together with his army; and many peoples will be with him; and they will come against Israel (see 38:3–6,16). Then, when this happens, God will rain down great judgement on Gog and his army and the peoples with him, and so God will be glorified (see 38:22–23). Thus, God draws out Gog to battle because he is against Gog (although Gog also acts by his own evil plan and will — see 38:10–11); and Gog and the peoples gather to a great conflict for judgement. Similarly, God is against the pope, and he is leading him out with all his followers, and all the peoples with him, in one final rebellion for judgement. In other words, God has purposed that the pope and the whole apostate church and godless world should gather in rebellion against him, to the end that they should be judged.]

Essentially, therefore, this sixth bowl judgement concerns the gathering of the godless world, in some form of collective opposition to God, to the final great battle between God and his enemies and to judgement. Moreover, it shows this gathering being orchestrated by anti-God forces (the devil, the beast and the false prophet), but ultimately happening in God's purpose. And, in view of certain significant developments of recent years (since the beginning of the twentieth century, and especially since the Second World War) there is much to suggest that we are seeing the fulfilment of this gathering in our own time. *(All of this is discussed more fully in 'Internationalism, Ecumenism & The End Times — Where ecumenism is leading the churches', 2018, by the same author.)*

Present-day indicators of the gathering

(a) First of all, very notable in our time (especially since the Second World War) has been a great emphasis on unity, co-operation, reconciliation and peace, together with growing international and religious unity and co-operation. In particular, recent years have seen the formation of a great many international bodies and organisations (such as the United Nations), and much more international co-operation in world affairs. There has also been the formation of the European Union with its goal of building a federal Europe. Similarly, in the religious sphere, we have seen the growth of both the church unity and interfaith movements, which are promoting unity and co-operation between the various Christian denominations and between all the world's religions (including Christianity). Thus, we are seeing a kind of gathering of the nations and peoples in our day — a gathering that is of worldwide scope, and that is catching up both the traditionally Christian and non-Christian nations.

Also of note is the motivation behind the current pursuit of international and interfaith unity. This is the belief that unity and co-operation between the world's nations and religions is the key to solving this world's problems, and to achieving peace and prosperity in the world. On the surface, this appears good. We live in a world blighted by such things as war, injustice, poverty, and environmental threats, and it is right that everything possible is done to alleviate such problems. Moreover, co-operation between international groups and governments can assist in this. However, the current pursuit of international and religious unity goes far beyond simply trying to prevent conflict or to help those who are suffering or in need. Instead, it is a proud, united attempt by man to 'fix' this world apart from God, by means of his own wisdom and effort. As such, it constitutes an act of great rebellion against and opposition to God. Essentially, it involves a denial of the fact that this world is fallen and lies under God's judgment, and that salvation and hope for this world lie only in and through the saving work of the Lord Jesus Christ; moreover, it is a work of great human autonomy and pride. (*See the note at the end of the chapter for a fuller explanation of this.)

That said, there is no doubt that those pursuing international and religious unity and co-operation sincerely believe they are on a wise and good course. Moreover, this notion is boosted by the fact that some good can come out of collective effort. In fact, however, terrible deception is at work here — especially deception of the world's political and religious leaders who are leading the peoples into unity. The fact is that the course being pursued by the peoples to solve the problems of this fallen world will not and cannot succeed, because man himself is totally unable to 'fix' this world's problems and bring in a better world. Not only that, as an act of rebellion against God and his purposes, it is putting man in conflict with God and is inviting his judgement. The world's leaders and peoples, however, are blind to this. (It is tempting to understand the conflict pictured here in Revelation in terms of a literal war. However, we need to remember that, fundamentally, this world is caught up in a great spiritual battle between God and evil forces which shows itself in many forms — not least the godlessness of society and its opposition to the true God and his ways.)

(b) Secondly, also of note is that, coinciding with and significant to the gathering of the nations described above, has been a notable rise in secularism in the West, and a notable increase in the standing and influence of the pope in both the political and religious spheres.

(i) First of all, a clear characteristic of recent times (and particularly the years since the Second World War) has been a great movement in the western world away from Christianity and towards secularism — with the outlook of individuals, and of society as a whole, becoming increasingly secular, humanistic, and even atheistic. So, we find ourselves in a time, in the West, in which the beliefs and morals of individuals and of society are being shaped less and less by Christianity and more and more by human reason and wisdom; also, we find ourselves in a time in which the prevailing outlook and mindset is characterised by a focus on this present world and present life, and by a confidence in human ability to solve man's problems and meet his needs. Moreover, as part of this, we have seen: Christian truth being increasingly doubted, questioned and denied; knowledge of the Christian faith and Christian history becoming very poor in once-Christian countries; and even increasing resistance to Christianity (with Christianity becoming more and more marginalised and discriminated against).

Equally notable, however, is that this same time has also been marked by an increased interest, in the West, in pagan and occult practices, and in eastern mysticism. Such a trend can seem incompatible with a secular outlook. However, it is understandable, because with the rejection of Christianity and growth of secularism has come a spiritual void that it was inevitable man would fill; and a large number have filled this with things occult and mystical. Thus, in many respects, a rise in secularism and in mysticism have gone hand in hand.

Thus we are, in a sense, seeing the power of the dragon at work promoting heathenism and secularism in the once-Christian West, and bringing the peoples of the West more and more under the sway of the devil. Moreover, this is playing a crucial part in the once-Christian nations being caught up in the growing internationalism of our day.

(ii) A further clear feature of recent times has been a notable increase in the standing and influence of the pope in the political sphere. As touched on when discussing the fifth bowl judgement, following the Reformation there was a significant decline in the political influence and temporal power of the papacy, which reached a low point towards the end of the 1800s. By then the pope was no longer exercising power over the rulers and nations of Europe as once he had done, and he had lost his temporal rule over Rome and the Papal States. Moreover, it seemed as if he would not recover from this. However, since then, the pope's political standing and influence have been on the increase.

A particularly significant development came in 1929, when the Italian leader, Mussolini, made a concordat (or agreement) with the Roman Church, called the Lateran Treaty. This resulted in the establishing of Vatican City as a sovereign city-state, with the pope as its sovereign head — a development which allowed the pope once more to exercise his claim to be a sovereign ruler and not subject to any other leader. Moreover, the years since then, and particularly since the Second World War (at the end of which the pope's credibility was not good), have gone on to see a marked, more general increase in the pope's influence in the affairs of this the world.

Of course, at the present time the papacy cannot openly and assertively pursue its designs for power as once it did. Also, how much political influence the papacy actually exerts is impossible to know, although undoubtedly it is more than is seen; certainly, the papacy can exercise considerable 'behind the scenes' influence via leaders and other influential people who are faithful Roman Catholics, and via the wealth of the Vatican. What is clear, however, is that since the establishment of Vatican City as a sovereign state, the Vatican has been establishing diplomatic relations with the world's nations, and it is now not uncommon for statesmen and leaders to seek an audience with the pope. Added to this, the pope is increasingly being viewed as a great leader and peacemaker, and he is increasingly speaking out about political and social issues and calling on the world's leaders to address such things as injustice, poverty and environmental threats.

Thus, we are, in a sense, seeing the power of the beast at work advancing the pope's political power and influence in the world, and giving him a voice encouraging the world's nations in solving this world's problems.

(iii) Along with this, recent years have also seen a notable advance in the standing and influence of the pope as a religious leader, and of the Roman Catholic Church as a church. Also, the pope is playing an increasingly significant part in the promotion of church and interfaith unity, and is even being looked to as a natural focus for both church unity and interfaith unity. This marks a significant change and development.

Until relatively recently most Protestant churches, even if they did not go as far as identifying the pope of Rome as the Antichrist of Scripture, rightly viewed the Roman Catholic Church as apostate, and therefore kept themselves separate from it. Moreover, the pope, as a religious leader, was held in no special esteem by the non-Christian nations and religions, and even his standing in Roman Catholic countries had diminished. At the same time, on its part, the Catholic Church defined Protestants as 'heretics', and it regarded the other religions as pagan religions leading only to damnation. Recent times, however, have seen the Protestant and evangelical churches changing their attitude towards the Roman Catholic Church and viewing it as a true church; also, they have seen these churches seeking unity with the Catholic Church. Equally, recent times have seen the Roman Catholic Church adopting an altered, more conciliatory stance towards those outside the Catholic Church, and it involving itself in both church unity and interfaith initiatives.

A number of things have played a part in these changes of stance by both Protestantism and the Catholic Church. First of all, a crucial factor has been a loss of doctrinal clarity and conviction within the Protestant/evangelical churches, accompanied by an ignorance of the issues involved at the Reformation (so, few churches now hold to a distinctly Protestant stance). This has led to many within the Protestant/ evangelical fold adopting an altered stance towards the papacy and Catholic Church. Moreover, this, in turn, has been crucial to another development that has shaped where we are today — the ecumenical movement.

The modern ecumenical movement began at the beginning of the twentieth century. From the outset, its aim was to promote a broad, all-inclusive church unity encompassing the Protestant churches, the Orthodox Church and the Roman Catholic Church. Moreover, more recently it has extended its scope to include the promotion of interfaith dialogue and co-operation. In the pursuit of these goals, the movement has been highly successful. Especially, it has played a significant part in the Protestant/ evangelical churches accepting the Church of Rome as a true church. It has also been a vehicle for the papacy and Roman Catholic Church to gain increasing prestige and influence both within the church and within the wider religious sphere.

Another crucial factor has been the Second Vatican Council (1962–65). At this Church Council, measures were taken to modernise the Catholic Church. The effect was to give the impression that the Catholic Church was changing (although there was no fundamental reform of doctrine), and to boost acceptance of the Catholic Church as a true church. Alongside this, the Church also adopted an altered, more conciliatory stance towards other churches and the other faiths, marking the beginning of greater involvement by the Catholic Church in church unity and interfaith initiatives. So, this Council played a significant part in the papacy and Roman Church gaining in acceptance, prestige and influence. (Other, more recent, factors have been the Catholic Charismatic movement, which has served to authenticate the Church of Rome, and the high profile of recent popes, particularly John Paul II.)

Consequently, today we find the pope and the Roman Catholic Church playing an increasingly leading role in promoting church unity and interfaith unity; also, we find the pope being increasingly looked to as a focus for religious unity. Thus, we are, in a sense, seeing the power of the false prophet at work, advancing the standing and influence of the pope and the Roman Catholic Church in both the church and the wider religious world, and promoting a church unity and interfaith unity in which the papacy is playing a prominent part.

Returning, then, to the imagery of the sixth bowl judgement: earlier we saw that depicted in verses 13 and 14 are Satan (represented by a symbol that also portrays him acting through a heathen power) and the papacy (represented in its political and religious power) together exerting an influence over the leaders of the Christian world and the non-Christian world; we also saw that this was with the purpose of gathering them (and thus their people also) in some kind of collective opposition to God, to the final great battle and the great day of God's judgement. And, comparing this with the recent developments outlined above, and taking note of the historical point we have reached following the first five bowl judgements, there is much to indicate that in these recent developments we are seeing the fulfilment of what is depicted here under the sixth bowl judgement.

Certainly, in the current pursuit of international and religious unity and co-operation in an attempt to solve this world's problems, we are seeing a kind of gathering of the nations and peoples in opposition to God and his purposes. Equally, in the rise of secularism in the West, and in the increasing standing and influence of the pope and the Catholic Church, we are, in a sense, seeing the power of the dragon, beast and false prophet at work. Therefore, there are grounds to conclude that we are living in the time of the sixth bowl judgement. Not only that, there is much to suggest that we are in the midst of Satan's last great effort in his rebellion against God.

An important question that remains is how far the international and religious unity of our day will develop. This needs to be considered because it is the belief of some (especially those who regard the Antichrist and his reign as still future), that we are heading for the establishing of a one-world government and one-world religious body, headed by the Antichrist; so, we should consider if this is the case. Certainly, a great, centralised, world political and religious system could issue from the growing international and religious unity of our day. However, the last chapters of Revelation do not depict such a thing appearing near the end. Moreover, as understood here, the reign of the Antichrist (the pope of Rome) does not lie in the future but is now past (we are now in the time of his judgement). Therefore, there would seem to be no real ground to be looking for the establishing of a one-world government and one-world religious body. Rather, it would seem more likely that we will see little more than the world's nations, and the world's apostate churches and false religions, having membership of and acting together in various international and interfaith political and religious bodies.

Whatever final form this international and religious unity ultimately takes, however, we might expect the pope to be a prominent and influential figure. Also, we might expect to hear much said about a new age of peace, safety and prosperity for mankind. Not only that, as these developments progress, we can anticipate that there will be an acceptance and tolerance of everything except the true church which, as it stands apart and faithfully proclaims the coming judgement of God and salvation through Christ alone, will be increasingly opposed.

Finally, in considering in detail the nature of the gathering depicted here, it is crucial that we do not lose sight of the fundamental point that this is happening in God's purpose, and it is a part of God's judgement. As noted above, this gathering is depicted under the sixth bowl of God's wrath, and thus it is part of God's judgement upon the papacy and upon all his enemies. Moreover, it is a gathering to "the battle of that great day of God Almighty" — a description which makes clear that the gathering and rebellion depicted here is to culminate not in a great victory for God's enemies, but in a day of God's judgement (that great day of God Almighty).

Therefore, if we are now seeing the fulfilment of the gathering depicted here, then it has to be concluded that such things as the rise of secularism in the West, the increasing standing and influence of the papacy, and the growing international and religious unity of our time, are happening as part of God's judgement. Essentially, these developments are part of a final great rebellion against God which is happening in God's purpose to bring the pope, and with him the whole apostate church and godless world, to a day of judgement.

Seeing this is important, because it helps us to have the right perspective on what is happening in our day. There can be a tendency to look at such things as the rise of secularism in the

West, the resurgence of papal power, and the all-embracing church and interfaith unity of our time, and to be dismayed and discouraged, and to think that the devil is getting the upper hand. However, if we understand that, in these developments, we are seeing the fulfilment of the sixth bowl judgement, and that God has purposed these things as part of his judgement of the papacy and all his enemies, then this will be strengthening. It will help us not to lose heart, but instead to be strong and full of confidence in the face of all these trends.

(NB: This godless world has always been destined for judgement; so, a question that all of this raises is why God has purposed this gathering in rebellion unto judgement when it would be perfectly just for God to judge the godless world without this. The answer would seem to be that this rebellion serves to make evident the antagonism of the world to God, and therefore to make apparent the justice of God's judgement.)

v15. Then, having given to John this revelation concerning the gathering of the peoples to the battle of that great day of God Almighty, Christ issues a direct warning to his people to be prepared for that day.

First of all, Christ announces and calls his people to be aware that he is coming as a thief. This is a reminder that his coming in judgement will be sudden, at a time we do not know; it is also a reminder of the danger of not being ready (see Mt 24:42–44).

Then, after alerting them to this danger, Christ shows his people what is needful to be prepared. He encourages them to watch and to keep their garments — to be vigilant and constantly on guard, and to be diligent to be walking in holiness (to be continuing in God's ways and truth) when he comes. Moreover, he encourages them to this by setting before them the consequences of doing or not doing this. The one who does this will be blessed — he will know the blessing and joy of those who walk with God. Conversely, the one who does not do this will walk naked and his shame will be seen — he will be exposed as unprepared and will be put to shame at this crucial time in the world's history (in fact, he will be like those outside the people of God). Whether the judgement in view here will come with Christ's actual return, or whether God is going to pour out some kind of judgement upon the papacy and world prior to this is not clear (this will be considered later). What is plain from Christ's statement, however, is the need for God's people to be prepared for that day by constantly being alert and walking in holiness of life.

The importance to us of what Christ says here cannot be over-emphasised. If we truly are in the days of the gathering to the battle of that great day of God Almighty, then these words are directly relevant to us and need to be heeded by us with great earnestness. We need to be making sure that we understand the time in which we live, that we are keeping constantly alert to all that is happening, and that we are keeping separate from all that is not of God and are walking in holiness of life. Moreover, we need to heed the warning of the consequence of not doing this — we will not be ready for this great day of judgment, and will be put to shame.

All the evidence is, however, that a very large proportion of the professing church (including the evangelical church) has no awareness of the significance of what is happening in our day, and is not prepared for what lies ahead. In fact, worse than this, a very large proportion of the church is actually caught up in the gathering, particularly through involvement in the church unity initiatives being promoted by the ecumenical movement (which is promoting unity and co-operation with the Roman Catholic Church and other churches that have departed from the faith). In short, rather than the church today being characterised by the watchfulness and holiness of life that is urged upon us here and that is so needed in our day, there is instead a woeful lack of alertness and discernment, and of commitment to walking in God's ways and truth.

However, mercifully, there is still the opportunity for us to heed Christ's warning and to make ourselves ready, and this we must now do. Prayerfully seeking God and depending on his grace, we must prepare ourselves for all that is to come by furnishing ourselves with truth, by not endorsing or involving ourselves in things such as the church unity being promoted by the ecumenical movement, by keeping alert, and by walking in holiness of life. Then, as the apostate churches and the world gather in their rebellion against God and are finally judged, we will be truly standing with God and will not be put to shame on that day.

v16. Following this, we are then told that "they [the unclean spirits] gathered them [the kings] together to the place called in Hebrew, Armageddon". So, having seen the kings and peoples being gathered to the battle of that great day of God Almighty (v13–14), we are now told the place to which they are gathered — to Armageddon.

Today, it not uncommon for Armageddon to be regarded as a literal place of conflict. However, in this context Armageddon is not meant to be taken as a literal site of battle; rather, it portrays something about the coming great battle, and it again shows us that the gathering depicted here is a gathering to judgement. Of note here is that John tells us that Armageddon is a Hebrew word. This prompts us to consider its meaning; and a common suggestion is that it means 'mount or hill of Megiddo'. If so, in this context the significance of this would seem to be that it was in the vicinity of Megiddo that God gave the Israelites a great deliverance and victory under the leadership of Deborah and Barak (see Judg 5:19) — a deliverance in which God drew out and subdued Israel's enemy, and their enemy was destroyed (see Judg 4:6–7,23–24). So, historically, Megiddo was a place of great conflict and judgement; and in line with this, Armageddon is symbolic of the final decisive conflict and final overthrow of all the forces gathered against God.

So, under this sixth bowl judgement, we see the enemies of God being gathered in one final great rebellion to judgement. This gathering is a work of evil forces, but it is part of God's preordained purpose. We are yet to see the full manifestation of this gathering against God, which will culminate in God's intervention in judgement. However, it does seem that we are seeing this gathering taking place in our day; and in the midst of this we must recognise what is happening, separate ourselves from all that is not of God and, heeding the words of Christ, endeavour to be constantly watchful and to walk in holiness of life.

The pouring out of the seventh bowl (16:17–21)

Having seen the peoples being gathered together to Armageddon, John might have expected to then see the final great battle itself. However, as already noted, this is not depicted until later; instead, next, under the seventh bowl, John is shown the judgement of Babylon — the Roman Catholic Church. Babylon's fall (her judgement) was announced earlier (see 14:8); now we are to see her great fall.

v17. So, John saw the seventh angel pour out his bowl. And this was poured "into the air". And "a loud voice came out of the temple of heaven, from the throne, saying, 'It is done!'"

Thus this seventh bowl judgement falls on the air; and this, most probably, signifies it falling on the domain of the devil, who elsewhere is described as the prince of the power of the air (see Eph 2:2). So, what is in view here is some judgement of the devil; and, in this context, it would seem to portray the devil's power being restrained and his purposes thwarted. The devil had engineered the rise of Babylon, and by it had deceived the world. Now he would be able to do this no longer; his activities were to be stopped — Babylon was to be brought down. Furthermore, the finality of this is made apparent in the proclamation coming from the temple, saying "It is done!" This is the voice of God announcing that this is the climax and completion of his judgement. The final judgement of Babylon, depicted here, is the finishing stroke — the climax and completion of the pouring out of God's wrath on this antichristian system.

v18,19. John then tells us "there were noises and thunderings and lightnings". These are symbols expressing the awesome power of God, and they instil a sense of awe and heighten the expectation of the great judgement to come. John also tells us "there was a great earthquake" (a symbol of great upheaval), one so great and mighty that it was of a kind that "had not occurred since men were on the earth". Moreover, he goes on to describe the effect of the earthquake — "the great city [Babylon] was divided into three parts, and the cities of the nations fell".

This clearly represents the final bringing down of Babylon. It would also seem to show Babylon's downfall involving not just the seat of power of this antichristian system but extending worldwide. So, under this last bowl judgement, we see finally coming to pass what was previously announced — the fall of Babylon (see 14:8). Moreover, fittingly this judgement is further described as great Babylon being "remembered before God, to give her the cup of the wine of the fierceness of His wrath". This, of course, does not mean that, before this, God had forgotten Babylon. Rather, this makes clear that this was now the appointed time for Babylon's judgement. God may have seemed to have overlooked Babylon's sin, but her judgement was awaiting his time; and this was now the time for God to pour out his judgement in fullness.

v20,21. John then tells us "every island fled away, and the mountains were not found". This picture of the earth's permanent landmarks disappearing, further depicts what a great upheaval the fall of Babylon will be.

He also tells us "great hail from heaven fell upon men, each hailstone about the weight of a talent" (a talent is around 34kg — so this is hail like great boulders, of an enormous size and weight). And he describes the response: "men blasphemed God because of the plague of the hail, since that plague was exceedingly great". This symbolises a terrible judgement falling upon men, and perhaps especially shows that for those associated with Babylon, her fall will be a crushing blow. The response to this judgement, however, is that men blasphemed God. Again we see God's judgement leading not to repentance but to the hardening of people's hearts. This is a judicial hardening, because it is God's purpose to judge those in opposition to him.

We come then to consider the possible fulfilment of all of this. As already noted, Babylon is a figure for the Roman Catholic Church. Thus what is depicted here is some great final judgement of the Church of Rome (which now has as its seat of power, Vatican City in Rome). Her judgement began at the time of the Reformation, but for a time, in spite of all her sins, she has been allowed by God to continue. However, she was always destined for final judgement, and this is depicted here.

Clearly, this is something to come in the future, and therefore we cannot say exactly what will happen. It is also not totally clear how this judgement fits in with the judgement of "that great day of God Almighty" (16:14) (whether or not it will be at that time); nor is it clear whether this judgement will coincide with Christ's return or whether some terrible disaster will befall the Church of Rome prior to this (these matters are considered later, in Chapter 19). Certainly, however, this depicts the bringing down of the Roman Catholic Church. Moreover, it would seem to show that this judgment will fall upon not just the seat of power of the Church of Rome but on the Roman Church worldwide, and that it will be a time of great upheaval and will be a crushing blow for those associated with her.

To say much more than this would be to engage in unwarranted speculation. Plainly, the actual fulfilment of this will not be known until it happens (which may or may not be within the lifetime of people living now). What we can be certain of, however, is that the Roman Catholic Church will fall. The importance to us of knowing this is that it should reinforce to us both the urgency of calling people out of the Roman Catholic Church, and the absolute necessity for us to keep separate from or to come out of any association with the Roman Catholic Church, so that we do not share in her judgement.

Note on the gathering of our day: Clearly, we live in a world blighted by such things as war and conflict, famine, poverty and injustice, and growing environmental threats. Such problems, of course, are nothing new. The difference today, however, is that in our age of rapid global communications, the global scale and impact of all these things is plainly evident. This global perspective has given rise to a global response. At the heart of this is the notion that the world must act together to tackle this world's problems, and that the key to overcoming the world's problems is international and interreligious unity and co-operation.

On the surface, this seems a good and sensible response to the challenges facing the world today (especially since the alleviation of human suffering is a good and worthy pursuit). However, a scriptural assessment of man's united attempt to overcome this world's problems and bring in a better world indicates that, essentially, it is not good. In fact, it constitutes an act of rebellion against and opposition to God. In order to see this, two things are necessary. The first is an understanding of what Scripture teaches us about this world's condition and God's solution to this world's need. The second is an understanding of the true nature of the solution that the world is pursuing.

First of all, Scripture is clear that, in the beginning, God created a perfect world — a world that was 'very good' (Gen 1:31). At the pinnacle of God's creation was man — a unique being who God created in his image, to enjoy a special relationship with himself, with his fellow man and with creation. As such, God created this world to exist in a state of harmony or peace — a state in which everything in creation, and all the relationships that man was created to enjoy, are as God intended.

Plainly, however, the world in which we live is not in this state of wholeness and peace; and the root cause is the fall, and man's rebellion against God. Soon after God created this world, which was 'very good', into God's creation came rebellion against him. First, Satan rebelled. Then man, under Satan's influence, rebelled: he disobeyed God (Gen 3:1–7). And, the consequence of man's rebellion against God has been a loss of peace/wholeness in this creation as all the relationships man was created to enjoy broke down and the whole world came under God's judgement. So, as we look at this world with all its wickedness, disharmony, exploitation, suffering and disarray, we are looking at a world which is far removed from all that God created it to be. Moreover, we are looking at a world where the root cause is the fall — it is man's rebellion against God.

Not only that, man himself is powerless to put things right. The reason for this impotence lies in the fundamental causes of all the wickedness and disharmony in this world: man's rebellion against God, his consequent inherent sinfulness, and God's judgement upon the world. These are things that man in his sinfulness will not acknowledge; equally, they are things that man is powerless to overcome. Consequently, man is without the ability to solve or eradicate this world's problems, and any attempts he makes cannot succeed. Rather, so long as this world goes on, there will continue to be godlessness and wickedness in the world, there will continue to be wars and injustice and want, and there will continue to be disorder in the creation, no matter what men do in an effort to put this right.

However, there is hope for mankind, and this lies in God's saving work in and through the Lord Jesus Christ. Fundamentally, this world has always been Christ's. Now, God is restoring all things in and through him. At the very heart of this is Christ's death on the cross (see Col 1:19–20; also Eph 1:7-10). By this, Christ atoned for man's sin and defeated the devil, and he bought for man forgiveness, redemption and reconciliation. Now, in and through Christ, God is saving men from their sin, he is re-establishing his rule, and he is restoring peace/wholeness once more. *In doing this, however, God is not patching up or restoring the present creation. Instead, in and through Christ, he is making all things new: he is doing a work of new creation (2 Cor 5:17; Rev 21:1–5). Moreover, he is not accomplishing this all at once, but in two stages — beginning in this present age and then completing his renewing work at Christ's return.*

This, then, is God's gracious plan of salvation for mankind. By it, God has wonderfully provided for man a salvation that is totally against man's deserving, and that man himself is powerless to achieve. Also, he has provided a salvation for this world — a world which, because of the fall, is in disarray and doomed, and which man himself cannot restore and save. It follows, therefore, that Christ is the hope of mankind. Particularly, it follows that the Christian's hope is not in man and his ability to 'save' the world and bring in a better world; rather, it is in Christ, his saving work, his return and the life to come.

Today, however, we are seeing the peoples of this world engaged in a very different plan to overcome this world's problems and, in a sense, rescue this world. This plan is for the world's nations and religions to come together and work together in tackling the problems that beset our world. However, no matter how sensible this whole approach might seem, or what good it accomplishes, the reality is that this grand plan of man is being pursued in opposition to God and his purpose for man. Essentially, what we are seeing is man, faced with this world's problems, pursuing his own solution independent of God and Christ: what we are seeing is him endeavouring to bring peace/wholeness to this world by means of, and trusting in, his own wisdom and power.

This great scheme of man stems from the fall when man set himself on a path of rebellion against God, and when man sought to be independent of God and to judge for himself what is wise and good (Gen 3:1–6). More significantly, it is typified in the building of Babel (Gen 11:1–9) — a grandiose project which is the prototype of all man's attempts, by collective effort, to control his own fortunes, and to make himself safe and secure. Fundamentally, in the building of Babel, we see men, in rejection of God's purpose for them, joining together and, by their own ingenuity and effort, creating their own society and religion. Moreover, we see them doing this to achieve for themselves safety and prosperity, and for their own glory. Thus, Babel stands as the first example of a collective project and endeavour by men to achieve peace and safety on earth — all carried out in independence of God and in pride, and all for the glory of man.

No doubt, to the builders of Babel this whole project seemed wise and good. However, it was not of God; it was opposed to God's will and purpose for them and was carried out in rebellion against and opposition to God. Consequently, it displeased God — a displeasure seen in God eventually judging this project by confusing their languages and scattering them into all the earth.

However, although God's judgement brought a scattering and separation of the people, this did not rid man of the tendency to try again to build a form of Babel. And this is very relevant to our time, when we see man engaged in another collective endeavour to secure peace and safety for mankind — ie, the pursuit of international and religious unity and co-operation as the key to overcoming this world's problems and bringing in a better world. Again, on the surface, this grand scheme of man appears wise and good. In fact, however, it has all the characteristics of the building of Babel. Particularly, it is being pursued in rejection of and opposition to God and his purpose for man: it constitutes a denial of the fact that this world is fallen and under God's judgement, and that salvation and hope for this world lie in and through the Lord Jesus Christ. Moreover, it is a work of human pride: it is being pursued out of a desire in man to control his own destiny apart from God; and it is being undertaken in the belief that man, by his own wisdom and effort, is capable of overcoming the problems that beset this world. So, it is something which ultimately glorifies man, as it stands as a monument to man's wisdom and ingenuity.

Given this, it must be concluded that, although God has allowed the world to pursue its course for some time, just as God eventually brought the building of Babel to a halt, he will do the same with this present great endeavour of man. Of course, even without God's intervention, this project of man cannot succeed because man himself cannot solve the evils and problems of this fallen world. However, we might also expect God, at some point, to intervene and bring man's great project to a halt. Whether this will be brought about by Christ's return, or by some other major event prior to this, is not clear. However, the final fate of Babel indicates that God will not allow this great endeavour of mankind to go on indefinitely. Rather, in due time, God will judge it and bring it to an end.

(Again, all of this is discussed more fully in 'Internationalism, Ecumenism & The End Times — Where ecumenism is leading the churches', 2018, by the same author.)

Chapter 17
The woman upon the beast

U nder the pouring out of the seventh bowl, John was shown the final judgement of Babylon (of the Roman Catholic Church). However, this was not all that Christ had to show John about Babylon's judgement; so now, as a new series of visions opens up, John is given further and fuller revelation concerning the wickedness and destruction of this great antichristian system.

The woman seated on the beast (17:1–6)

v1,2. After seeing the judgement of Babylon depicted under the seventh bowl, John tells us that then one of the angels who had the seven bowls came and talked with him, saying to him, "Come, I will show you the judgement of the great harlot who sits on many waters, with whom the kings of the earth committed fornication, and the inhabitants of the earth were made drunk with the wine of her fornication." From verse 5 it is clear that this harlot and Babylon represent the same entity; thus, John is again to be shown the judgement of Babylon, now depicted as a harlot — an image that further displays the great wickedness of this worldly antichristian system, and that makes clear that its judgement is just.

The imagery of a harlot portrays one who is sexually immoral, and in the Old Testament is used, in the main, to describe the unfaithful people of God (eg, Ezek 16:15ff; 23:1ff; Hos 2:2ff). Here, this represents a false church — one which is unfaithful to Christ, which professes to belong to him but is given to idolatry and worldliness. However, this is not just any false church but the great false church of Antichrist. This, we are told, is the great harlot who sits on many waters — who has sway over the nations (see v15). This is the great harlot with whom the kings of the earth committed fornication — this is the one who allured the kings of the earth, so that they joined in her sins against God, and joined themselves with her in some kind of unholy alliance. And this is the great harlot who made drunk the inhabitants of the earth with the wine of her fornication — this is the one who intoxicated the peoples with her idolatry and worldliness, and seduced them to join with her in her wickedness. So this harlot depicts not merely a false church, but the great false church of Antichrist that is given to idolatry and worldliness, that holds sway over the nations, and that drew the rulers and peoples to share in her sins. And it is for all this wickedness that this great harlot is to be judged.

Here, then, we have another depiction of the Roman Catholic Church (the church of Antichrist), now portrayed as a harlot. And this harlot is an accurate representation of the Roman Church which professes faithfulness to Christ but is given to idolatry and worldly religion; which (especially in the Middle Ages) held sway over the nations; which has seduced kings into an unholy alliance with her; and which, by means of her alluring idolatries and practices, has made the peoples senseless and drawn them away to share in her sins. For all of this, the Roman Catholic Church is being judged.

v3. Having summoned John to see the judgement of the great harlot, the angel then carried John away in the Spirit into the wilderness, where John was shown this harlot. We will remember that the wilderness was the place that God had prepared for his church, where he would protect her and provide for her during the time of the reign of the Antichrist (see 12:6,13-14). This is a place apart from the apostasy of the Roman Catholic Church; and it is only in this position that we will see this harlot for who she is.

And John tells us what he saw. He says he saw "a woman sitting on a scarlet beast [scarlet is a colour of splendour] which was full of names of blasphemy, having seven heads and ten horns". This beast bears resemblance to the beast from the sea, described in chapter 13 (see v1), which represented papal Rome (the papal dominion). Thus this great harlot is portrayed associated with papal Rome, and having her seat there — which, of course, is true of the Church of Rome.

v4. John also tells us that the woman "was arrayed in purple and scarlet, and adorned with gold and precious stones and pearls". Thus this woman displayed great status, splendour and riches. These are things that the world loves and finds desirable; so, all her attractiveness consists in worldly status, splendour and riches, and she is powerfully attractive to those with worldly and sensual minds. Also, she had in her hand "a golden cup full of abominations and the filthiness of her fornication". Thus this woman is portrayed holding something that seems very desirable and good; however, her attractive, impressive golden cup is, in fact, full of abominable and filthy things — it is full of her idolatries and impurities which she is enticing others to partake of. So there is strong delusion involved here — this woman has something that seems good and desirable, but it is exceedingly evil.

Again, this is an accurate representation of the Roman Catholic Church, portraying its worldly and sensual allure by which it draws people into its sins. This allure lies above all in the Roman Catholic religion, which is one of great ritual and richness and pomp and beauty. Thus it is a very sensuous religion and very attractive to unsaved mankind; and it is by means of this that the Roman Catholic Church draws men to herself and so draws them to share in her idolatrous and worldly religion. Moreover, the Roman Catholic Church also has great worldly power and wealth; and it has been by means of this power and wealth that the Roman Church has attracted to herself the rulers and merchants of the earth (see chapter 18), thus drawing them into an unholy alliance with her and into her sins.

v5. John then adds, "and on her forehead a name was written: MYSTERY, BABYLON THE GREAT, THE MOTHER OF HARLOTS AND OF THE ABOMINATIONS OF THE EARTH".

This name reveals something further about this woman. First, the visibility of her name (on her forehead for all to see) indicates the open guilt and shamelessness of this woman. Then, each part of her name has something more to show us.

The initial term "Mystery" introduces her name, and it indicates that the significance of her name and her identity is not apparent to all, but is known only by divine revelation. Thus, it shows us that, although her sin is open for all to see, to the worldly (including those only nominally Christian) her name will be hidden, and they will not know the true identity of this one — they will think this is a true church. Also, however, it encourages us to know that true believers will know the identity of this woman.

Her name is then given as "Babylon the Great". This draws a resemblance between this woman and Babylon of old, which was noted for its idolatrous pagan religion. Thus the church represented by this woman, that gives the appearance of being a Christian church, is shown in fact to be the home of idolatrous paganism. This is true of the Roman Catholic Church — her religion is not truly Christian, but essentially is paganism in a Christianized form. By the name "Babylon" it is also made clear that this harlot represents the same entity as the great city, whose fall has already been announced and depicted (see 14:8; 16:19).

She is also termed "the Mother of Harlots and of the Abominations of the Earth". This depicts this woman as the origin of all the idolatries of the apostate churches and of the Christian world as a whole. Thus, the Roman Catholic Church is shown to be not just the repository of idolatrous paganism, but also the source of all the idolatries of Christendom.

v6. Lastly, John tells us that he saw the woman "drunk with the blood of the saints and with the blood of the martyrs of Jesus" — he saw her intoxicated from persecuting and killing God's people. The mention here of martyrs (witnesses) in addition to saints may show that in carrying out this persecution she was not ignorant of the truth — a witness had been made. Moreover, the drunkenness of the woman indicates she had killed a great many of God's people, and had found great pleasure in this. This plainly portrays the Roman Catholic Church's persecution of the true church, and perhaps especially the severe persecution of the true church in the centuries prior to and at the time of the Reformation, when thousands of true believers were cruelly killed.

John then adds that when he saw this woman, he "marvelled with great amazement". Here John's wonderment was not merely because this pictured great wickedness and terrible persecution; John would have known that until Christ returned, the world would be full of wickedness and it would cruelly persecute the church. Rather, he marvelled because this was a church — a great false church, displaying great worldliness, full of idolatry and intoxicated from persecuting the people of God.

The meaning of the woman and the beast (17:7–18)

v7. Quickly, however, the angel questions John's amazement at seeing this woman, asking, "Why did you marvel?" No doubt, if we had seen what John saw, our first response would have been, as his was, to marvel with great amazement. But this woman should not cause amazement. False religion always has been, and always will be, amongst the people of God and characterised by all worldliness and fierce opposition to the true church. So, we should not be surprised when we encounter apostasy in the church, or when we suffer fierce opposition from those who profess to be Christians; particularly, we should not be amazed at the great sin and fierce opposition of the Roman Catholic Church.

The angel then undertakes to tell John "the mystery of the woman and of the beast that carries her, which has the seven heads and the ten horns". So now the identity of the woman and the beast is to be revealed. What follows, however, is not a plain unveiling of their identity, but more symbolic portrayals. Nevertheless, as these are followed through, the identity becomes clear.

v8. First, the angel explains to John that the beast he saw "was, and is not, and will ascend out of the bottomless pit and go to perdition". As already noted, this beast bears resemblance to the beast from the sea in chapter 13. In that description of the beast we were told that one of his heads was as if it had been mortally wounded, and his deadly wound was healed (see 13:3). Now we are told that the beast was, and is not, and will ascend out of the bottomless pit. These two descriptions convey the same idea — that this beast represents a power that is a kind of resurrection or revival of a power that once existed and then ceased to exist. And, as already discussed in the comments on chapter 13, this beast represents the papacy and its dominion in the world, which arose as a kind of revival and continuation of the old Roman emperor and Empire (the papal dominion, centred at Rome, ascended out of the ruins of the Roman Empire and occupied its place).

Also of note here is that the revival of this beast is described in terms of it ascending out of the bottomless pit. This shows this beast to be associated with evil forces and to be an instrument of Satan. It also identifies it with the beast in chapter 11 (see v7) which was shown persecuting the true church before the Reformation. Equally of note is that this beast is said to go to perdition. This shows that this beast is destined for destruction. Moreover, the fact that its appearance and destruction are linked together in one statement, without any details in between, stresses that destruction is the beast's certain end (from its appearance, this was its only end). Thus this makes clear the Satanic origin and certain final destruction of the papal system.

The angel then adds, "And those who dwell on the earth will marvel, whose names are not written in the Book of Life from the foundation of the world, when they see the beast that was, and is not, and yet is." This again echoes the words of chapter 13 (see v3) and shows the unbelieving world's response to the papacy being one of great wonder (which was especially the case during the Middle Ages). The comfort to us is that those who are bedazzled are only those whose names are not written in the book of life. This gives us confidence that the true church will not be taken in.

v9,10. The angel then goes on to give John further insight into the identity of this beast, making clear the need of wisdom (wisdom from God) in order to understand. So again we see that the meaning of these things is not plain for all to see; but we are also encouraged to know that God's people, who have God's wisdom, will understand these things.

First the angel explains, "The seven heads are seven mountains [which could also be termed hills] on which the woman sits." These seven mountains/hills point to Rome, the city on seven hills. Thus this beast is shown to be a great power governing from Rome. And here the woman sits; she resides at Rome — this is the seat of her influence.

Then John is told, "There are also seven kings. Five have fallen, one is, and the other has not yet come. And when he comes, he must continue a short time." These seven kings (which would seem to follow one other) most probably represent the seven forms of Roman government that existed during the development and history of the Roman power. In John's time five were past (kings, consuls, tribunes, decemviri, dictators), one was currently in existence (pagan emperors), and one was yet to come (Christian emperors).

v11. Next, the angel further explains, "The beast that was, and is not, is himself also the eighth, and is of the seven, and is going to perdition." This shows us that the beast, which was shown to be a kind of revival of the fallen Roman Empire, is a further type of government from Rome. This, of course, has been fulfilled in the papacy, which rose up in the place of the deposed Roman emperors (then Christian) and exercised great dominion from Rome. And this is the power whose end is perdition/

destruction. This shows us that nothing will follow this stage in the career of the beast — this is the final manifestation of its power, and then it will be destroyed.

v12. John is also told that the ten horns which he saw "are ten kings who have received no kingdom as yet, but they receive authority for one hour as kings with the beast". Some take the view that these kings are to appear near to the very end, and for a time will zealously serve the interests of the papacy. However, another interpretation, which would seem to be better, is that these ten kings represent the kingdoms that the Roman Empire broke up into when it fell (see 13:1 for the same imagery). In John's time these kings and kingdoms were still future (they had received no kingdom as yet); but when they came (following the fall of the Empire in the fifth century), for a short time they ruled with the beast — they were not under the power of the papacy but simply ruled over their lands alongside the pope, who by then had control of certain lands in and around Rome, and later of certain provinces in Italy. However, things were soon to change, as described in the following verses.

v13,14. John is then told that these kings "are of one mind, and they will give their power and authority to the beast". After a time of free rule, the rulers of the lands of Europe, caught up in a common delusion (they were of one mind), began to submit themselves to the pope and to serve the interests of the papacy.

He is also told that these (the kings) "will make war with the Lamb" — a consequence of their submission to and service of the papacy was that these rulers opposed the true gospel and persecuted the true church. (In many instances the papacy's fierce persecution of the church was not carried out directly, but through the agency of temporal rulers and authorities who lent themselves to the persecution carried out by the pope.) However, the angel adds, "the Lamb will overcome them, for He is Lord of lords and King of kings; and those who are with Him are called, chosen and faithful". So, we are assured that the victory would lie with Christ and the people of God, first because Christ is over all and all are subject to him, and also because his people are called and chosen by him, and kept faithful.

v15,16. Having explained these things, the angel then explains to John the meaning of the waters which he saw, where the harlot sits (see v1) — these are "peoples, multitudes, nations and tongues". So, attention is again drawn to the power exercised by the harlot (by the Roman Catholic Church) over the peoples and nations.

However, John is then told that the ten horns (the ten kings) which he saw on the beast "will hate the harlot, make her desolate and naked, eat her flesh and burn her with fire". This depicts the rulers, after a time of subjecting themselves to the papacy and serving its interests, coming to hate the Roman Catholic Church and turning against it, and laying it waste and destroying it. So we see that the Roman Catholic Church is to fall at the hands of these rulers — God's purpose is that they are to be the instrument of her judgement.

Those who take the view that these kings are to appear near to the very end, naturally see this turning against and destruction of the Roman Catholic Church as entirely in the future. However, if we take these kings to represent the kingdoms that the Roman Empire broke up into, then it would seem that what is depicted here has to some degree been being fulfilled since the time of the Reformation, although it is yet to reach a climax (the Roman Catholic Church is yet to be totally destroyed). Certainly, at the time of the Reformation, those nations that became Protestant turned against the Roman Catholic Church and eliminated it from their lands. Moreover, following the Reformation there was a reaction against the Roman Catholic Church even in those countries that remained Roman Catholic. In many of these countries there was a strong reaction against the Church's power and influence in temporal matters, which led to such actions as the restriction of the Church's powers and activities, the confiscation of her property and money, and in some cases actual church burning. Thus there has already been some reaction against the Roman Catholic Church. It would seem, however, that what is described here is yet to be fully fulfilled; and this passage would seem to lead us to expect that in the future there will be further hostility towards the Roman Catholic Church (as an institution), perhaps especially by the leaders of Europe, that brings her final downfall.

That said, a pertinent question to ask at this point would be how this relates to the last three bowl judgements, which also depict God's bringing down of the papacy and the Roman Catholic Church. Considering these in turn, first under the fifth bowl judgement we saw God's judgement falling upon the throne of the beast/papacy and his rule or kingdom being brought down. And this concerned the papacy's loss of political influence and temporal power during the centuries following the Reformation — which, notably, happened at the hands of the rulers and peoples of Europe, who turned against the Roman Catholic Church (as outlined above). Then, under the sixth bowl judgement we saw Satan and the papal system, through deception, gathering the leaders of the Christian world and the rest of the world in some form of collective rebellion against God, to the final great battle and to judgement. And, in discussing this it was suggested that we are seeing at least the beginnings of this in our own day in the increased standing and influence of the pope and the Roman Catholic Church, and the trends towards political and religious unity. If this is so, then it explains why, in our day, the hostility previously shown towards the Roman Catholic Church seems to have ceased. Finally, under the seventh bowl judgement we saw the final judgement and downfall of the Roman Catholic Church, which is yet to come. And the fact that here, in verse 16, this is shown taking place at the hands of the kings, suggests that at some time there will be a renewed turning against the Roman Catholic Church, perhaps especially by the leaders of Europe (now gathered into the European Union), that finally brings her down.

Thus the last three bowl judgements would seem to cover the period of the kings' hostility towards the Roman Catholic

Church, while also making sense of this present time when hostility towards the Roman Catholic Church seems to have ceased. They also are compatible with the notion that in the future there will be further hostility towards the Roman Catholic Church that will bring her final downfall.

v17. Having described the kings' submission to the beast and their subsequent antagonism to the harlot, the angel then adds, "for God has put it into their hearts to fulfil His purpose, to be of one mind, and to give their kingdom to the beast, until the words of God are fulfilled". This makes it clear that all of this is happening in the preordained purpose of God. It was God's purpose that the rulers should submit themselves to and serve the purpose of the papacy — they collectively were judicially blinded and hardened to do this. Moreover, this was to the end that, at the time that God had ordained, they would resent this subjection and would turn against the Roman Catholic Church and bring it down, thus serving as his instrument of her judgement.

v18. Finally, in case there is any doubt about the identity of the harlot (the great false church in view here), the angel makes clear her identity with Rome. The angel tells John that the woman whom he saw "is that great city which reigns over the kings of the earth". From John's perspective, Rome was the great city that held sway over the nations. Thus, this harlot (this great false church) is identified with Rome — finally making clear that she is the Church of Rome, which from Rome (the seat of her power) has exercised power over the rulers and peoples of Christendom.

In summary, the Roman Catholic Church perfectly fulfils the description of the harlot given here. Moreover, what is explained here about the beast and the harlot is being fulfilled in the history of the papacy and the Roman Catholic Church. The papal dominion rose up as a kind of revival of the old Roman Empire. In the Middle Ages the Roman Catholic Church held sway over the nations of Europe, and the rulers submitted themselves to the papacy and served its purposes, especially in the persecution of the true church. However, from the Reformation onwards the rulers turned against the Roman Church and rejected her power over them — which marked the beginning of her demise. However, we are yet to see the full downfall of the Roman Catholic Church; and what is depicted here suggests that although, at present, hostility towards the Roman Church seems to have ceased (which can be explained by the sixth bowl judgement), in the future there will be renewed hostility towards her, ending in her final downfall. It must be said, however, that since this concerns things yet to happen, time alone will reveal if this is to be the manner of the Church of Rome's downfall.

Chapter 18
The fall of Babylon the great

Following on from the explanation of the woman and the beast, we come in this chapter to the final judgement of Babylon and the response of the world to this. In this chapter, the imagery turns back to that of Babylon the great city (the imagery used under the seventh bowl, see 16:19), here combined with descriptions that were applied (in chapter 17) to the harlot. This switching and mingling of imagery is no ground for confusion since it all concerns the same entity — the Roman Catholic Church.

The fall of Babylon the great (18:1–8)

v1. After being told of the judgement of the harlot at the hands of the ten kings, John then saw "another angel coming down from heaven, having great authority". The description of this angel as having great authority stresses that what he is to pronounce will most certainly happen. We are also told, "the earth was illuminated with his glory". This indicates that the pronouncement of this angel is for all the earth — it is something that all the earth needs to know.

v2. And the angel cried mightily with a loud voice (so all could hear), saying, "Babylon the great is fallen, is fallen, and has become a dwelling place of demons, a prison for every foul spirit, and a cage for every unclean and hated bird!" The announcement that Babylon is fallen repeats the announcement recorded in chapter 14 (see v8) which, in the historical framework of Revelation, came at the time of the Reformation. When discussing this it was noted that these words echo Isaiah's proclamation of the fall of literal Babylon (see Is 21:9). It was also noted that the fall of Babylon does not refer to its wickedness but to its judgement; also, the past tense (fallen) does not mean that its judgement has happened, but it expresses that it will most certainly take place (it is as good as done). Thus this angel is announcing the certain coming judgement of Babylon — of the Roman Catholic Church. This judgement began at the time of the Reformation but is to reach a climax at the end, and this is what is now being announced.

Moreover, the angel adds that Babylon has become a dwelling place of demons, a prison for every foul spirit, and a cage for every unclean and hated bird. Some take this to be a description of Babylon's wickedness and a ground for her judgement. However, although certainly Babylon is the harbour of all kinds of evil, this description forms part of the announcement of Babylon's judgement (Babylon is fallen and has become a habitation of these foul things); so it is better understood as imagery depicting a state of complete desolation (cf. Is 13:19–22; also Jer 51:37, which describe Babylon as becoming the habitation of various creatures). At that time there was the notion that evil spirits and hateful birds inhabited deserted places and ruins; thus, Babylon's inhabitation by these things depicts a state of desolation and further depicts her judgement.

v3. The angel then announces the grounds of Babylon's judgement. The first two grounds echo what was said in the previous chapter (see 17:1–2; also 14:8). Firstly, "all the nations have drunk of the wine of the wrath of her fornication" — the nations have been seduced into her sinful and worldly ways, which are bringing God's judgement. Also, "the kings of the earth have committed fornication with her" — they have been drawn to her, and have joined in her sins and allied themselves with her. To this is then added, "the merchants of the earth have become rich through the abundance of her luxury" — the merchants of the earth, attracted by her great wealth and opulence, have become involved with her and enriched through her. So we see that Babylon's judgement is to be severe because not only has she herself been unfaithful to God, but she has drawn others to share in her sins, captivating them by her idolatries and by her worldly splendour, power and riches.

Again this is an accurate representation of the Roman Catholic Church, which has drawn the nations to share in her sins, which has drawn rulers into an unholy alliance with her, and which, with all her wealth, has been involved in all sorts of worldly trade. This was especially true of the Roman Catholic Church during the Middle Ages, but it is still true today — and it is for drawing others to share in her sins that she is to be severely judged.

v4,5. Having heard Babylon's judgement announced, John then heard another voice from heaven saying, "Come out of her, my people, lest you share in her sins, and lest you receive of her plagues. For her sins have reached to heaven, and God has remembered her iniquities." This is a straightforward call for the people of God to separate themselves completely from Babylon — from the Roman Catholic Church. It also sets forth the reasons why this must be done: it is needful so that God's people do not participate in her sins and receive of her judgements; it is also vital because Babylon's sins are so great that they have, in a sense, reached up to God for vengeance, and the time for God's wrath has now come (see 16:19). Of course, this call is one that has been relevant since the time of the Reformation, when God's judgement of the Roman Catholic Church began; moreover, it is a call that should have been being sounded ever since that time. However, it is a call especially relevant to the time of God's final judgement of Babylon, with which we are specifically concerned here.

Before going on it needs to be stressed how vital it is that this call is sounded out and heeded in our own day, when it seems that we are in the time leading up to the final judgement of the Roman Catholic Church, and when the ecumenical movement has drawn many true Christians into fellowship and association with the Roman Catholic Church. These verses make it clear that these Christians are in great danger of being drawn into her sins, and sharing in her judgement. Thus, while there is still time, such people need to recognise the sins of the Church of Rome and see that it is under God's judgement; also they need to turn from any of its sins that have polluted their lives; and they need to separate themselves from the Church of Rome completely and without delay, before the fullness of God's wrath is poured out. We must not underestimate the allure of this worldly system. The fact that this call is necessary indicates that it is possible even for the elect to be bewitched by the Roman Catholic Church and to become entangled in her sin. It also suggests that there may be some elect even within the Roman Catholic Church itself. However God, who is faithful, has given this call; and we can have hope that, if this call is sounded out by those who have understanding, it will be effectual and, by God's grace, his people will hear and come out.

v6,7. Having called God's people out of Babylon, the angel then continues, "Render to her [Babylon] just as she rendered to you, and repay her double according to her works; in the cup which she has mixed, mix double for her." This is an instruction to repay Babylon for her sins — for her deeds against the church, and for her idolatry and sinfulness by which she seduced people and led them astray (cf. Jer 50:14–15,29). Moreover, repaying her double and mixing her double conveys the idea that Babylon's sins have been very great and warrant a severe and full punishment (it is as if an eye for an eye is not sufficient — her sins are so great that a more severe punishment is warranted).

The angel then adds, "In the measure that she glorified herself [considered herself and presented herself as great] and lived luxuriously [gave herself to pleasure], in the same measure give her torment and sorrow". Moreover, he goes on to make clear the great extent of her glorying and self-satisfaction: she says in her heart, "I sit as queen" — she believes she is supreme over all and destined to rule the world; "and am no widow" — she believes she truly is the church/bride of Christ, and will not entertain the thought that she is bereft of his favour; "and will not see sorrow" — she believes that she is unassailable and indestructible, and no evil will befall her. So we are shown the great measure of Babylon's pride, presumption and complacency; and in the same measure, God's people are to give her anguish and grief.

All of this cannot possibly refer to the church in any way taking revenge on or inflicting punishment upon the Roman Catholic Church; and it certainly does not involve feeling or showing any enmity towards Roman Catholics. Rather, we should regard these verses as depicting what the attitude of God's people to the Roman Catholic Church (as a system) should be: we should see them as a call to the true church to oppose the Roman Catholic Church (as a system) with an intensity that befits the immensity of her persecutions, sinfulness and pride. Essentially, this is a call to oppose this system (which we do by proclaiming the true gospel, and exposing the Church of Rome's sin and error), and to do this with great vigour, out of a deep concern for God's glory and for righteousness and truth.

v8. The angel then adds, "Therefore [because of her wantonness and pride] her plagues will come in one day — death and mourning and famine." Because of her blinding sin and pride, her judgement will be to her a sudden and totally unexpected event. Self-deceived that she is a great, favoured, unassailable church, and totally blind to her sin and judgement, when judgement falls upon the Church of Rome this will come with a terrible unexpectedness that only adds to the misery this brings. The severity and finality of her judgement is then indicated — "she will be utterly burned with fire". The certainty of this is also made clear — "for strong is the Lord God who judges her". God will certainly inflict on the Roman Catholic Church her deserved judgement.

The world mourns Babylon's fall (18:9–20)

v9,10. With the finality and certainty of Babylon's judgement having been made clear, the world's reaction to

Babylon's fall is then described, and various groups are mentioned (see Ezek 26:15–18; 27:27–36, where similar imagery is used in relation to the fall of Tyre). First to be mentioned are "the kings of the earth who committed fornication and lived luxuriously with her". These are pictured, when they see Babylon's utter downfall, standing at a distance for fear of her torment, weeping and lamenting for that great and mighty city, distressed at the suddenness of her judgement. This portrays the rulers who associated themselves with Babylon (with the Roman Catholic Church) being exceedingly sorrowful and distressed at her great and sudden fall. However, their sorrow and distress is not for Babylon herself but is essentially for themselves: it is because they benefited from her (they lived luxuriously with her), and now this is lost; it is because, having been closely associated with her, they fear sharing in her judgement (so they stand at a distance); and it is because the suddenness and completeness of the fall of this great and mighty city is an unnerving blow to their own confidence and pride in their own position and security. It is also notable that certainly this is not a sorrow of repentance.

v11–13. We are then told that the merchants of the earth also will weep and mourn over Babylon, "for no one buys their merchandise anymore". And we are then given a long list of their merchandise, which is a list of costly and highly valued goods.

Here there are differences of view concerning who these merchants represent. Some people note that many of the goods listed were things used in the Jewish tabernacle or temple; so they take these merchants to represent those who gained from peddling the Church of Rome's religious merchandise — eg, statues, crucifixes, vestments and so on. Others take this to be a straightforward reference to merchants — to those who traded in this world's wealth and goods (in which case "bodies and souls of men" may indicate the exploitation of people for financial gain). Understood like this, this long list of merchandise reveals more about the worldliness and wealth of the Church of Rome — it shows her to be extensively caught up in worldly trade, herself becoming rich by it, and making others rich. Whichever understanding we adopt, however, we see again (as with the kings) that the sorrow of the merchants is not a sorrow for Babylon herself; rather, it is a sorrow springing from the consequence for them — no one buys their merchandise any more. They became rich by her (see v15), and financial loss, not concern for Babylon, is the cause of their distress.

v14. Following this, there is then a statement which would seem to be addressed to Babylon herself — a statement that, with her destruction, all the rich and splendid things Babylon desired and loved have been lost beyond recovery. This makes even clearer the worldly desires and concerns of this great system — her heart is set predominantly on the riches of this world (and not on heavenly things and on the spiritual riches that cannot be lost or destroyed).

v15–17a. The merchants who became rich by her are then portrayed, in similar fashion to the kings, standing at a distance for fear of her torment, weeping and lamenting for that great, splendid, wealthy city, distressed that in one hour such great riches came to nothing. Of note, however, is that there is an important difference between the lament of the merchants and that of the kings. In their lament, the kings mention the greatness and might of the city (see v10) — this is what principally impressed, concerned and profited the kings. In contrast, the merchants speak of the city's greatness, splendour and wealth — this is what principally impressed, concerned and profited them. However, like the kings, the merchants are not showing sorrow for Babylon, but they are sorrowful and distressed at the consequences for themselves. Their sorrow and distress is for their loss of riches; it is because they have been associated with Babylon and fear sharing in her judgement; and it is because the sudden and total fall of one so rich is a blow to their own sense of security and importance.

v17b–19. Finally, mention is made of "every shipmaster, all who travel by ship, sailors, and as many as trade on the sea" — a category of people whose inclusion indicates the international extent of Babylon's (of the Church of Rome's) dealings. These similarly are pictured, at the sight of Babylon's total destruction, standing at a distance mourning and lamenting the fall of that incomparable and great city, distressed at the suddenness with which she has been made desolate. Again, however, the distress and mourning of these seafarers and traders is not for Babylon herself. Rather, it is because of their loss of wealth (they became rich by her wealth); it is because of fear of sharing in her judgement; and it is because the sudden and total destruction of this incomparable and great city makes them fear for themselves.

All of this pictures the effect of Babylon's fall on those who, bewitched by her power, splendour and wealth, and motivated by self-interest, involved themselves with Babylon, shared in her worldly pursuits, and gained by her power and wealth. For such as these, her fall will be shocking and painful because of the worldly loss it brings, and because of the fear it strikes in their hearts. When this great system is brought down, those who have loved what she loved, and have profited from her, will have cause to fear.

Applying this to the Roman Catholic Church, this would seem to show that her fall will have political and financial repercussions in the world, and it will shake all those who have been politically and financially associated with her and have profited from this. Moreover, this is a reminder to us of the great worldliness of the Roman Catholic Church, and particularly that it is not just a religious body but it is also a political body, and it has vast wealth and financial dealings throughout the world. No doubt, the full extent of the Church of Rome's political and financial involvement is not seen. However, this portion of Scripture suggests it is great, and that her fall will send shock waves throughout the world.

v20. As a contrast to the lamenting of the world, heaven and the holy apostles and prophets (representing the people of God) are then called to rejoice over the judgement of Babylon, because in this God has avenged the wrong done to his church by her. This rejoicing is not a vindictive response, or a pleasure at the misery of individuals. Rather, it is a rejoicing that this evil system has been brought down, out of a gladness that justice has been done and right has triumphed. This shows us the attitude we should have to God's future judgement of the Roman Catholic Church (as a system). We are not to be sorrowful about this, as the world will be; rather, out of a concern to see righteousness and justice prevail, we are to be glad that this antichristian system will be brought down.

The finality of Babylon's fall (18:21–24)

v21–23a. In conclusion, the finality of Babylon's fall (already indicated in v8) is again made clear. John tells us, "Then a mighty angel took up a stone like a great millstone and threw it into the sea, saying, 'Thus with violence the great city Babylon shall be thrown down, and shall not be found anymore.'" This depicts Babylon's ruin being unrecoverable — she will be utterly brought down never to rise again (cf. Jer 51:63–64). So, it expresses the finality of God's judgement of the Roman Catholic Church.

There then follows a list of things, all of which are a part of city life, which the angel pronounces will be heard or done in the city no longer (cf. Jer 7:34; 16:9; 25:10–11). The picture portrayed here is one of desolation with an air of finality (these things will be found in her no more); and again, it symbolises the totality and finality of God's judgement of the Roman Catholic Church.

23b,24. Last of all, the reasons for Babylon's judgement are again given, reinforcing the fact that her judgement is just. The first reason stated is, "your merchants were the great men of the earth". This does not immediately seem like a reason for

Babylon's judgement, but it may mean that she brought forth those who had the greatest influence in world affairs, and who presided over and influenced this world's system. The second ground for her judgement is, "by your sorcery all the nations were deceived" — by all her bewitching seduction she deceived the peoples, thus drawing them into her sins. Thirdly, "in her was found the blood of prophets and saints, and of all who were slain on the earth". This, of course, makes her persecution of the true church a ground for her judgement. However, it seems to go further than this and to portray her having a hand in much wider bloodshed (wherever her influence reaches). Certainly, applying this to the Church of Rome, it is the case that during her history she has persecuted and killed not only true believers, but others also (eg, Jews). Moreover, many of the bloody wars and revolutions that broke out in Europe in post-Reformation times were a reaction against the tyranny of the Church of Rome. Plus, there is evidence of Catholic Church involvement in other bloody conflicts (eg, the Balkans conflict in the 1990s). To her account is far more bloodshed than simply her terrible persecution of the true church.

Thus, in this chapter, there is depicted the complete and final downfall of the Roman Catholic Church (which now has its seat at Vatican City in Rome, and is spread worldwide). This chapter also portrays her downfall causing great distress and having considerable repercussions in the world. Of course, all of this is yet to come, and so we do not know what the precise fulfilment of these things will be (consideration will be given later to how this relates to the judgement of "that great day of God Almighty", see 16:14, and to the return of Christ). Nevertheless, this chapter is important for us today. First of all, the fact that God has given this detailed prediction of the final and complete fall of the Roman Catholic Church indicates that this is something God wants us to know is to happen and to keep in view. Equally relevant to us is the vital call that this chapter contains, which urgently needs to be heard and heeded in our day (v4) — "Come out of her, my people, lest you share in her sins, and lest you receive of her plagues."

Chapter 19
Christ triumphant

Rejoicing in heaven (19:1–10)

v1–3. Having been shown Babylon's total and final fall, John then heard a great multitude in heaven praising God and rejoicing in Babylon's fall. In their outburst of praise, this great multitude first sounds out a loud "Alleluia!" (Praise ye the Lord). Then they ascribe to God salvation, glory, honour and power; and they declare him true and righteous in his judgements, because he has judged the great harlot who corrupted the earth with her fornication, and has avenged her slaughter of his people (again, we see that those sins of the harlot that above all provoke God's judgment are her corrupting idolatry, and her cruel persecution of the true church). Then, repeating their "Alleluia", this great multitude rejoices at Babylon's total and final destruction ("her smoke rises up forever and ever" is imagery showing that Babylon will be destroyed completely, never to rise again).

It is difficult to tell whether this great and rejoicing multitude in heaven represents the angels or the church or both. Since the church features in the next verse, it may represent the angels; but whichever it is, this rejoicing is, in a sense, the answer to the call for heaven and God's people to rejoice over Babylon's judgement (see 18:20).

v4. Upon hearing this rejoicing, John also saw the twenty-four elders and the four living creatures fall down and worship God who sat on the throne, saying, "Amen! Alleluia!" When considering chapter 4, we saw that the twenty-four elders signify the whole church of God, and the four living creatures are a symbol of God's merciful purpose to redeem men. We also saw that their joint worship before the throne links together the church's worship with the redemption we have in Christ. Now, here, using this imagery, the whole church is pictured, through God's redemption in Christ, affirming the praise of the great multitude and their rejoicing over Babylon's judgement.

All of this again helps us to see how we should be viewing and responding to the coming total and final judgement of the Roman Catholic Church. From this we see that when we think about her coming judgement, we should do this keeping in view that her judgement is a true and righteous judgement of God, and recognising that in her fall God will be glorified (it will be a great manifestation of his salvation, glory, honour and power). These are important truths that need to shape our attitudes and prayers. Moreover, this picture of the elders falling down to worship along with the living creatures also prompts us, when considering the coming judgement of the Church of Rome, to maintain a due sense of humility and reverence before God; it reminds us that we have escaped this judgement not because of any merit in ourselves, but only through the redeeming mercy we have received in Christ.

v5. Next, John heard a voice coming from the throne, saying, "Praise our God, all you His servants and those who fear Him, both small and great!" The one speaking here is not identified, but the description of the voice as coming from the throne indicates that we must regard this as a call originating from God. Most likely this is the voice of an angel, sounding out a call from God for all God's people, both small and great, to join in the praise (see v9–10, which indicate that the one speaking to John in this vision is an angel). So we see that the coming judgement of the Roman Catholic Church is something that all believers should be anticipating and welcoming — not only those who have a prominent part to play in the service of God's kingdom, but all who serve and reverence him.

v6. As if in answer to this call, John then heard the sound of a vast company of worshippers, loudly saying, "Alleluia! For the Lord God Omnipotent reigns!" So the note of praise continues, now with praise being offered that the all-powerful sovereign God has exerted his royal authority and reigns. And again, this relates to God's judgement of Babylon — of the Roman Catholic Church. The Roman Church has exercised, and still exercises, great power (both temporal and spiritual) in this world. But God is the one who is almighty over all; and his bringing down of the Roman Catholic Church will both manifest his sovereign power and authority, and be an outworking of this. And this is a cause of great rejoicing — that in God's judgement of the Roman Church, his glory and kingdom will be manifested and advanced.

v7,8. John also heard these worshippers sounding out an exhortation, "Let us be glad and rejoice and give Him glory, for the marriage of the Lamb has come, and His wife has made herself ready." In Scripture, the marriage relationship is one of the key figures used to describe the relationship between God and his people. Here, "the marriage of the Lamb" symbolises the union of Christ and his church, and it points forward to the time of Christ's return and the resurrection, and to the church's full salvation in Christ.

And of note here is the term used for Christ — he is called "the Lamb", reminding us that his sacrificial death is the ground of this coming salvation (see Eph 5:25–27). Also notable is what is said about the church (his wife). She is said to have made herself ready; moreover, her wedding clothes are then described — "to her it was granted to be arrayed in fine linen, clean and bright, for the fine linen is the righteous acts of the saints". Here, in the statement that the church has made herself ready, we must not find any suggestion of the church making herself fit for Christ. Rather, her wedding garment of fine linen, clean and bright, is the gift and grant of Christ (it was granted to her to be arrayed in fine linen); thus it would seem to signify the totally righteous state, free from all sin, which will be the blessing of God's people when their full salvation has come. (NB: This picture of the glorified church, arrayed in the clean, bright linen of holiness, stands in stark contrast to the harlot — the great false church —

who has been pictured clothed in garments of gaudy colours and adorned with gold and jewels, depicting her great worldliness.)

In these verses, therefore, using the imagery of marriage, we essentially have an exhortation to be glad and rejoice and give God glory, because the church's full salvation has come. And of note is that this exhortation follows on immediately from the rejoicing over Babylon's fall. This could indicate that the church's full salvation will follow on from Babylon's fall. Alternatively, the announcement at this point that the marriage of the Lamb has come, may serve to parallel the announcement of Babylon's fall (Babylon is fallen) — in which case it shows us that just as the downfall of Babylon (the Roman Catholic Church) is certain, so the future glorification of the church also is certain. In either case, this exhortation encourages us to look forward to the church's full and final salvation, and to do this with assurance and great gladness, giving God all the glory.

v9. The angel who is speaking with John then instructs him, "Write: 'Blessed are those who are called to the marriage supper of the Lamb!'" Here, the imagery changes from the church being portrayed as the Lamb's wife, to the church being portrayed as wedding guests invited to the wedding feast. These called ones are, of course, the elect, who Christ effectually calls so that they accept the invitation to come. And these are pronounced "blessed" — happy and spiritually rich are all those who have answered the gospel call and who have a share in the church's glorious destiny. (NB: Here there is another contrast: those called to the marriage supper of the Lamb stand in sobering contrast to those who will be found at the supper of the great God, described in 19:17–18, which, as we will see, concerns God's judgement to come upon the world.)

The angel then affirms, "These are the true sayings of God." It might seem unnecessary to affirm something that is so central to the believer's faith — that is, the church's coming full salvation in and through Christ. Nevertheless, the angel stresses that these are truths of God, not to be doubted. And it may be that this was

stressed to set our eyes more firmly on our glorious destiny —
sight of which can be easily lost, and sight of which plays a vital
part in us standing firm in the midst of all the trials we are called
to endure in this life.

v10. John then tells us that he fell at the angel's feet to
worship him. From this we see how overwhelming these
revelations were for John, and what an impact they must have
made on John's mind and heart. However, quickly John is
rebuked by the angel: "See that you do not do that! I am your
fellow servant, and of your brethren who have the testimony of
Jesus. Worship God! For the testimony of Jesus is the spirit of
prophecy." Thus the angel reminds John that he was merely a
fellow servant, called to give testimony to Christ; and he exhorts
John to worship God. This reminds us that God alone is to be
worshipped; especially, it reminds us that when we hear the
glorious truth about Christ proclaimed, this is to the end that we
might glorify and worship God and not give inappropriate
honour to the messenger. It also sets before us the important
truth that all true speaking of God's word is centred on
proclaiming the Lord Jesus Christ. And this was what the angel,
as God's messenger, had done, as a fellow servant of God's people
who have the testimony of Jesus.

The rider on a white horse (19:11–16)

With the rejoicing over Babylon's judgement and the
announcement of the marriage of the Lamb, one might think that
the climax has been reached. However, John has not yet been
shown anything depicting the final great battle — the battle of
that great day of God Almighty, when God's enemies will be
finally judged. Under the sixth bowl judgement the gathering of
the nations to this battle was depicted (see 16:12–16), but from
that point to this the focus has been on the judgement of
Babylon. Here, however, we now see this great battle itself.

v11. First, John is shown Christ going out to battle; and it is notable that this comes before we see Christ's enemies gathered to make war. This is because this is Christ's great battle and his great victory.

John tells us he saw "heaven opened, and behold, a white horse. And He who sat on him was called Faithful and True, and in righteousness he judges and makes war." This clearly is imagery depicting the Lord Jesus Christ going out as a great conqueror and victor to make war on his enemies. Moreover, the description of Christ given here adds to this picture, and every part of it wonderfully exalts Christ.

First, he is named "Faithful and True" — a description which expresses his constancy, his faithfulness to his people, and his faithfulness in fulfilling all his purposes and promises. To this is added, "and in righteousness he judges and makes war" — which makes clear that the acts of judgement he is now to carry out are wholly just.

v12. Next we are told, "His eyes were like a flame of fire" (see 1:14) — this symbolises his penetrating insight, and perhaps here especially shows that he sees and knows all the wickedness and the evil designs of his enemies; "and on His head were many crowns" — this shows that it is he, and not the beast and the kings of the earth, who is sovereign over the nations. Also, "He had a name written that no one knew except Himself." The names ascribed to Christ form part of God's revelation to us of Christ's being. This name that is hidden from us reminds us that Christ's attributes can never be fully comprehended by us. It also prompts us to be cautious concerning how this imagery of Christ judging and making war causes us to think about God — only Christ knows what it is to him to enact these judgements on his enemies.

v13. Also, "He was clothed with a robe dipped in blood". This mention of 'blood' naturally makes us think of the blood of Christ's sacrifice (ie, his saving death, which is the basis upon which Christ was exalted over all, and is fulfilling all God's purposes for this gospel age). However, in this context it is probably better to understand this as the blood of his enemies, staining his clothes as a result of him treading the winepress of God's wrath (see v15, also Is 63:1–4); so, this blood points to the judgement he is to enact. And "His name is called The Word of God" — this is a name for Christ which expresses that he is the one who reveals God and who accomplishes the will of God; and Christ will do both of these things in this final act of judging his enemies.

v14. John then describes others riding out with Christ. He tells us, "And the armies in heaven, clothed in fine linen, white and clean, followed Him on white horses." It is not clear whether these armies following Christ are the angels or the saints or both (elsewhere in Scripture both are described accompanying Christ when he comes to judge his enemies — see 2 Thes 1:7–8; Jude v14–15). Very probably, here they are the angels, who previously have been shown engaged with Christ in warfare (see 12:7). And these, like Christ, are going forth on white horses, showing that they are going forth to a great victory. Only Christ's robe, however, is stained red with blood, reminding us that the victory will be Christ's alone.

v15. John also observes, "Now out of His [Christ's] mouth goes a sharp sword, that with it He should strike the nations. And He Himself will rule them with a rod of iron. He Himself treads the winepress of the fierceness and wrath of Almighty God." This is all imagery of Christ's judgement of his enemies. Specifically, his striking of the nations with the sword coming out of his mouth (which represents the word of God), in this context, would seem to depict Christ fulfilling his word of judgement. His ruling them with a rod of iron shows that Christ has absolute authority over the nations and he cannot be resisted. His treading the winepress of God's wrath points to the complete overthrow of his enemies. So this makes clear that Christ's coming out with his armies to war, is a coming out to judge his enemies. Moreover, the imagery here leaves us in no doubt that Christ will have the victory, and the victory will belong to him alone (he himself will do these things).

v16. Finally, we are told "He has on His robe and on His thigh a name written: KING OF KINGS AND LORD OF LORDS". This expresses the fact that Christ is the Lord over all — he is the supreme ruler. This also shows us that in this victory Christ will be expressing his dominion over all. It is this that has been and is being contested by Satan and the beast and the earth's rulers, and in this great judgement Christ's dominion will be manifest.

The beast and his armies defeated (19:17–21)

v17,18. After seeing Christ and his armies riding out, John then saw an angel "standing in the sun". It is difficult to know what this signifies — it may simply place this angel at the level of this material creation, and at a point suitable for commanding the birds. And this angel cried out to all the birds that fly in the midst of heaven, "Come and gather together for the supper of the great God [a supper prepared by him], that you may eat the flesh of kings, the flesh of captains, the flesh of mighty men, the flesh of horses and of those who sit on them, and the flesh of all people, free and slave, both small and great." Essentially, this is an invitation to the birds of the air to come to the great battle and to share in the spoil — to feed on the flesh of the slain. It depicts this final battle leaving the enemies of God as a feast for the birds, and is imagery for a terrible slaughter (similar imagery is found in Ezekiel for the judgement of Gog — see Ezek 39:4,17–20). Thus we see that the battle to come will end in terrible judgement of the enemies of God — from the least to the greatest.

v19. With the certain end of this battle having been brought into view, John then saw "the beast, the kings of the earth, and their armies, gathered together to make war against Him who sat on the horse and against His army". This depicts the papacy (depicted in its political power) and the nations joined together in some form of collective opposition to Christ; and it concerns the end point of the gathering depicted under the sixth bowl judgement (see 16:12–16). There we saw Satan (depicted acting through heathen or secular power) and the papacy (represented in its political and religious power), by means of deception, gathering the kings to the final great battle and to judgement. Now here we see the end point of this — we see the papacy and the nations actually gathered together to make war against Christ and his forces.

This, then, raises the question of what the fulfilment of this will be. Of course, we cannot know the precise fulfilment of what is depicted here because it concerns things yet to happen. However, when discussing the gathering depicted under the sixth bowl it was suggested that we are seeing the fulfilment of this gathering in our own day, and that it is being fulfilled in the growing international and religious unity and co-operation of our time (which has as its goal achieving peace and prosperity in the world, and which constitutes a kind of collective rebellion against God). If this is right, then the likelihood is that the end point of this gathering, which we see here in chapter 19, will be some form of international and interfaith unity — probably having the pope as a prominent figure, and probably expressing great antagonism towards the true church of Christ. Such a thing would constitute a fundamental challenge by the papacy and the nations to the kingdom of God; also it would constitute a fundamental contrast and clash between all that is opposed to God (the papacy, godless government, and all false religion) and the true church of Jesus Christ. Clearly, however, only time can tell what precisely is to happen.

v20,21. In conclusion, John was then shown the outcome of this confrontation. And it is notable that having seen the beast and the kings and their armies gathered to make war, there is then no description of any war itself; rather, the imagery passes immediately on to God's judgement of his enemies. The whole end of this gathering to battle is that God is bringing his enemies, and especially the beast, to judgement; and this is what is immediately portrayed.

First we are told "the beast was captured, and with him the false prophet who worked signs [attesting miracles] in his presence, by which he deceived those who received the mark of the beast and those who worshipped his image" (this description of the false prophet identifies him as the beast from the earth — see 13:11,13–14). We are then told their fate: "These two were cast alive into the lake of fire burning with brimstone." This depicts the utter destruction of the beast and the false prophet — it depicts the whole papal system, political and religious, being brought to a complete and permanent end.

Also we are told, "And the rest [the kings and their armies, who were gathered with the beast] were killed with the sword which proceeded from the mouth of Him who sat on the horse. And all the birds were filled with their flesh." This is a picture of Christ fulfilling his word of judgement, and great judgement falling upon the nations.

Again, then, we come to the question of what the fulfilment of this will be. Clearly, we are dealing here with the climax of God's judgement of the whole papal system, and his bringing of this to a complete end. It also seems that we are concerned here with some decisive and very great judgement falling upon the nations. However, exactly what is to happen, and what form these judgements will take, is not clear. What should be said, however, is that the climactic nature of these events does suggest that we may be dealing with events that will take place at the time of the return of Christ. In support of this notion is the teaching of Paul in 2 Thessalonians where, describing the end of the man of sin (the Antichrist/the pope of Rome), he describes this in terms which seem to associate this with Christ's return (see 2 Thes 2:8). However, we have to place against this what we have previously been shown about the judgement of the Roman Catholic Church. Depicted as the fall of Babylon, this was shown to take place at the hands of the ten kings (see 17:16), and to be mourned over by the world (see 18:9ff); and this would suggest that the fall of the

Church of Rome will happen in time, prior to the return of Christ. Clearly, since there can be no discrepancies in Scripture, all of this must somehow harmonise. And perhaps, put all together, it indicates that, at a point in time just prior to Christ's return, the Roman Catholic Church will be brought down by hostile forces, sending shock waves through the world; then Christ's return will quickly follow, at which time the whole papal system will be brought to a complete and permanent end, and some terrible end will befall those then living on the earth. And so all the enemies of Christ will be dealt with once and for all.

Having said all of this, it must be stressed again that only time can reveal what actually is to happen. The importance to us of what is depicted here is that it sets before us, to encourage us, the certainty that ultimately Christ will have the victory, and his church will be delivered from her enemies. At the same time, however, it also reminds us that this world is destined to suffer some terrible judgement — a sobering fact which should spur us on to greater devotion to Christ, to greater holiness of living (separated from all false religion and all worldly ways), and to greater concern to preach the gospel while there is still time.

Finally, if it is right that we are living in the time of the gathering to this final great battle, then we have to conclude that the judgement depicted here must be relatively close. This does not mean, however, that this generation of Christians (or even the next) will necessarily be the generation that is involved in these climactic events.

Chapter 20
Satan bound and loosed

Interpretation of the millennium

Having seen the end of the beast and the false prophet, the focus in this chapter turns to the judgement of the dragon/Satan. Here, first we see Satan being bound for a thousand years, and his power to deceive the nations being curtailed (v1–3). Then we are shown those who had been martyred, and who had not worshipped the beast, reigning with Christ for a thousand years (v4–6). This is then followed, when the thousand years have finished, by Satan being released, and him mounting a final rebellion against God, which culminates in his judgement (v7-10). There then follows the last judgement (v11–15).

Over the years, a great deal has been made of the thousand-year period described here in verses 1–6 (a period commonly termed 'the millennium'). Therefore, before going on to consider this chapter, it would be appropriate to mention the main interpretations of this. Some see this thousand-year period, during which Satan is bound and the saints reign with Christ, being fulfilled in a glorious reign of Christ and his saints on this earth after Christ's return (the premillennial view). Some see it being fulfilled in a time of great progress and triumph of the gospel towards the end of the gospel age, before the return of Christ (the postmillennial view). Others see this thousand-year period as signifying the whole gospel age, from the death and resurrection of Christ to his return, when this world will end and there will be a new heaven and earth (the amillennial view); accordingly, verses 1–6 are said to depict, first, the curtailing of Satan's power to keep the nations/Gentiles in darkness (v1–3), and then, the saints reigning with Christ during this gospel age (v4–6). There are, however, problems with each of these interpretations.

The premillennial view is problematic in that there is no clear support for this view in the rest of the New Testament; in fact, the rest of the New Testament indicates that the second coming of Christ will mark the end of this world and bring in the eternal state of things.

The postmillennial view is similarly problematic in that the rest of the New Testament contains no plain teaching that there will be a time of great progress and triumph of the gospel just before the end; in fact, the main thrust of the New Testament is to warn of terrible apostasy in the last days (although such warnings do not mean there is no place to pray or hope for revival).

The amillennial view also poses difficulties: firstly, during this gospel age, Satan clearly has been active deceiving the nations, something which Revelation actually pictures in chapter 13 (which concerns papal Rome); secondly, the imagery of the saints reigning with Christ speaks not of all the saints, but only those who have been martyred by the beast (v4); lastly, in this chapter the thousand-year period does not culminate in Christ's return but in Satan being released, and him going out to deceive the nations and lead them in a great rebellion against God (v7-10). So, this view is problematic.

All of this forces us into a position of having to take a fresh look at this chapter, and the best approach is to remind ourselves of the point we have reached in the unfolding of events. In the previous chapter we saw the papacy and the nations gathered to make war against Christ and his forces, and then the whole papal system and the nations being judged. Moreover, when discussing this, it was suggested that this judgement is related to Christ's return. If this is so, then this indicates that in this present chapter (as happened in chapters 12 and 13) we must be going back over time already covered, looking at this from a different perspective. And, what seems most probable is that here we are covering again the time of God's judgement of the papacy and the Roman

Catholic Church (which began at the Reformation and is to reach a climax at the end), but now from the perspective of the judgement of Satan.

God's judgement of the papacy and the Roman Catholic Church (which has been the central theme from chapter 14 onwards and reached a climax in the last chapter) is also, in a way, a judging of Satan and curtailing of his power. The whole papal system, since the fall of pagan government and religion in the Roman Empire, has been Satan's great instrument for holding sway over the nations and persecuting the church; and just as Satan was judged in the downfall of paganism in the Empire, so Satan is being judged in God's judgement of the papacy and Roman Catholic Church. However, since seeing the rise and reign of the papacy in chapter 13, no further mention has been made of Satan (except in 16:13, as the dragon), even though everything depicted since then concerning God's judgement of the papal system has, in a sense, also been a judging of him. In view of this and the contents of this chapter, it would seem, therefore, that the best way of approaching this chapter is to regard it as covering again the time of God's judgement of the papacy and the Roman Church, but now from the perspective of Satan's judgement. This is the approach that will now be pursued, conscious that this is a very difficult chapter, and that many would understand it differently.

Satan bound for 1000 years (20:1–3)

v1–3. Having seen God's judgement of the whole papal system and of the nations, John then saw "an angel coming down from heaven, having the key to the bottomless pit and a great chain in his hand". And this angel "laid hold of the dragon, that serpent of old, who is the Devil and Satan, and bound him for a thousand years; and he cast him into the bottomless pit, and shut him up, and set a seal on him, so that he should deceive the nations no more till the thousand years were finished".

This binding of the dragon and incarcerating him in the bottomless pit depicts Satan being restrained in the exercise of his power; and we are told that, specifically, this concerns him being allowed no longer to deceive the nations. The multiplicity of titles given to him (the dragon, that serpent of old, the Devil and Satan) may show that with all his power and subtlety, Satan was not able to prevent this. The period for which he is bound — a thousand years — must be regarded as symbolic, but what it signifies is not readily apparent (part of the difficulty is that this is a period of time vastly longer than any other time period given in Revelation). Some have suggested that since a thousand is ten cubed, it may be a number expressing completeness; if so, it shows that Satan will be bound for a perfect period — for the exact time preordained by the all-wise God, who is fulfilling his perfect purposes in this earth. Alternatively, it may be that the thousand years of Satan being bound, and the "little while" mentioned in verse 3, during which Satan is released to do his worst, stand as a contrast. And so the thousand years of Satan's binding shows that God's power and control over Satan is boundless and limitless; whereas the "little while" shows that when God allows Satan to act, this is limited by God and is only to the extent that it serves God's purpose. Whatever this thousand years means, however, essentially what is pictured here is Satan, for a certain time preordained by God, being restrained in the exercise of his power, so that he can deceive the nations no more until the time preordained by God has finished.

We are then told, "after these things he must be released for a little while"; moreover, later it is made clear that with his release he will go out to deceive the nations in all parts of the world, to gather them together to battle (see v7–8). So this shows that after the time during which Satan is no longer allowed to deceive the nations, he will be allowed to do this once more. Again, however, it is clear that this is all in God's perfect plan — the statement, "he must be released for a little while" makes clear that this is to serve God's purpose, and is for a time that is entirely under God's control and limited by him.

We come then to consider the fulfilment of this. And if we follow the approach that we are covering again the time of God's judgement of the papacy and the Roman Church, then it would seem that this restraining of Satan, so that he should deceive the nations no more, took place at the time of the Reformation and concerns the curtailing of his power to deceive the peoples by means of Roman Catholicism. Prior to the Reformation, by means of the great deception that is the Roman Catholic religion, Satan had trapped the peoples in false religion. Not only that, by means of the false claims of the papacy to supreme temporal and spiritual power, Satan had been gathering the peoples together under the authority of the pope of Rome, and thereby holding sway over the nations. At the time of the Reformation, however, when the true gospel was regained and widely proclaimed, Satan's hold over the peoples was broken.

The Reformation was a decisive turning point when many individuals and nations were set free from the false gospel of Rome, when the papacy and Roman Church were exposed for what they are, and when many nations and states rejected the pope's jurisdiction in their lands. Moreover, the Reformation marks the beginning of several centuries characterised by the true gospel being widely known and preached, and by seasons of significant progress of the gospel (associated with this were widespread revivals and world missions). That said, it is true that after the Reformation many people remained deceived and trapped in the errors of Rome, and the Roman Church also spread beyond Europe. However, there is no doubt that the Reformation marks a time when Satan's great plan to deceive the peoples, and to gather them into a great entity under the power of the papacy, was curtailed.

(NB: Support for the above interpretation is found in the fifth trumpet judgement — see 9:1–12, and the comments on this. There we saw the bottomless pit being opened, and coming from the pit the great flood of demonic deception that gave rise to the Roman Catholic religion and the papacy. Moreover, this deception was depicted as presided over by Satan. This is harmonious with the view that the imprisoning of Satan in the bottomless pit, so that he should deceive the peoples no more, concerns the curtailing of his power to deceive the peoples through Roman Catholicism — which began with the Reformation.)

However, as we have seen, this restraint of Satan was to be only for a time ordained by God, at the end of which Satan would be released for a little while and allowed to deceive the nations once more. And all the evidence is that the time of Satan being restrained has now passed, and that we are now in the time of Satan being allowed to mount a final rebellion against God. This will be discussed when we come to verses 7–10.

The saints reign with Christ 1000 years (20:4–6)

v4. Having seen the binding and imprisoning of Satan for a thousand years, John then saw a scene depicting something else happening during the thousand years. He tells us he saw "thrones, and they sat on them, and judgement was committed to them". Then he saw the souls of those who had been executed for their witness to Jesus and for the word of God, who had not worshipped the beast or shown allegiance to him. And these "lived and reigned with Christ for a thousand years".

Here, a seeming difficulty is that John begins his description of what he saw with an unidentified "they". However, viewing this verse as a whole, "they" would seem to be those mentioned afterwards, who had been put to death for their faithful witness to the truth of Christ, and who had refused to show allegiance to the beast/papacy (see 13:15). These are they who sat on thrones — a symbol of being accorded great honour. These are they to whom judgement was committed — which may mean that justice was done for them (they had been put to death, but were vindicated in being raised up to reign with Christ), or it could mean that judgement was placed in their hands (in the sense that their vindication was a condemnation of their enemies). And these, we are told, lived and reigned with Christ for a thousand years. So we see the true end of these faithful ones — they had been put to death in ignominy, but John saw them living and having great honour with Christ during all the time of Satan's power being curtailed.

In view here would seem to be the true believers who, during the time of the papacy's ascendancy, witnessed to the truth of Christ and refused to show allegiance to the papacy, and were put to death because of this. And these are portrayed living and having honour with Christ during all the time of Satan's power being curtailed.

Clearly, this vision contains great encouragement for all who are called to suffer and die for Christ, by making clear that death will not be their end, but they too will live and reign with Christ. However, in this context, it may also serve a more specific purpose. Of note is that the next thing to be portrayed is Satan's final rebellion; therefore, it may be that this picture of these martyred saints living and reigning with Christ is intended particularly to encourage those who will face persecution and death in the midst of this. Certainly, as we will see below, this time will involve some final great onslaught against the true church.

v5. To this, John then adds, "the rest of the dead did not live again until the thousand years were finished". It is difficult to know what is meant here by "the rest of the dead" (as distinct from these martyrs who had held to the truth of Christ and had not worshipped the beast). Commonly, it is understood to refer to the unbelieving dead; however, this does not seem entirely satisfactory in this context, because to call these "the rest of the dead" in distinction from these martyrs does not really make sense. Nor does it make sense to see this as referring to those believers who have died but were not martyred, since all who die in Christ go immediately to be with the Lord. Since the central subject here is those who have been martyred for their stand for the truth, and the main purpose would seem to be to encourage those who will suffer in Satan's final rebellion, "the rest of the dead" could simply refer to the rest of the martyrs, who will be put to death in Satan's final rebellion (to call these "the rest of the dead" may relate to the fact that with their death the number of those to be martyred will be completed — see 6:9–11).

Then (referring back to the fact that those who were martyred, lived and reigned with Christ), John also adds, "this is the first resurrection". So, the passage of the souls of these martyrs to live and reign with Christ (which is the blessing of all who die trusting in Christ) is termed here "the first resurrection". These ones may have been killed, and their bodies placed in a grave or destroyed, but their souls had gone to be with Christ, dwelling in his presence.

v6. In conclusion, the great blessedness of those who have part in this first resurrection is then stressed. They are "blessed and holy" — they have great blessing and holiness in Christ's presence. Also, "over such the second death has no power". The second death is a term Revelation uses for the final fate to be suffered by the wicked — a fate of everlasting punishment. And those who have part in this first resurrection are safe from this, and this fate cannot overtake them. Rather, "they shall be priests of God and of Christ" — they shall be numbered among those worshipping before God's throne; and they "shall reign with Him a thousand years". All of this, of course, describes blessings that belong to all who die in Christ. However, here this is particularly said of those who held to the truth, and refused allegiance to the papacy, and were killed because of this. And, it would seem it is said especially as an encouragement and help to those who are to suffer in Satan's final great rebellion.

Satan's final rebellion and overthrow (20:7–10)

v7,8. Satan's final rebellion and his overthrow are then pictured. Here, first we are told that when the thousand years have expired, "Satan will be released from his prison and will go out to deceive the nations which are in the four corners of the earth, Gog and Magog, to gather them together to battle, whose number is as the sand of the sea".

From this we see that, at the end of the time of Satan being restrained, Satan will be allowed by God to deceive the nations once more: he will resume his work of deception with the objective of gathering the nations together in some kind of collective rebellion against or opposition to God. Moreover, the description of the nations as "in the four corners of the earth" shows that this will be a worldwide collective rebellion. Also, the description of those gathered being in number "as the sand of the sea" depicts them being a seemingly overwhelming and unassailable force. Furthermore, the names given here — Gog and Magog — are also significant. These names take us back to the account in Ezekiel of the attack by Gog and his allies on Israel, and God's judgement of Gog (see Ezek 38:1–39:20). And from this it would seem that, here in Revelation, Gog and Magog are figures for the enemies of God. Moreover, in the attack on Israel by Gog, we see that it was God who engineered this to bring Gog to judgement — he drew out Gog and his allies against Israel because it was his intention to judge Gog. This indicates that here Gog and Magog are figures not simply for the enemies of God, but they also symbolise God's enemies being drawn out by God to battle, for judgement.

Thus, what we have depicted here is Satan going out to deceive all the nations, in order to bring them together in some kind of final great rebellion against or conflict with God. We also see, however, that this is to happen in God's purpose, and is all part of God bringing his enemies to judgement. And, if we follow the approach that we are covering again the time of God's judgement of the papacy and the Roman Catholic Church, it would seem that what we are again concerned with here is the gathering to Armageddon and the battle of that great day of God Almighty (pictured earlier in chapters 16 and 19), but now with special focus on Satan's part in this. In those earlier chapters, first we saw Satan and the papal system, by means of deception, gathering the nations to the final great battle (see 16:12–16 — the sixth bowl judgement); then we saw the papacy and the nations gathered together to make war, and being judged (see 19:19–21). Moreover, we noted that in this God was bringing out the papacy, and all his enemies, in one final rebellion for judgement. Now we see the same event depicted as Satan's final great deception and rebellion.

v9. We are then told, "They [the nations gathered by Satan] went up on the breadth of the earth and surrounded the camp of the saints and the beloved city." (cf. Ezek 38:9,16). This shows the nations, which have just been described as a vast force, taking up a position of hostility towards the church of God; thus it shows the church facing vast and formidable opposition that would seem to overwhelm it. At the same time, however, there is also help and encouragement for the church here in the way it is described. Here, the church is termed "the camp of the saints", which may be a reference to the encampments of God's people during the wilderness wanderings, where God dwelt in the midst of the camp; or it may picture a military encampment, in which case there is a reminder here to the church to be ready and equipped to stand. It is also called "the beloved city", which is a figure for the true church that God loves and watches over, and which stands in contrast to that great city Babylon that God was against and judged; so there is also assurance here of God's love for and protection of his beleaguered people as they face this vast enemy.

So, from this verse we see that in Satan's final great rebellion (probably towards the climax of it) the people of God will suffer at least the threat of great persecution, if not some great persecution itself. However, the very next thing we are told is, "fire came down from God out of heaven and devoured them". So, again, as in 19:19–21 (where we see the beast and his allies gathered to make war), no actual war is depicted; instead, the picture of the nations assembled against the church is followed immediately by God's intervention in judgement — fire came down from God out of heaven and devoured them (cf. Ezek 38:22). This depicts some terrible judgement falling upon the nations. It also shows God delivering his people — God will fight this final great battle for his people, and the hostility of the nations will be ended by some decisive intervention and judgement of God. The church's part will be simply to stand firm, strong in the Lord and looking to him for deliverance.

v10. After seeing God's judgement falling upon the nations, we are then told, "the devil, who deceived them, was cast into the lake of fire and brimstone where the beast and the false prophet are". Thus we see that at the climax of this final great rebellion, Satan too will be judged. And here he is shown suffering the same fate as the beast and the false prophet — being cast into the lake of fire and brimstone. Moreover, it is added, "they will be tormented day and night forever and ever", making clear that the terrible punishment of these enemies of God will be permanent and enduring.

Thus, Satan's final rebellion is shown to end in some terrible judgement falling upon the nations, and Satan himself being finally judged. And harmonising this with God's judgement of the papacy and the Roman Catholic Church, this would seem to overlap with the events depicted in 19:20–21, where we saw the whole papal system being brought to a complete and permanent end and the nations being judged. Thus we see that at that time Satan also will be judged, and a final end will be brought to all his rebellion against God. Moreover, the climactic nature of these events again suggests that we are dealing here with events related to Christ's return.

Finally, something should be said about how this relates to our present time. When discussing the sixth bowl judgement, it was suggested that we are now living in the time of the gathering to the final great battle; also, it was suggested that we are seeing at least the beginnings of this in the increasing influence of the papacy and the Roman Catholic Church, and the trends towards international and religious unity and co-operation. If this is so, and given that the gathering spoken of here (in v8) concerns the same events, it follows that: the time of Satan's binding is now past; we are now living in the time of Satan's final great rebellion and deception; and the present increasing papal influence and growing international and religious unity are part of this. It also has to be concluded that a time of great opposition and persecution lies ahead for the true church (for those who are holding to and witnessing to the truth of Christ, and who are standing distinct from apostate religion and from this godless world).

We may not, of course, be those who have to endure Satan's final great onslaught against the church. However, whatever the coming years may hold, it is vital that we now furnish ourselves with all the resources that God has provided to enable his people to stand. We must also learn from what is depicted here, however, that the battle will not be the church's but God's, and he will deliver his people from their enemies.

The last judgement (20:11–15)

v11. Having seen God's final judgement of the devil, and some terrible end befalling the nations, John then saw a scene depicting the last judgement — that awesome event that will take place at the return of Christ, when every individual will be judged and the eternal fate of all people will be finally sealed.

John tells us he saw "a great white throne and Him who sat on it". Here, it is not clear whether this is God the Father seated upon the throne (as elsewhere in Revelation — see 4:2–3; 5:1,7), or the Lord Jesus Christ (to whom all judgement has been committed — see Jn 5:22). In either case, as we have seen before, God's throne symbolises God's power and dominion; and here, God/Christ upon a great white throne symbolises God executing judgement in great majesty and holiness, and it portrays the purity of his judgement. Moreover, John adds that from his face "the earth and the heaven fled away. And there was found no place for them". This signifies that the end of this world has come and the old order of things has ceased. And now all that is in focus is God's judgement — which will seal the eternal fate of all people.

v12. John then saw "the dead, small and great, standing before God" (some manuscripts have "standing before the throne"). This is a scene that is unpleasant to contemplate — all mankind, from the least to the greatest, standing before God to be judged; however, what is depicted here is a coming awful reality that we must give thought to. Moreover, although in these verses the focus is very much on the judgement and fate of the wicked, we must keep in view that believers are not exempt from judgement, but all will be judged on that day.

Then we are told, "books were opened. And another book was opened, which is the Book of Life". John does not say what these first books were; but a common understanding, which has much to commend it, is that these consist of a book containing a record of the deeds of all men, and a book recording the moral law (a book containing the righteous requirements of God, by which men's deeds are judged). The contents of the Book of Life, however, is plainer — this book records the names of all those who have been saved by and belong to Christ. Of course, on the day of judgement there will be no literal books opened. What this makes clear is that God knows all the things that every person has done (all their thoughts, words and actions), and all is taken into account in the judgement (nothing is overlooked). It also shows that God knows all those who belong to Christ, and this too is taken into account.

We are then told, "the dead were judged according to their works, by the things which were written in the books". This shows that this last judgement will be conducted with absolute justice on the basis of the deeds men have done, measured against God's moral law (his righteous requirements for man). The sobering thing is that all people, judged by the works they have performed, will be found guilty before God. The only escape from this will be that a person's name is found in the Book of

Life — that he belongs to Christ, and is numbered among those who have been redeemed and justified in and through him.

v13. John then tells us, "The sea gave up the dead who were in it, and Death and Hades [the abode of the dead] delivered up the dead who were in them." This is a way of indicating that all will be included in this judgement and none will be omitted. Those who have been lost in the sea, or have died and gone to the abode of the dead, may seem to have been lost from sight and forgotten; but on that day all who have ever existed will appear before God. And again the basis of God's judgement is made clear — "they were judged, each one according to his works".

v14,15. We are then told, "Death and Hades were cast into the lake of fire". This depicts death and Hades being utterly and permanently destroyed — these are, in a sense, as opposed to God's perfection as his great enemies the beast and the false prophet and Satan, and they will suffer the same fate. It is then added that the lake of fire "is the second death" (see also 21:8) — a term that Revelation uses for the final fate of the wicked, a fate of eternal punishment.

Finally, we are told, "anyone not found written in the Book of Life was cast into the lake of fire". This shows that at the judgement, all who do not belong to Christ will suffer the final fate of being consigned to everlasting punishment and destruction (which for man means not extinction, but ruin — a total loss of both bodily and spiritual well-being away from the presence of the Lord — see also 2 Thes 1:9). What this will be in reality is impossible to envisage and is, in many ways, too awful to contemplate. Nevertheless, this is the very real fate of the wicked. Moreover, it is the deserved fate from which all who belong to Christ have been saved. The knowledge of this can only serve to increase our gratitude to God and our wonder at his marvellous mercy and grace. It should also spur us on to preach the gospel of Christ, who alone saves men from this terrible end.

Chapter 21
The new Jerusalem

All things made new (21:1–8)

After seeing the last judgement, and the wicked cast into the lake of fire, John is now shown the final destiny of God's people. Here we are concerned with the eternal state of things, and the future life and blessing of the church.

v1. First, John tells us he saw "a new heaven and a new earth, for the first heaven and the first earth had passed away" (see 20:11). The new heaven and new earth represent the new perfect order of things to come (see 2 Pet 3:10–13; also Is 65:17; 66:22). Scripture is clear that when Christ returns, this present world with all its sin and imperfection will pass away, and God will bring in a new order of things in which is found only godliness and righteousness. John also notes "there was no more sea". In this context, this would seem to indicate the absence of trouble or turmoil or evil (all of which are associated with the sea, eg, Is 57:20–21; Jer 49:23; Rev 13:1). Thus, it reinforces the purity and peace of the new heaven and earth.

v2. Then, John saw "the holy city, New Jerusalem, coming down out of heaven from God, prepared as a bride adorned for her husband". This is an image of the glorified church — the church as it will be when its full salvation has come. And this is depicted as coming down out of heaven from God, showing that it is a creation of God by his grace. It is also described as "prepared as a bride adorned for her husband" — this is the church made beautiful with all holiness, the fruition of its union with Christ.

v3. Also, John heard a loud voice from heaven announcing the dwelling of God with his people. This is expressed in a number of ways which together magnify and emphasise this greatest blessing of the church ("Behold, the tabernacle of God is with men, and he will dwell with them.... God Himself will be with them"). This sets before us the certain future blessing of immediate and unhindered communion with God (this is, in a sense, the fellowship of Eden restored). Moreover, also announced here is the covenant relationship between God and his people (they shall be His people and God Himself will be their God). This relationship, which we now enjoy in Christ, will reach its perfection and fullness when the church is perfected and God dwells amongst his people. Then, God's love towards his people will be fully manifested to them, and God's people will express towards God all the love and honour that is his due.

v4. John also heard this voice announcing the blessed relief ahead for the people of God: "God will wipe away every tear from their eyes; there shall be no more death, nor sorrow, nor crying. There shall be no more pain." This expresses God comforting his people and relieving them of all affliction and grief; and it shows God's people having the great blessing of never again knowing sorrow and pain. And the reason there shall be no more pain is that "the former things have passed away". All the trouble and sorrow we now have to bear is associated with this fallen world. It is associated with such things as the sinfulness of others and our own remaining sinfulness, with the disorder in the physical creation (bringing famines, earthquakes etc), with sickness and, of course, death. When this world has passed away, however, and the church has entered into her future blessing, all trouble and sorrow will have passed away and will be known no longer.

v5. After this, John then heard the one who sat on the throne say, "Behold, I make all things new." This is an affirmation from God that he will bring in this blessed new order of things. John is then told, "Write, for these words are true and faithful." John was to write this affirmation down because it was the true word of God and would certainly come to pass. Here is encouragement for the church to set its sights on the blessed life to come and wait for this with confident expectation.

v6. Another pronouncement then follows, "It is done! I am the Alpha and the Omega, the Beginning and the End." This is a further affirmation from God that he will bring in this blessed new order of things. It is done — it is as sure as if it were already done. And it is sure because he is God, from everlasting to everlasting, the origin and Lord of all; so, the work of salvation that he has begun, he will most certainly bring to completion. This repeated stressing of the certainty that God will bring in this future blessed state for the church highlights what an important truth this is to the people of God, and how vital it is that we have the fullest assurance of it. A full assurance of our heavenly destiny will help us to stand in all the trials we have to endure and will greatly affect the way we live our lives in this present world.

Then, by way of further assurance, a wonderful promise follows: "I will give of the fountain of the water of life freely to him who thirsts." This is a promise of abundant life and continuous satisfaction in the presence of God, with man's deepest spiritual needs met. And this is for those who thirst — those who long for God and his righteousness. This describes the true believer: those who have been saved, and have a foretaste of the life to come, will know a great longing for God and his righteousness. And this is a promise that this longing will be satisfied, and in the life to come God's people will know fullness of life and satisfaction in God's presence.

v7. The promise of God then continues, "He who overcomes shall inherit all things, and I will be his God and he shall be My son." This is a sure promise that those who overcome in all the trials and temptations of this life, and remain faithful to the end (which, by God's grace, the believer will do), will enter into all the blessings God has for his people in and through Christ. Some of these have already been expressed here — immediate and unhindered fellowship with God, freedom from all sin and sorrow and pain, and a fullness of life and satisfaction. And this inheritance is one that can never be lost because it rests on the believer's special relationship with God as his son — a most sure relationship that will never be annulled or forfeited.

v8. By way of contrast, however, John is then reminded of the fate of the wicked. They will have no part in this future blessing; rather, they "shall have their part in the lake which burns with fire and brimstone, which is the second death" — their due end will be everlasting punishment away from the presence of God. This will be everything that is the very opposite of the blessing the church will know in God's presence. The sight of this should not detract from the sight we have just been given of the future blessing of the church, but serve to heighten it. It reminds us of the fate from which we have been saved by Christ, and it can only increase our gladness at and anticipation of what is to come.

The new Jerusalem (21:9–27)

v9. John then tells us that one of the seven angels who had the seven bowls came and talked with him, saying, "Come, I will show you the bride, the Lamb's wife." This parallels the call at the beginning of chapter 17, "Come, I will show you the judgement of the great harlot" (see 17:1). With that call, John was shown the judgement of the false church of Antichrist. Now he is to be shown the future glory of the true church of Jesus Christ.

v10,11. Having summoned John, the angel then carried John away in the Spirit to a great and high mountain (cf. Ezek 40:2). This high mountain may simply have been a suitable vantage point from which John could view the church, which is to be pictured as a vast and glorious city descending from heaven (great cities are best viewed from a high vantage point). However, it may also point to the fact that the future glory of the church will be seen only from an exalted standpoint, by those whose sights are on things above — on the things of God, and not the things of this world (see Col 3:2).

Then, from this vantage point, John was again shown "the great city, the holy Jerusalem, descending out of heaven from God, having the glory of God" (see v2). And he describes her light as "like a most precious stone, like a jasper stone, clear as crystal". Essentially, what John saw descending out of heaven was a vast and impressive city shining with a brilliance such as is seen when light passes through a clear precious stone; furthermore, he describes this city as "having the glory of God" — it was radiating the glory of God. This sets before us the fact that the church is destined to have a great glory, but also that all the glory of the church will be from God. When the church is glorified and God's people are perfectly conformed to the image of Christ, it will be God's glory that the church will display through all eternity.

v12,13. Then, continuing his description of the city, John tells us, "Also she had a great and high wall with twelve gates, and twelve angels at the gates". And concerning the gates, he tells us they had "names written on them, which are the names of the twelve tribes of the children of Israel: three gates on the east, three gates on the north, three gates on the south, and three gates on the west" (cf. Ezek 48:31ff). Isaiah, describing the city of God, speaks of God appointing salvation for walls, and her walls being called Salvation (see Is 26:1; 60:18), and it would seem right to apply this to the imagery here.

Thus, the great and high wall of the city shows the church safe and secure through the salvation that there is in Christ. The salvation we have in Christ is an eternal salvation that eternally secures to us the future blessedness depicted here. Moreover, the gates in the wall show that there is a way into the heavenly city, and this way is through the salvation that there is in Christ. It is only through Christ that people will have a part in this glorious future for the church, and all who have trusted in him will most certainly be brought into this.

Furthermore, the twelve angels at the gates would seem to portray the gates being guarded, and so point to the fact that there will be control over who may enter. Not everyone will enter into this future blessing, but only those permitted by God (which will be those saved by Christ, whose names are written in the Lamb's book of life — see v27). Moreover, the arrangement of the gates — three on each side of the city (east, north, south, and west), with the names of the twelve tribes of Israel written on them — indicates that it will be the true Israel of God that will enter into the new Jerusalem, consisting of people gathered out of all the nations of the earth. All who have been saved by Christ out of the nations of the earth will most certainly have their place in the heavenly community of God's people.

v14. John then adds, "the wall of the city had twelve foundations, and on them were the names of the twelve apostles of the Lamb". This shows the wall being founded upon the truth which the apostles laid down in the church — the gospel of Christ and him crucified. It is through the gospel of Christ that people are saved and are secured for this heavenly destiny.

v15. John then tells us that the one who talked with him "had a gold reed to measure the city, its gates, and its wall". In chapter 11 (v1–2) we saw John receiving a reed and measuring the true church of God, with its life ordered by God's ways and standards. This measuring of the heavenly Jerusalem — fittingly, by an angel with a gold reed — similarly shows that this is the true church, established by God and conformed to his glory.

v16. John then describes the shape and dimensions of the city. From the description John gives, we learn that the city he saw was a perfect cube of enormous size (each side is twelve thousand furlongs or stadia, which is in the region of one thousand five hundred miles); moreover, both the shape and the size would seem to be significant. Regarding the shape — depicted as a cube, the city is the same shape as the Most Holy Place in the temple, where God dwelt (see 1 Kgs 6:20). Thus this would seem to show that this city is a place where God dwells; so this again sets before us the certain future blessing of immediate and unhindered fellowship with God. Regarding the size — the figure of twelve thousand may indicate completeness (it is the number of the tribes of Israel multiplied by ten cubed), showing that the full number of God's people (the perfect and complete number chosen by God from all eternity) will have their part in this future blessing. Moreover, the huge size of the city would seem to indicate that the total number saved will be vast. It may seem to us that few are saved, but in eternity we will find ourselves among a great multitude redeemed by Christ (see 7:9-10).

v17. Having described the shape and dimensions of the city, John then tells us that he (the angel with the gold reed) measured its wall; and John gives the measurement — "one hundred and forty-four cubits [which is in the region of two hundred and sixteen feet], according to the measure of a man, that is, of an angel". Although previously the wall of the city was described as great and high (see v12), this measurement for the wall is clearly out of all proportion to the vast size given for the city itself (it is very small compared with the height of the city). However, since all of this is symbolic, it is what this signifies that is important. And again, the number given would seem to indicate perfection or completeness. Moreover, the small measurement given for the wall, when compared with the height of the city, would seem to depict that there is perfect safety inside this city and it needs no defence. Thus this sets before us the future blessing of a life of peace and safety, with nothing that would threaten or harm us (all ours through the salvation there is in Christ).

v18–21. Having given the dimensions of the city, John then describes the materials of which the city was made. The wall was of jasper; the city was pure gold, like clear glass; the twelve foundations of the wall were adorned each with a different precious stone (these are named); the twelve gates were twelve individual pearls; the street of the city was pure gold, like transparent glass. Here there is no need to try to attribute specific meaning to the different materials listed. The thing to note is that the city is built of brilliant and costly materials, showing it to be something glorious. The church in its future heavenly state will have a great glory, which we have seen is God's glory displayed in the glorified saints.

v22,23. John then tells us of two things which the city did not have. First, he says he saw "no temple in it, for the Lord God Almighty and the Lamb are its temple". In the literal, earthly Jerusalem, the temple was the place where God dwelt amongst his people, and where the people came to worship by means of certain sacrifices and ordinances given by God. In the new Jerusalem, God will dwell directly amongst his people. Again this points to the immediate communion with God that will be enjoyed by the church in its future heavenly state. The mention here of the Lamb, however, reminds us that this will still be only on the basis of the saving work of Christ.

Also, we are told, "the city had no need of the sun or of the moon to shine in it, for the glory of God illuminated it. The Lamb is its light." This shows that in the future heavenly state, God and the Lord Jesus Christ will be an everlasting source of knowledge and grace to the saints. Then the church will enjoy the blessing of truly knowing God and dwelling in his favour.

v24. John then adds, "the nations of those who are saved shall walk in its light, and the kings of the earth bring their glory and honour into it" (cf. Is 60:3,5). All those who are saved out of the nations will enter into this heavenly blessing. Amongst these will be some who on earth have known great honour and glory. However, when these enter in they will not add to the glory of the church, for its glory is from God. Rather, all the glory and honour which they had, which was only theirs by the bestowal of God, will, in a sense, be laid down and swallowed up in God's glory.

v25. John also tells us, "Its gates shall not be shut at all by day (there shall be no night there)." The gates of a city were always shut when darkness came, to protect the city, which also meant that after dark none of its citizens could enter. In this city, however, there will be no darkness, and in the perpetual day the gates will never be shut. This again points to the peace and safety that will be enjoyed by God's people in the future heavenly state. It may also indicate that all those who God, through Christ, is bringing to this heavenly destiny will certainly enter in — none will find themselves shut out.

v26,27. Lastly, we are told, "they shall bring the glory and honour of the nations into it. But there shall by no means enter it anything that defiles, or causes an abomination or a lie, but only those who are written in the Lamb's Book of Life." This shows us that all that is excellent and honourable in this world will have a place in the city, but everything that is ungodly will be totally excluded; also it shows us that nothing that would defile the city (which the wicked would do) will be allowed to enter, but only those saved by Christ. This is a picture of purity, free from any mixture. In this world, God's people dwell among the ungodly and unbelieving, and they have in their midst those who are merely nominally Christian; also, they still have in their lives the old sinful nature from which they are yet to be totally liberated. The glorified church, however, will be the community of God's holy people, cleansed from all sin and separated forever from the ungodly and unbelieving.

Chapter 22
Come Lord Jesus

The river of life (22:1–5)

v1,2. Having seen the design and glory of the new Jerusalem, the angel then showed John "a pure river of water of life, clear as crystal, proceeding from the throne of God and of the Lamb". This reminds us of a vision seen by Ezekiel of water flowing from the temple (see Ezek 47:1–12; also Zech 14:8). Water is a symbol for the source of all life; and here the pure river of water of life proceeding from the throne of God and of the Lamb depicts God and the Lamb as the source of all the church's life. Moreover, mention here of the Lamb, again reminds us that all the life that the church will enjoy in heaven comes through Christ's saving work.

With his attention having been drawn to this river, John then notes, "In the middle of its street [the city's street — see 21:21], and on either side of the river, was the tree of life, which bore twelve fruits, each tree yielding its fruit every month." What John describes here is difficult to picture; but essentially it is portraying that at the heart of the city was the tree of life, being watered by the river of life flowing from the throne of God, and bearing a continual and abundant supply of fruit. This cannot fail to remind us of the garden of Eden, and it shows that in the future heavenly state the church will enjoy a continual and abundant supply of life from God. We are also told, "the leaves of the tree were for the healing of the nations" (cf. Ezek 47:12). Here it is probably best to regard these leaves as health-giving — as bringing wholeness to and promoting the well-being of God's people in both their personal and communal life. And so, essentially, all of this shows us that in its future heavenly state the church will enjoy a fullness of life and wholeness which comes as a continual supply from God.

v3. The future blessed state of the church is then further described in the fact "there shall be no more curse [accursed one or thing], but the throne of God and of the Lamb shall be in it". This shows that in heaven the saints will enjoy total freedom from all that is evil. And this is because God will rule there, and where God rules there will be nothing that is in opposition to his perfection and will. Rather, there "His servants shall serve him" — there his people will be wholly given up to God, and perfect obedience and service will be rendered to him.

v4. We are also told, "they shall see his face" — in heaven the saints will see the glory of God. This great blessing which was denied to Moses (see Ex 33:18–23), in heaven will be the privilege of all God's people and will be the pinnacle of the church's blessedness. Also, "His name shall be on their foreheads" — forever the church will be God's, and will be wholeheartedly devoted to him.

v5. Finally, we are again told, "There shall be no night there: They need no lamp nor light of the sun, for the Lord God gives them light." Again, this shows that the saints will dwell in the light of God, knowing God and enjoying his favour. Also, we are told, "they shall reign forever and ever". We must not see in this any suggestion of the saints ruling over anyone (who would their subjects be?); rather, this expresses the blessed and exalted state of God's people in the life to come. And this will be forever and ever because Christ has secured for us an everlasting salvation.

With this, there ends the sight that John was given of the future glorified church and its blessed state. All of this is to be contemplated by us who belong to Christ. This is our destiny, and a contemplation of these things will serve to increase our hope and strengthen us in all the trials we have to endure. It should also cause us to strain towards the goal, and to seek to experience in this life a greater measure of what will be ours in full measure in eternity. Above all, it should move us to praise and glorify God, who through Christ has saved us from all the consequences of our sin and is bringing us to this glorious destiny.

Conclusion of the book (22:6–21)

With this vision of the glorified church, the climax of Christ's revelation to John of things to come has been reached. What follows are some final things that were said to John as a conclusion to the whole revelation.

v6. First, the angel who has been showing these things to John, affirms, "These words are faithful and true." Here it is difficult to know if this refers to the last things John was shown or to the whole prophecy. Probably we should take it to be both — to be a final ratification of the truth and certain fulfilment of all that John has been shown, and particularly this last vision of the future blessed state of the church. To this John then adds, "the Lord God of the holy prophets sent His angel to show His servants the things which must shortly take place". This echoes what John said in his introduction to this prophecy (see 1:1). And this statement emphasises that although John received this revelation through an angel, this angel was sent by the Lord God who spoke through the prophets — thus it is a revelation from him and will assuredly come to pass. Moreover, here we are reminded that this is a revelation of things that must shortly take place — things affecting the church that were soon to unfold.

v7. John then hears words addressed directly to him by Christ: "Behold, I am coming quickly! Blessed is he who keeps the words of the prophecy of this book." At the very beginning, John directed our attention to Christ's return (see 1:7). Now, at the end, our attention is again called to this. Christ's return is something that we need always to have set before us as a concrete hope. It is everything that human history is headed towards; and it is the certain and sure hope of the church that will usher in our eternal blessing and that puts everything else into perspective.

Moreover, also repeated here is the promise of blessing for those who keep the words of the prophecy of this book (who retain them in their hearts and live by them) (see 1:3). When considering this before, it was suggested that those who do this will be blessed in being prepared for and strong in the midst of all that is to happen. Now, repeated in this context, there is the suggestion that they will also be blessed in being more ready for Christ's return — they will be more eagerly looking for it, and it will not take them by surprise.

v8,9. John then confirms it was he who saw and heard these things. We have already had confirmed the divine origin of all that John was shown (see v6). Now, here, John vouches for the truth of what he has written — he himself saw and heard what he has recorded.

Moreover, John adds that when he heard and saw, he fell down to worship before the feet of the angel who showed him these things, and was rebuked by the angel for doing this. It may seem surprising that John should have done this again having already been rebuked for doing this (see 19:10); however, it shows us how overwhelming these revelations must have been — what an impact they had made on John's mind and heart. We, of course, can never see them as John saw them; but this reminds us that we must really contemplate all that is revealed in this book, that by the revelation of God's Spirit, the truth may really impact our hearts and minds. And this must be to the end that we worship God (that we honour and obey God) who has revealed these things and will surely bring them to pass.

v10. John is then instructed by the angel, "Do not seal the words of the prophecy of this book, for the time is at hand" (cf. Dan 8:26; 12:4,9). The sealing or not sealing of prophecy relates to whether the things prophesied are far in the future or soon to happen, and whether their fulfilment will be for a long time hidden or shortly known. In this case John was told not to seal the words of the prophecy because the time was at hand — the things prophesied were soon to take place (which also meant that this prophecy was to be studied carefully, watching for the prophesied events to happen). And, as we have seen, this prophecy does not deal with events that in John's day were to unfold far in the future; rather, it has been being fulfilled in the unfolding history of the church age since the time of John.

v11. To this, the angel then added, "He who is unjust, let him be unjust still; he who is filthy, let him be filthy still; he who is righteous, let him be righteous still; he who is holy, let him be holy still." This reminds us that throughout the time of this prophecy, from John's day to the return of Christ, there will be unjust and wicked people (those who reject God's word and walk in ungodly ways), and righteous and holy people (those who are saved by Christ and walk in his ways); and it seems to show each being given by God to continue in his course until his fate is finally sealed at Christ's return. This, however, is not meant to lead us to a resignation about the fate of men which dampens our concern to preach Christ that some may be saved. Instead, it should serve to encourage the saints to press on in righteousness, and to know that whilst unrighteousness will continue, the church also will continue (God will always have some in this world who belong to him), and God will keep all who are his to the very end.

v12,13. Then, again, Christ speaks directly to John. "And behold, I am coming quickly, and My reward [in the sense of recompense — what is due] is with Me, to give to everyone according to his work." Thus again Christ proclaims his coming, calling our attention to this. In this instance, however, he does this pointing us to the last judgement, when all men will be judged by what they have done, and each will receive his due reward. All of this prophecy must be seen against a backdrop of Christ's return and the reality of the last judgement — that sobering time when both the unrighteous and the righteous will be judged, and the final fate of all people will be sealed. This is the great climax towards which everything is leading.

Christ also adds, "I am the Alpha and the Omega, the Beginning and the End, the First and the Last" (see 1:8). These titles show Christ to be the one, eternal God, and so to be the origin of and Lord of all things. It is as such that he can judge all men and determine their final end.

v14,15. With the last judgement in view, the fates of the righteous and the wicked are then contrasted. First, we are told, "Blessed are those who do his commandments, that they may have the right to the tree of life, and may enter through the gates into the city." Those who do his commandments are those who, by God's grace, have been saved and have proved their salvation by obeying his commandments. Their certain reward will be that they will have a share in the glorious destiny of the church, and will enjoy a fullness of life dwelling in God's presence forever.

Also, however, we are told, "But outside [the city] are dogs and sorcerers and sexually immoral and murderers and idolaters, and whoever loves and practices a lie." Those who have lived in wickedness and loved falsehood (not the truth of Christ) will have no part in the glorious destiny of the believer. Rather, they will be completely and forever excluded from the presence of God and from the life which comes from him. Again, sight of the fate of the unsaved is not meant to dampen our anticipation of the blessing to come; rather, it should heighten it as we see what our end would have been if Christ had not saved us. We should also take this as a warning to examine our lives to see that we are amongst those who will enter in — who are proving our salvation by the fact that we obey Christ's commands, and are not walking in the ways of this world.

v16. Jesus then affirms to John that he sent his angel to make known the revelation to his people — the angel has spoken by Christ's authority. Although this revelation came to us by means of an angel, we are to be in no doubt that it is a revelation from the Lord Jesus Christ (see 1:1); so, it is to be received as such by us, and to be fully believed and obeyed. Jesus then describes himself as "the Root and the Offspring of David" (see Is 11:1,10).

He is the Messiah who was to come from David's line — one who is both divine and human (both the origin/root of David, and his offspring/Son). He also describes himself as "the Bright and Morning Star". The morning star heralds a new day. Christ is the one who is the promise of, and who will bring in, the perfect day of God — life in his presence, knowing him and walking in his favour. Our hope of a glorious future lies in Christ, who has secured this for us and will bring it to pass.

v17. As this whole revelation reaches a conclusion, there then comes from the Spirit and the church a call to men to come to Christ and receive life — "The Spirit and the bride say, 'Come!'" We also see those who come being exhorted immediately to join in the call — "And let him who hears say, 'Come!'" Finally, there is a gracious invitation to those who thirst, and to all who desire, to come and take the water of life freely.

This sets before us the fact that through all the time of the things prophesied in this book it is God's purpose, by his Spirit, to bring men to Christ; it is also a prompt to the church to be constantly issuing the gospel invitation so that by means of God's word and his Spirit people may come to Christ and have life. The prophecy of this book makes clear that the gospel age will see varied events which we need to be aware of and to understand. But, this call reminds us of the constant duty of the church, whatever else may be happening, to preach the gospel of Christ and to call people to come to him and receive the gift of eternal life. And this the church must do with urgency while there is still time, because Christ is coming back, and then God's time of opportunity for men to be saved will be ended.

v18,19. There then follows a solemn warning to all who hear the words of the prophecy of this book: "If anyone adds to these things, God will add to him the plagues that are written in this book; and if anyone takes away from the words of the book of this prophecy, God shall take away his part from the Book of Life [some manuscripts have "tree of life"], from the holy city, and from the things which are written in this book." We must not, of course, add to or take away from anything in the Scriptures. Here, however, just as a special blessing was attached to knowing and living by the words of this book (1:3), so a special curse is attached to adding to or taking away from this book of Revelation. The prophecy of this book has an important part to play in the church remaining faithful to God through all the various developments of this gospel age, and it is vital it is not tampered with. It must not be added to — with this prophecy, God's revelation of what is to happen in this gospel age is complete, and what is recorded here must not be added to by way of any new revelation. Any who do this will certainly go astray and find themselves suffering the judgements that God is enacting on those who do not believe and obey his word. Equally, we must not take away from it — we must not deny or dilute or evade what is written. Any who do this will be in peril of finding that they have no part in the blessings to come for the church.

v20. Then, the Lord Jesus Christ who has testified to these things affirms again, "Surely I am coming quickly." So, as this book draws to a close, Christ again sets our sights on his return; and this would seem to be significant. After Christ had commissioned his disciples and then ascended into heaven, his disciples were pointed towards his return (see Acts 1:6–11). This was the great future event on which they were to keep their eyes set as they carried out the task of taking the gospel to all nations. Now, having unveiled the major events of this gospel age (developments we need to be aware of and watch for) Christ also points us to his return. This is the great future event towards which everything else ultimately is heading; and this is something we must keep in view, as we also watch and seek to understand the time in which we live.

John then responds to Christ's words: "Amen. Even so, come, Lord Jesus!" So, John affirms his coming and prays for it. And we too must be truly believing that Christ is coming back; and we too must be looking for, longing for, praying for and gladly anticipating his coming. His coming is the blessed hope of the church, for it will bring our full and final salvation. And the promise of his coming is to be answered by us with faith and longing and expectation.

v21. John then ends with a blessing: "The grace of our Lord Jesus Christ be with you all. Amen." This, of course, is a typical end to a letter (which this book is — see 1:4). However, it is more than that. It is a prayer and expression of desire that the believers will know God's grace/blessing in their lives; as such, it is set forth by John to encourage them that God's blessing is theirs. Moreover, it has something important to say to us as this book concludes. It reminds us that our salvation is of grace from beginning to end. It also reminds us that it is God's grace (grace that will be abundantly given) that the church needs if it is to walk rightly and to stand firm in the midst of all the events depicted here. So, John concludes by looking for grace for all God's people. And we should not leave this book without seeing the need to depend constantly on God's grace in Christ as, understanding the time and looking to Christ's return, we seek to walk in faithfulness to God and to bear witness to Christ in our day.

Summary

Having looked at each chapter in some detail, we end with a brief summary of the book, and some concluding comments concerning our response to all that is happening in our day.

Foundational to the interpretation of Revelation offered here is the belief that Revelation is a prophecy of the major events affecting the church in the gospel age. Also foundational is the belief that the events and developments depicted are centred on the progress of the Roman Empire and of the pope (the Antichrist) and his dominion, and the church's relationship with these. Moreover, the primary goal has been to help the people of God to understand how our present time fits into the unfolding purposes of God so that we might be better equipped to serve God and to stand in the midst of the testing days in which we live.

In view of this, in this summary the emphasis will be on outlining the history covered by Revelation — which is centred on, and carried forward by, the opening of the seven seals, the sounding of the seven trumpets, and the pouring out of the seven bowls of God's wrath. It should be reiterated, however, that Revelation is not simply a linear catalogue of events. Rather, around and between the seals and trumpets and bowls are other visions that furnish us with additional insights. Some of these go back over the time previously covered, but with a slightly different emphasis or perspective; others picture the safety and blessedness of the church in the midst of the events signified, for the encouragement and strengthening of God's people. However, since the main concern here is to outline the history covered by Revelation, in this summary these other passages and chapters will be commented on only briefly.

Chapter 1. The book begins with John's introduction and greeting *(v1–8)*. There then follows a glorious vision of Christ in the midst of his churches, in which Christ instructs John to write down the revelation, and to send it to the seven churches in Asia (v9–20).

Chapter 2. This is then followed by Christ's messages to the seven churches in Asia:

to Ephesus (v1–7) — which had lost its first love;

to Smyrna (v8–11) — which was enduring persecution;

to Pergamos (v12–17) and to Thyatira (v18–29) — which were tolerating false teaching and teachers, and compromising with the world;

Chapter 3. to Sardis (v1–6) — which had a reputation for being alive but was dead;

to Philadelphia (v7–13) — which had remained faithful;

and to Laodicea (v14–22) — which was lukewarm.

These messages are not just messages to the named churches, but they are messages for every church of every day. They serve both to prepare us to receive Christ's revelation of things to come, and to strengthen us to stand firm and to maintain our witness in all the trials we have to face. They also serve to give us insight into the major errors, dangers and trials confronting and affecting the churches during the gospel age.

Chapter 4. After Christ's messages to the churches, the focus then turns to heaven, and we are shown a glorious vision of God upon the throne, and of worship around the throne — a vision which displays God's majesty, glory and sovereign rule (v1–11).

Chapter 5. Also, we are shown Christ receiving from his Father a scroll sealed with seven seals, which symbolises the preordained purposes of God for this gospel age, which God will bring about (v1–14). So, the scene is set for John to be shown the things that, in God's sovereign purpose, were to come.

Chapter 6. The opening of the first six seals — after this, the unfolding of events then begins with the opening of the first six seals. These cover the time from John's day until the reign of the Emperor Constantine in the fourth century, when the

Empire became a Christian empire; and they concern events to do with the pagan Roman Empire, which was the world of the early church. As understood here:

The first seal *(the rider on a white horse) (v1–2)* — this concerns the Roman conquest of the ancient world. By John's day the Roman power had been conquering and was already in the ascendancy; however, for some time there was continued conquest and expansion. (The vast Empire, with its peace and its good organisation, provided the ideal environment for the rapid initial spread of the gospel and growth of the church in the world.)

The second, third and fourth seals *(the rider on a red horse, on a black horse, and on a pale horse) (v3–8)* — these concern the troubles that later befell the Empire, beginning towards the end of the second century. As the power of the Empire reached a great height, God did not allow it to be at ease in its pride and seeming invincibility, but he brought a time of crisis marked by war, economic chaos and other trouble. This was the beginning of the Empire's decline.

The fifth seal *(the martyrs under the altar) (v9–11)* — this concerns the persecution of the early church by pagan Rome. This was especially severe in the second half of the third century and beginning of the fourth century, and in part arose out of the crisis in the Empire. The Christians were seen by the state to be disloyal, and in the attempt to restore the Empire out of the chaos into which it had fallen, many Christians were killed. This seal, however, shows these martyrs in a place of safety and blessedness with God.

The sixth seal *(a scene of cosmic disturbance) (v12–17)* — this concerns the fall of paganism in the Empire. This happened in the fourth century when the Empire became Christian. The fall of pagan government and religion in the Empire was a great judgement of God on the pagan Roman world, which God judged for its wickedness and its cruel persecution of the church. (It also brought great change for the church. Essentially, the church found itself in a whole new situation — its world was no longer a pagan empire headed by pagan emperors, but a Christian empire with Christian emperors. With this, came an end to the severe persecution the church had been suffering at the hands of Rome. At the same time, however, it also marked the time when there began to be a large number of nominal Christians in the church; it also brought the beginning of state involvement in church affairs.)

Chapter 7. Having seen the opening of the sixth seal, and reached the time of the Empire becoming Christian, there is next a short interlude before the seventh seal is opened and we are shown the events associated with this. In this interlude come two visions depicting the safety and blessedness of the true believers in what was to come.

First there is a vision showing God's keeping power *(the sealing of the 144,000) (v1–8)*; then comes a vision showing the heavenly destiny of the church *(the multitude from the great tribulation) (v9–17)*. These visions were understood to show that in the midst of the Christianized world, God knew who were his people, and that through the judgements to come upon the world and the trials that lay ahead, God would keep his people safe, he would give them power to overcome, and he would bring them to their heavenly home.

Chapter 8. The seventh seal *(v1–6)* — after this interlude, the unfolding of events then continues with the opening of the seventh seal. This ushers in a further series of events (a series of judgements) revealed under the sounding of the trumpets.

The sounding of the first six trumpets — these cover the time from when the Empire became a Christian empire (in the fourth century), to just prior to the Reformation (in the sixteenth century). When discussing this, it was noted that this was the time of the rise and reign of the papacy; it was also noted that, while the papacy is not depicted here, these trumpet judgements concern events that were important to the papacy's rise to supremacy over Christian Europe in the Middle Ages. As understood here:

The first four trumpets (*the striking of the earth, the sea, the rivers and the heavenly bodies*) (*v7–13*) — these together concern the fall of the Roman Empire which came to an end during the fifth century. This was a great and just judgement of God upon an Empire that had devoured and trampled the nations, and that, in pride, thought it would never end.

Chapter 9. The fifth trumpet (*the first woe — the locusts from the pit*) (*v1–12*) — this concerns the great flood of deception that engulfed the Christian church and world after the Empire became Christian (deception which caused the church to fall away from the faith, and which gave rise to the Roman Catholic religion and Church). By this time the gospel had gone forth into the world, but many had not believed it; so, God gave the peoples over to this great flood of deception, which was of the devil but was first of all a judgement sent by God on those who refused to believe the truth of Christ.

The sixth trumpet (*the second woe — the hoards from the Euphrates*) (*v13–21*) — this concerns the overrunning of Christendom by the followers of Islam. This began in the seventh century when Islamic armies swept out of Arabia, and it then continued with the rise of Turkish power in the eleventh century. It resulted in much of the church being wiped out and, eventually, in the fifteenth century, it brought the final end of the Empire in the east. The conquering by Islam of a large part of Christendom was a great judgement of God on the apostate Christian world. However, the hardness of people's hearts was such that even this terrible judgement did not cause the people to turn from their idolatry and error.

Having seen the sounding of the sixth trumpet (which brings us to the time just prior to the Reformation), as with the opening of the seals there is then another interlude before the seventh trumpet is sounded.

Chapter 10. In this interlude, first John is made ready to receive and pass on the visions he is to be shown following the sounding of the seventh trumpet — visions depicting terrible things to happen in the earth, and involving things it would be unpleasant and painful to know *(the angel with the little book) (v1–11)*.

Chapter 11. Then, again, the focus turns to the church. And we are shown: first, the faithful witness of the true church during all the time of the great apostasy of the church and the reign of the papacy in the Middle Ages *(the two witnesses) (v1–6)*; then, the terrible persecution of the true church by the papacy and the Roman Church just prior to the Reformation *(the witnesses killed) (v7–10)*; and finally, God's powerful intervention at the Reformation, when many were saved and God raised up once more a church of true believers, witnessing to Christ *(the witnesses resurrected) (v11–13)*.

The seventh trumpet *(the third woe) (v14–19)* — having reached the point of the Reformation, there then comes the sounding of the seventh trumpet. This heralds the pouring out of the seven bowls of God's wrath. However, unlike before (when the trumpet judgements immediately followed the opening of the seventh seal), in this case the pouring out of the bowls does not immediately follow. Rather, before the history is carried forward again, there are some further intervening visions (chapters 12-14). These take us back over the time already covered (the time from John's day to the Reformation), and they especially bring into focus Satan's activity and the papal dominion.

Chapter 12. In these intervening visions, first we see Satan's attempt to destroy the early church through the pagan Roman Empire, and Satan's defeat in the downfall of paganism in the Empire *(the dragon and the woman) (v1–12)*. This concludes with a depiction of God's protection of and provision for his people in what was to follow *(the woman takes refuge in the wilderness) (v13–17)*.

Chapter 13. Then we are shown Satan's new instrument, the papacy — first depicted in its political power *(the beast from the sea) (v1–10)*, and then in its religious power *(the beast from the* *earth) (v11–18)*. And, particularly, these depict the papacy's dominion over Christian Europe in the Middle Ages.

Chapter 14. After this, by way of contrast, there is then a vision of Christ and his true kingdom and church *(the Lamb and the 144,000) (v1–5)*.

This is then followed first by an announcement of God's judgement of the Roman Catholic Church, together with words of encouragement for the saints *(the proclamations of the three angels) (v6–13)*. Then come two visions depicting souls being saved out of apostate Christendom, and apostate Christendom being judged *(the two visions of reaping) (v14–20)* — which were understood to relate to the time of the Reformation.

Chapter 15. Having been brought again to the time of the Reformation, we then have the introduction to the pouring out of the seven bowls of God's wrath *(v1–8)*. And, with this, the scene is set for the unfolding of events to continue.

Chapter 16. The pouring out of the seven bowls of God's wrath — these bowls cover the period from the Reformation, through our present time, on to the final events of this age; and they deal particularly with God's judgement of the papacy and the Roman Church. As understood here:

The first four bowl judgements *(poured on the earth, on the sea, on the rivers and on the sun) (v1–9)* — these together concern the Roman Church being turned over completely and irreversibly to all its corrupting and deadly doctrines and practices (causing it to become only a source of darkness and harm and death to those having a part in it). This judgement befell the Roman Catholic Church and its followers at the time of the Reformation, when the Roman Church resisted the Reformation and reaffirmed its apostate position. It is a judgement that has continued, and that has affected all who have been part of the Roman Church ever since.

The fifth bowl judgement *(poured on the throne of the beast) (v10–11)* — this concerns the diminution of papal political and temporal power during the centuries following the

Reformation. This was part of God's judgement on the papacy, which proudly and blasphemously had claimed and endeavoured to exercise supreme power over the nations.

The sixth bowl judgement *(the drying of the Euphrates and gathering of the nations) (v12–16)* — this depicts Satan (acting through heathen power), and the papal system, gathering the whole world in some kind of collective rebellion against God to the final great battle (to Armageddon and the battle of that great day of God Almighty). Here it was suggested that we are seeing the fulfilment of this in our own day in the growth of secularism in the West, in the growing standing and influence of the pope and the Roman Catholic Church, and in the growing international and religious unity and co-operation of our day. It was also stressed that this is all part of God bringing the pope, and with him the whole apostate church and godless world, to a day of judgement.

The seventh bowl judgement *(the fall of Babylon) (v17-21)* — this concerns the final judgement of the Roman Catholic Church. This, of course, is an event which is still future, and therefore we cannot say what precisely is to happen. However, Revelation makes clear that the Church of Rome is destined to suffer some final great judgement, when it will be brought to a complete and permanent end.

So, the bowls of God's wrath carry us through to the very final events of this age and to the climax of God's judgement.

Having seen the pouring out of the seventh bowl, and having been brought to the final events of this age, there then follows a number of visions which give further insight into these climactic times (chapters 17–19).

Chapter 17. First, having been shown the final judgement of the Roman Catholic Church, there then comes a further and fuller depiction of her judgement. In this, first we are shown more clearly the great wickedness of this antichristian system *(the harlot sitting on a scarlet beast) (v1–6)*, following which we are given further insight into her identity *(v7–18)*.

Chapter 18. Then we are again shown her complete and utter destruction *(the fall of Babylon, the great city)* *(v1-8,21-24)*, with which we are also shown the world's response to her fall — a response of great mourning *(v9–19)* (which notably is followed by a contrasting call for heaven and God's people to rejoice over her — *v20*).

Chapter 19. This then climaxes in a scene of great rejoicing in heaven over her judgement *(v1–10)*.

After this, there then follows a depiction of the final great battle — the battle of that great day of God Almighty. Under the sixth bowl, we were shown the gathering to this battle. Now, here, the battle itself is depicted (when again we see the papal system being judged). First we are shown Christ and his armies riding out to battle *(the rider on a white horse) (v11–16)*. Then we see the papacy and the nations gathered in opposition to Christ and his forces, followed by the whole papal system being finally judged and some terrible judgement befalling the nations *(the beast and his armies defeated) (v17–21)*. So again we are shown the very final events of this age and the climax of God's judgement.

Chapter 20. Lastly, the focus having been on God's judgement of the Roman Catholic Church, the focus then turns to Satan; and as a conclusion to the revelation of things to come, we are then taken back again over the time of God's judgement of the papacy and the Roman Catholic Church, but now from the perspective of Satan's judgement.

First, we are shown Satan being restrained in the exercise of his power so that he should deceive the nations no more *(Satan bound for 1000 years) (v1–3)* — which was understood to relate to the Reformation, and to concern the curtailing of his power to deceive the peoples by means of Roman Catholicism. Next, we are shown the saints who were martyred during the time of the papacy's ascendancy, living and having honour with Christ *(the martyrs reign with Christ 1000 years) (v4–6)*. Then, again we see the final great battle — but now depicted in terms of Satan's final rebellion and overthrow *(v7–10)*.

After this, with the climax of God's judgement having again been reached, there is then a depiction of the last judgement *(the great white throne) (v11–15)*.

Chapter 21. Finally, come visions depicting the final destiny of God's people — the future glory and blessing of the church *(21:1–22:5)*.

Chapter 22. The whole book then ends with some final things that were said to John, which conclude with a final affirmation of Christ's return *(v6–20)*.

Concluding comments

One of the main purposes served by the book of Revelation is that it provides us with a perspective on the history of the church age and on the future, and it enables us to see where we are in the unfolding purposes of God for this age. Equally, it helps us to understand the significance of the events and developments of our time, and how we should respond. It is fitting, therefore, to end this study of Revelation by highlighting again where our day fits into the prophecy of Revelation, and by considering how we should be responding to the developments of our day.

1. In this interpretation of the book of Revelation it has been suggested that we are in the time of the sixth bowl judgement, and that this is being fulfilled in the growing international and religious unity and co-operation of our time, the rise of secularism in the West, and the increasing political and religious power of the papacy and the Roman Catholic Church.

This means that:

(i) we are in the time of God's judgement of the papacy and the Roman Catholic Church (which the bowl judgements concern); and

(ii) more precisely, we are in the time of the gathering of the world to the final great battle (depicted under the sixth bowl judgement), when God will finally judge the papacy and the Roman Catholic Church, and when some terrible judgement will befall the nations.

It follows that such things as the godless religious unity of our time, the rise of secularism, and the increasing power of the pope and the Catholic Church, are not reasons to think that the devil is being victorious and getting the upper hand (although that is how it can appear). On the contrary, they are happening in God's preordained purpose as part of God bringing all his enemies — the devil, the pope, the whole apostate church and godless world — to a day of judgement.

2. Given all of this, it goes without saying that how we respond to these developments is crucial. And, as mentioned above, the book of Revelation itself helps us to see what our response should be.

a. Firstly, heeding Christ's call, "Come out of her, my people..." (18:4), we need to separate from the Roman Catholic Church. Particularly, this means keeping apart from ecumenical activities, initiatives or bodies that are promoting an all-inclusive unity which includes the Roman Catholic Church. Of course, in saying this it is not being suggested that a believer should have nothing to do with someone who is a Roman Catholic. What is meant here is separation from the Roman Catholic Church as a religious body, particularly through ceasing involvement in ecumenical activities and organisations that include the Roman Catholic Church as if it were a true church of Jesus Christ. As well as this, there is a need to examine ourselves to see if we have in any way been led away into Romish beliefs or practices and, if so, to turn from these.

This is not to imply that separation from the Roman Catholic Church will be an easy or straightforward step to take. On the contrary, separation is likely to be costly: it is likely to provoke hostility, and accusations of being judgmental or unloving or of causing division in the church. Added to this, deciding what action to take in response to the compromise of ecumenism may not be simple. Today, most churches are committed to ecumenism in principle and/or in practice, including most evangelical churches. This means that many believers who see the need to be separate from the Catholic Church may be faced with a difficult choice between either remaining where they are while keeping out of ecumenical events, or leaving and joining a non-ecumenical church that may not be local. Nevertheless, God has called us to come apart from the Roman Catholic Church so that we do not share in her sins and receive of her judgements; so, this must be worked out in practice, no matter how difficult or costly that may be.

Furthermore, equally important is that, with humility and love, we share the gospel with Roman Catholics so that they might be saved; also, that we call them out of the Roman Catholic Church. Such witness has been stifled by the ecumenical movement and urgently needs to be carried out. Again, this will not be an easy task, but it is something that must be done out of concern for those trapped in the deadly darkness of the Church of Rome. (Here we must not forget the Anglo-Catholics in the Church of England, who have embraced most of the Roman Catholic religion, and also need to hear the true gospel.)

b. Secondly, heeding Christ's words that are spoken in the context of the sixth bowl, "Blessed is he who watches and keeps his garments..." (16:15), we need prayerfully to keep alert to all that is happening, looking to God for wisdom and grace to stand; also we need to build ourselves up in the faith, and to walk in holiness of life. Only then will we be strong and able to stand in the midst of all that is now happening and all that lies ahead.

Furthermore, conscious that many Christians (including many in evangelical churches), are not watching and keeping their garments, we need to devote ourselves to prayer for the church — praying that God will bring his people into a place of separation from the Roman Catholic Church and all its error, and that he will build up his church to stand. Equally, as the opportunity arises, we need to speak to other believers about the true nature of the Roman Catholic Church, in the hope that they will see the truth and do what is needful. Again, doing this will not be easy. However, it is something that we can do in faith, knowing that God, who is faithful to his people, is calling his people to be separate and wants his people to be ready for all that is to come.

c. Finally, as we were reminded at the very end of the book, in the midst of all of this we must fulfil our constant calling to share the saving gospel of God's salvation in Christ with all who do not know Christ (22:17) (which includes a good number within the Protestant/evangelical churches). Also, we must keep our sights on Christ's return (22:7,12,20), which, whether it is to be in this generation or not, is a continual source of comfort, strength, hope and joy to the church of God. So, it should be kept in view as we endeavour to make Christ known and to walk in faithfulness to him in this testing time in which we live.

In conclusion, we should not end without remembering the special blessing associated with this book of Revelation: "Blessed is he who reads and those who hear the words of this prophecy, and keep those things which are written in it..." (1:3). The book of Revelation has been given that we might understand the time in which we live; that we might be strong and stand firm; and that we might have hope. Thus it has a vital part to play, both now and in the days ahead, in us glorifying God, fulfilling his purposes, and knowing the personal blessing that comes from walking with God in holiness and truth. Moreover, in a day when many seemingly true believers are stumbling through a lack of understanding, Revelation has a crucial part to play in helping them to stand. So, let us all heed and keep (remember and live by) the things that Revelation shows us, and help others to do the same — knowing that this book of Revelation has a vital part to play in the church being faithful to God and being a true witness to the world in the midst of the dark and perilous time in which we live.

oOo

Finally, acknowledgement must be given of the help and insight afforded by the following commentaries:

"Matthew Henry's Commentary on the Whole Bible", Hendrickson Publishers, 1992.

"Matthew Poole's Commentary on the Holy Bible", Hendrickson Publishers, 1982.

"Tyndale New Testament Commentaries" — "Revelation" by Leon Morris, Inter-Varsity Press, 1983.

"The War with Satan — An Explanation of the Book of Revelation" by Basil F C Atkinson, 1940, Protestant Truth Society.

oOo

**Other books by the same author
(the 'Blessed Is He Who Watches' series)**

Antichrist Revealed
Described in Scripture...fulfilled in the papacy

A Little Leaven Leavens the Whole Lump
The leavening of modern evangelicalism

Righteousness Exalts a Nation
Britain's hope for a better future

Internationalism, Ecumenism & the End Times
Where ecumenism is leading the churches

Also see our website:
http://www.blessedishewhowatches.org.uk

To contact us:
contact@blessedishewhowatches.org.uk

About the author: Carol White lives in Teddington, Greater London. She was converted in 1980 after spending 28 years as a convinced atheist. Her church affiliation has been with Baptist and Independent Evangelical churches.

Blessed is He Who Watches

Printed in Poland
by Amazon Fulfillment
Poland Sp. z o.o., Wrocław